W H A T

A B O U T

TOMOR-

R O W ?

What About Tomorrow?
An Oral History of Russian Punk from the Soviet Era to Pussy Riot

© Alexander Herbert, 2019

Cover painting by Matt Gauck | MattGauck.com
Design by Joe Biel

Visit or write for catalog:
Microcosm Publishing
2752 N Williams Ave.
Portland, OR 97227
www.Microcosm.Pub

ISBN 978-1-62106-404-6
This is Microcosm #342
This edition © Microcosm Publishing, 2019

First Published September 15, 2019
First printing of 3,000 copies

For a catalog, write or visit:
Microcosm Publishing
2752 N Williams Ave.
Portland, OR 97227
www.Microcosm.Pub

To join the ranks of high-class stores that feature Microcosm titles, talk to your rep: In the U.S. **Como** (Atlantic), **Fujii** (Midwest), **Book Travelers West** (Pacific), **Turnaround** in Europe, **Manda/UTP** in Canada, **New South** in Australia, and **GPS** in Asia, India, Africa, and South America.

If you bought this on Amazon, I'm so sorry because you could have gotten it cheaper and supported a small, independent publisher at www.**Microcosm.Pub**

Global labor conditions are bad, and our roots in industrial Cleveland in the 70s and 80s made us appreciate the need to treat workers right. Therefore, our books are made in the U. S.

Library of Congress Cataloging-in-Publication Data

Names: Herbert, Alexander, author.
Title: What about tomorrow? : an oral history of Russian punk from the Soviet era to Pussy Riot / Alexander Herbert.
Description: Portland, Oregon : Microcosm Publishing, 2019. | Includes bibliographical references.
Identifiers: LCCN 2019013236 (print) | LCCN 2019014576 (ebook) | ISBN 9781621060789 (e-book) | ISBN 9781621064046 (pbk.)
Subjects: LCSH: Punk rock music--Russia (Federation)--History and criticism. | Punk rock music--Soviet Union--History and criticism.
Classification: LCC ML3534.6.R8 (ebook) | LCC ML3534.6.R8 H47 2019 (print) | DDC 781.660947--dc23
LC record available at https://lccn.loc.gov/2019013236

W H A T
A B O U T
TOMORROW?

An Oral History of Russian Punk
from the Soviet Era to Pussy Riot

ALEXANDER HERBERT

Microcosm Publishing
Portland, Ore

Contents

"The love of soil and what grows on it is not acquired by sketching with a paintbrush— it is only in its service; and without loving it, how paint it?"

– P. K.

INTRODUCTION

By all accounts punk arrived in Russia around 1978, the same year that Johnny Rotten and Malcolm McLaren's project to expose the contradictions of the capitalist rock establishment imploded. Like their British counterparts, Russian punks were confronting their own socio-economic stagnation, cultural monotony, and using the music to express their skepticism of the status quo. They certainly managed to do that and more; in a little less than forty years Russian punk survived the failure of the experimental socialist state that held a monopoly on cultural expression, economic bankruptcy of the post-Soviet years, and an intense neo-Nazi movement. Today Russian punk confronts a number of issues that were always latent, but overshadowed by these other concerns (for better or for worse). A ubiquitous patriarchal mentality, an unequal distribution of wealth between the capital and the provinces, and the increasing encroachment of a Western dominated culture industry confront Russian punk rock more than anything else in the waning age of Putin.

The book in your hands tells the story of punk's long history in Western Russia, particularly Moscow and St. Petersburg, with only one chapter on punk in the provinces and one small section generously compiled by Vladimir Kozlov on Siberian Punk. To include all of Russia east of the Ural Mountains and all the post-Soviet space would necessitate a substantially larger volume.

Unlike the majority of oral histories that address a particular scene or limited time period, this book aims to tell the span of a nation's punk history, and is thus structured differently than other scene histories. Punk rock is a subculture notorious for its know-it-alls and their love for the obscure, and they will have a field day here noting that Purgen or Sektor Gaza didn't receive enough attention, or something like that. However, my hope is that by not dwelling on one single subject or one particular band, the reader can more easily see the larger narrative, and do further research on their own.

From the outset I sought to explore what punk meant in Russia over time. If we define punk rock in the broadest sense as a nonconformist social identity with an unorthodox (but coherent) music style, then the entire rock pantheon of late Soviet Russia would have to be included. The rock bands Akvarium and Kino were equally rebellious in their earlier years, but their sound is unfamiliar and perhaps unpleasing to the punk rocker's ear.[1] Those bands also embodied a sound that many of Russia's first punks vehemently rejected. With that in mind, the bands discussed in this book play music akin to what the West defines as punk rock, but I am fully cognizant of the potential problems of ignoring cultural relativity. In so far as some definition is needed in order for this book to exist, I don't believe many will protest my decision.

The conversations that form the bulk of the book took place from 2013–2017. As most researchers realize after diving headfirst into a big project, the nesting doll of sources is endless, and the deeper one goes the easier it is to get lost. Some people refused to talk (in one noteworthy case, a woman involved with the Leningrad Rock Club scene told me to "go to hell" before questioning even started). The more cordial participants who refused to give their two cents referred me to previously published interviews or texts. A citation is included in those cases so that the reader knows when someone other than myself conducted the interview. I hope this recognition pays sufficient homage to those whose work made many parts of this book possible.

In every interview I encouraged the actors to tell their own stories, which I then put in an order that made narrative sense, without my own commentary. As a lifelong fan of punk rock, my only goal was to give something back to the scene that helped shape

1 *Akvarium*—Aquarium; *Kino*—Cinema.

me and let the participants do the talking. Still, I am fully aware that the interviews I chose to include and exclude contribute to the way I want to tell the story, and how I want to understand punk. I invite anyone dissatisfied with my structure of events to tell the story themselves. At least this book begins a discussion.

No matter where it has emerged, punk rock's commercial potential has never undermined the fact that it provides an important outlet for creative expression and youth empowerment. In Russia, as in anywhere else, punk managed to create a space where people could release aggression and vent their frustrations with a culture, society, and state that seemed alien to them. That is precisely what gave punk as a musical style and scene its staying power worldwide. It is also what makes it virtually inaccessible to academic researchers who have long since outgrown their "adolescent" angst and idealism.

While Western youth in the 1970s had a lot to be dissatisfied with—racial and gender inequality, the post-World War Two world order, the nation-state, and urbanization—at least they could voice their displeasure. In the Soviet Union, criticism of the regime was heavily monitored and punished, forcing many, especially those who did not like state-socialism, to fall in line with the rest. The conditions that made punk possible in the West (a burgeoning music industry, privately owned clubs, sex shops) simply did not exist in the Soviet Union. Contrary to popular opinion, the Ramones wanted to *Rocket to Russia* so that they could bring punk rock to radios throughout the evil empire, where everybody assumed that, in theory, "punk" couldn't exist.

The Ramones were not alone in the way they imagined the social dynamics of Cold War culture. The great novelty of the Clash's *Ivan Meets G.I. Joe* was that it was their attempt to broadcast Western punk's exceptionalism by putting Soviet imagery and politics into a musical context that completely parodied everything the Soviet Union was said to be. It was as if they took a decrepit grandpa (*dedushka*) and put him in the middle of a Harlem b-boy floor: out of context and beyond the style. Truthfully, as I hope this book shows, Ivan's dance moves were much more sophisticated than anyone in the West imagined.

In lieu of starting each chapter with a comment, thereby disrupting the flow of interviews, I wish to outline the book here.

Part One deals with the rise of punk rock in Leningrad in the final decade of the Soviet Union. Andrey "Svin" Panov and friends discovered punk rock through clandestine means that empowered them with an alternative to what they perceived to be the monotony of Soviet life.[2] As counterculture penetrated Russia's historic window on the West, the Soviet Union faced a crisis of confidence leading to Gorbachev's *perestroika* and *glasnost*, which relaxed the social straightjacket in an attempt to overcome economic stagnation.[3] Both reforms changed the face of rock in Russia seemingly overnight, as amateur bands formally excluded from the official houses of culture and concert venues confronted and embraced a new openness. The last part of this section, provided by Vladimir Kozlov, addresses the rise of Siberian Punk, a phenomenon worthy of its own book. My decision to ask Vladimir for a contribution stems from the fact that any attempt I could make in researching that topic would pale in comparison to what he's already done.

Part Two continues the narrative of Leningrad in its transition to St. Petersburg following the breakup of the Soviet Union. The 1990s witnessed one of the most socially and economically difficult decades for Russia. No longer could Soviet censorship hold back the flood of anger and angst germinating in a generation that witnessed the overthrow of its birth country, and

---

2 *Svin*—pig.
3 *Perestroika* (restructuring)—political movement for democratic reformation in the USSR during the second half of '80s; *glasnost* (publicity) is associated with increased government transparency as a result of democratic reforms in the second part of 1980's.

amateur bands created a new scene in places like club TaMtAm in St. Petersburg and the Jerry Rubin Club in Moscow. For readers wanting to hear more about what was going in Moscow in the late 80s and early 90s, flip to Max Kotchetkov's article on the "'Moscow Rock Laboratory' Revisited," which details a legendary Soviet institution that promoted underground music in the capital. I also asked Max to reflect on its demise and whether Moscow punk is missing anything without the Rock Laboratory.

The next chapters finally transition out of St. Petersburg and into Moscow and the provinces. Part Three presents a number of perspectives on the rise of Moscow-based punk as the center of commercial music and demonstrative showmanship (and show-womanship). Combining the new cultural influences from the West with the Soviet legacy, Moscow musicians defined the new standards of Russian punk rock for succeeding generations.

Punk rock was a fairly well-known and bloated subculture by the first term of Putin's Russian Federation. But with that recognition came problems. The anti-fascist movement (its height in 2003–2008, roughly) denoted a stint of prolonged violence and aggression between self-proclaimed punk rockers and those labeled as fascists—neo-nazis, *gopniki*, and nationalists.[4] The anti-fascist movement was born with strong ideological foundations and advocated straight-edge and vegan lifestyles, complemented by popular mutual aid initiatives. After numerous murders and street brawls, the Russian Government created the Tsentr po Protivodeystviu Ekstremizmu, or Tsentr "E," to tame both fascists and anti-fascists through a series of laws that never clearly defined extremism.[5]

---

4 *Gopniki* is a generic term for Russian thugs. They do not denote any homogenous or conscious social group, but rather a collection of pseudo-Russian nationalists prone to drunken bouts of arbitrary violence and bigotry.
5 *Tsentr po Protivodeystviu Ekstremizmu* (Department for Combating Extremism), *Tsentr "E"*— Center "E".

Part Four is a very brief chapter comprised of interviews from a number of musicians and fans from cities in Western Russia—Kazan, Kirov, Izhevsk, Nizhny Novgorod, Ufa, and Arkhangelsk. The task in this chapter was not to include every band and node of provincial punk history, but to provide paradigmatic snapshots of how punk rock arrived and evolved outside the capitals. For a more focused and comprehensive narrative, the reader can skip to the final section of that chapter, "A Brief History of Punk in Izhevsk."

That leads us to Part Five, which briefly paints a picture of what punk rock looks like today in Russia. In almost every way it is not dissimilar to the United States. However, there is a recent tendency to retreat from Western models of punk aesthetics and to rediscover the gems of Russia's punk past. The Leningrad and Siberian legends are being rediscovered, re-mastered, and redistributed to a generation of punk rockers that admittedly lost the reigns of its own indigenous sound and spirit. From bands that seek to maintain something distinctively Russian, to those that sing in English for larger audiences, and those who revel in the absolute underground, punk rock in Russia today is structurally like that in the United States, but perhaps more dignified by its forced start.

The final section of Part Five addresses the modern phenomenon of Pussy Riot. Whether or not to include them in this book posed a serious quandary for a number of reasons, not least of which is their non-involvement in the DIY music culture described throughout the book. The vast majority of my interviewees (all but one, in fact) did not consider them to be a part of the Russian punk scene, but acknowledged the importance and bravery of their protests. "The Paradox of Pussy Riot" argues that there are valid reasons for their inclusion and exclusion from this history, but I am unwilling to decide either way. Before their protests, they had never been seen at shows, never released a punk single, and were generally never heard of. But it cannot be denied that their actions catapulted the idea of Russian Punk into Western consciousness. In compiling the book, I believed that the paradox was too complicated to leave to oral history, and therefore required a more direct explanation.

The appendices represent my best attempt to let active participants in the scene reflect on the history themselves. Tommy Dean, an American if I ever met one, was fascinated by the life of Fedor "Begemot" Lavrov in the Soviet Union, and spent a good amount of time talking to him and compiling an article to pay homage to a true legend. Of the years I spent involved in Russia's punk-rock scene, I have never met any individuals more knowledgeable and respected than Kirill "George" Mikhailov and Maksim Dinkevich. Their reflections on the St. Petersburg and Moscow scenes are to a certain extent the most valuable to be had.

For the reader's convenience I have included a list of characters in the order they appear at the end of every part. I have also retained the transliteration of band names in the text so as to ease the searches of non-Russian speakers. Experts will notice some discrepancies in the transliteration of names, and that is due to the participant's preference more than my own caprice. Before setting you off on your way, my final recommendation is to search for the bands that are mentioned and give them a listen. There is no better context to the narrative than the music itself. You might find that you thoroughly enjoy much of it, and maybe you will even pick up on what makes Russian punk special.

ACKNOWLEDGEMENTS

There are a lot of people to thank for making this book possible. I owe my largest debt to my best and longest friend, Tommy Dean, who listened to me talk about Russian punk rock after spending a quarter of a year in Nizhny Novgorod, and then another half a year in Moscow. It was him who dared me to act on my impulsive, partially inebriated line "I could write a book about it." After leading a successful crowdfunding campaign to raise money, Tommy accompanied me to Russia in the summer of 2014 to help conduct interviews.

None of the research was possible without the generous donations I received. In particular, Eric and Christine Kovac, Sergey Khabaroff, Tero Viikari, Aristides Rudnick, Rolando J. Garcia, Ralph Brandi, Francois Apatride, Donna Dean, Ted Herbert, Kate Shepard, Eve Adams, Alicia McCarthy, Dan Doyle, Ivan Antonuyk, Kevin Dunn, Ian Williams, Jo-Ann Bergantino, Jay Johnson, and Samantha Barchard deserve special attention. I also must thank Indiana University's Russian and East European Institute, led by Mark Trotter and Padraic Kenny, which granted me a modest amount of summer research funding. This project would have been impossible without all your financial support.

After coming home with over 75 interviews in audio recordings, and a more or less equal number of typed interviews and fanzines, balancing the translations with my own academic work became the most arduous part of the entire process. Without the help of certain friends, I could not have finished the translations in a timely fashion. Alexander Mitnikov, Masha Balova, Jacob Khorev, and Maxim Rohr, I am forever grateful to you for making the hardest task a little less difficult.

Some people deserve special recognition for being guides, providing moral support, and endowing me with a sense of purpose. Especially Fedor Lavrov, who responded to my late night messages, eased my anxieties, found the impossible-to-find people, and helped correct some potentially deal-breaking mistakes. Joanna Stingray, an amazing participant in the Soviet Union's rock scene, provided her own personal pictures, bringing the Soviet punk scene to life for us. Any research of Leningrad Rock cannot be complete without visiting her website, found in the bibliography. I'm convinced that no one knows more about contemporary Russian punk rock and rock music than Maksim Dinkevich, who patiently directed me toward new bands and new people to interview. While I originally refrained from including any provincial cities, I have to thank Sasha Shmakov for imploring me to visit Izhevsk to document the scene he was so proud of. Kirill "George" Mikhailov also deserves recognition for getting me in to St. Petersburg's very tight-knit scene. Finally, Alex Mitin and his best friend Bagi Boev went out of their way countless times to get me in the same room with bands like Distemper and Tarakany!, who had better things to do than talk to a lowly American researcher.[6] This book was also not possible without these punks.

After I had compiled and ordered the interviews, I met Dasha Kholobaeva, who double-checked my translations and transliterations and made sure everything was consistent. Unexpectedly, in the summer of 2017 Aaron Cometbus stayed with me in St. Petersburg and looked over the first chapter of the book and guided me through the publication process. At Microcosm Publishing, Elly Blue pushed me to dig deeper into questions of gender in the scene, and Joe Biel patiently read my compulsive and often lengthy emails.

Last, but certainly not least, in the middle of composing Part One my partner gave birth to our beautiful daughter. Not only was I pushing through a pile of doctoral work and translating interviews, but I also had to learn how to be a dad. I don't think anyone can be as patient as Kerry has been through the process, and I like to believe that only she would have put up with the amount of time I spent nose-deep in books and my laptop. While it looked like I was wasting time on social media, I was actually reaching out to people, sending questions, and tying up loose ends. This book, as the culmination of hours spent and days absent, is dedicated to her.

---

6 *Tarakany!*—Cockroaches!

PART ONE:
LENINGRAD PUNK 1979-1988[7]

Going crazy all day
The reason is one that
I do not share
I don't know what to do

Delirium
Delirium

—Andrey "Svin" Panov

1.1 Avtomaticheskie Udovletvoriteli and Andrey "Svin" Panov[8]

Aleksey "Ryba" Rybin: Nobody thought about Soviet power. Power was distant and we did not dare reach for it. Sometimes the power manifested itself on the black-and-white television and in the street. There you could see people mumbling, wandering meaninglessly, standing, sitting, smoking, and glancing sideways at each other, and they were the Soviet power themselves. But we had boiling hot young blood, and it was necessary to leave the house for the street, where you were met with thousands of eyes illuminated from inside with the same public opinion. On the streets, at work, in the subway, buses, cinemas, restaurants, cafeterias, near the beer

---

7 Because many of the people involved in Leningrad's early punk scene are either unavailable for interview or uninterested in remembering their past, many of the commentaries from this chapter have been taken from previous interviews. All interviews not conducted by the author have been properly footnoted and cited. All translations are the author's own unless otherwise stated.

8 *Avtomaticheskie Udovletvoriteli*—Automatic Satisfiers.

stands, Soviet power was pervasive, stupid, and pointless; escaping from the absurd rules was impossible.

Twenty years ago my country was like a giant theater of the absurd. But nobody seemed to be about changing anything. People simply followed the preset rules: get up before dawn, hop on the jumping bus, and squeeze between the warm, humid crowd exuding the same "after yesterday" smell. You had an hour to get to work and you were there until sunset. People knowingly engaged in this pointless and useless routine.

We were young, and this inkling of mindless work didn't exist in us. We listened to rock and roll and didn't give a shit about anything. We were lucky. We heard rock and roll a little earlier than the others and loved it more than others. Why it happened and why it all affected us differently—I don't know. Maybe it's some kind of pathology.[9]

Svin and Friends, 1970s–1980s, Yufit Collection

9 Aleksey Rybin in Ilya Stogoff, *Anarkhia v RF* (Saint Petersburg: Amfora, 2007), 19–20.

Yevgeny "Yufa" Yufit: There was no punk rock in 1976. I met Andrey "Svin" Panov on the street, and we had a lot of common interests, primarily the grotesqueness of Soviet society, black humor, and provoking innocent bystanders. One of our favorite provocations consisted of shoveling snow in the nude in front of glass windows. The police would show up, but we'd run in different directions, knowing all along that we were leaving tracks in the snow.

At that time, the only source of music information was a shortwave radio that I would use to listen to the BBC. In 1977 I heard a new group—the Sex Pistols— and I remember telling Svin, "In England there are idiots just like us!" Svin never played music, but he was an ideologue.

Yevgeny Titov: In 1976 Svin met Yufit. At that time Yufit was listening to "enemy" radio stations like the BBC and Radio Free Europe, despite the government's attempt to block those broadcasts. Yufit was trying to record the music too, so maybe it was him that told Svin about punk rock and the Sex Pistols.

I must say that at the time, in the late '70s–early '80s in the USSR, many "advanced" audiophiles listened to hard rock like Deep Purple, and considered it very progressive music. But it was a country where even the Beatles were banned, and of course, it was hard to imagine that people could be so disillusioned and fed up with traditional hard rock. Therefore, nobody really understood Yufit and Panov's passion for this "stupid and primitive" music. In the Soviet Union, even hard rock barely existed.

It was around 1978 when I entered the university. I studied one thing, and then another, and all along I was reading a lot in the libraries. I really liked the theory, you know, that every human being aspires toward justice and fairness, especially throughout youth. I was an idealist, so to say. I realized that whatever was said was a lie, and that it didn't correspond with reality, so I wanted to know what people in other countries thought about it. We didn't have access to much information back then.

Fedor "Begemot" Lavrov: I got into punk rock while listening to the radio. It was the BBC or Voice of America—I think it was the BBC. They used to run 20 minute shows once per week. They played all the top songs, and in between Paul McCartney and some other shit they played The Clash. In fact, I think the very first was "She's so Modern" by The Boomtown Rats. It started like "Ow ow ow ow ow!" and when I heard it I realized that there is music that sounds totally different, music that is really fast and expressive. The vocalists are not vocalists at all—they can shout, they can scream. The drummers were fantastic. The second song I heard was probably "Do You Wanna Dance" by the Ramones.

Anyway, Mezhdunarodnaia Panorama aired once a week, I think on Sundays, and one time in 1977 they had some video of London punks—it was totally outstanding![10] You have to understand that there was nothing even remotely related to punk in Russia back then.

Svin, 1989, Valery Potapov

---

10   *Mezhdunarodnaia Panorama*—International Panorama was a program that aired in the USSR, which, as the name suggests, updated Soviet citizens to a very tailored rendition of international culture and affairs. It is surprising that it showcased London punks in 1979, although not entirely unlikely by that time.

Olga Korol-Borodiuk: Andrey [Svin] heard that in England there were people walking around with pins on their clothing calling themselves "punks."

Leah Panova: Andrey's father Valery went abroad to Israel, probably sometime in 1973. People around him started becoming nasty because his father immigrated to an enemy country. His school teacher called him to the board in front of the whole class and said that his father was a traitor. I went to the director of the school and said, "How can you let her get away with that?" He responded, "I understand your concern Leah, but I cannot dismiss her for it. We can't tell a teacher what to say and what not to, and your husband, frankly, did immigrate to Israel…"

After dropping out of school, Andrey took a course on selling radios. It was here that his passion for music began.

Andrey "Svin" Panov: I had a neighbor upstairs, we lived in the same building since childhood. He told me that his friend or schoolmate was studying at the Serov Art School and that they had a band called Palata #6, three people.[11] They were also punks— having fun and so on. He said he would introduce me to them, and I had just left the theater institute and had nothing better to do; I was sitting in, playing guitar, and searching for a band. I had just stopped collecting music and instead began buying gear to play myself.

I started working at a home sound equipment store as a sales guy because I was a music fan. Tape recorders were very rare at that time, they were actually sold "under the table," and the salesmen earned a commission from every sale.

Everything began when Yufit brought Monozub, also known as Punker, to my work for a job. Monozub later became a cool band manager, but during Soviet times his dad held a post at

---

11 Serov Art School was later renamed as Rerich Art School, also known as Tavricheskaia Art School; *Palata #6* is also the title of a short story by the famous Russian writer Anton Chekhov (*Palata Nomer Shest*—"Ward no. 6.").

the Communist Party's Committee in Leningrad, in the department of ideology. Anyway, Monozub was the first to tell me about underground Soviet rock. One night he called me and said there were some bands playing illegally, writing good stuff. He asked, "Do you write lyrics?" I said I used to write something that I thought were lyrics. He asked, "Can you play?" I replied no. He said, "You must learn! It's very easy to form a band—we will find some guys and start!" [12]

Aleksey "Ryba" Rybin: To get rock records, you could only go to the *tolchok*, which was located in the store Yuny Tekhnik on Chervonnogo Kazachestva Street.[13] It was an important place in the USSR where you could buy real things during the Brezhnev era.

Anyway, I started going to that market after school—it was the only place where I could freely express my interests. Rather than thinking about the future, taking an example from your parents and building a career, I thought about one thing—how close am I to Saturday? Saturday was the day when I could look at and maybe even buy records.

I wanted to have so many albums but always lacked money. In addition to albums, I traded jeans, perfume, chewing gum, and cigarettes. It seems harmless now, but back then you could end up in prison for doing such things.

The hardest thing was to find the Soviet equivalent of a record with the same number of tracks as the Western original. Leningrad music fans in those years could recall from memory the names of all the songs on any album in the last 20 years. If the number of tracks on the record didn't match up, then they knew it was a fake right on the spot. Therefore, we preferred not to risk it and we changed the labels on the vinyl. We would put artificial breaks into records. For example, we changed the breaks on one

Stogoff, *Anarkhia v RF,* 28.
tolchok—flea market; *Yuny Tekhnik*—Young Technician.

record of Brezhnev speeches and we sold it as "Wish You Were Here."

I met Andrey through my classmate and business partner, Voldemar.

"It's so cool! He has so many disks at home," said Voldemar. He was referring to about 20 records Andrey had at home.

To meet such a man would have been a great honor, but time passed and Voldemar hadn't introduced me to him. Finally, he agreed to take me to meet Svin at his house on Kosmonavtov Street on the sixth floor. Voldemar rang the doorbell, and a granny opened the door. She was short with grey hair.

"Are you looking for Andrey? I'll call him."

She stepped back and closed the door. We stayed on the stairs, I looked at Voldemar and we agreed to wait.

Andrey Panov a.k.a. "Lake" [Svin's first nickname] came out a minute later. He was tall, long haired, a moderately thick guy. His stomach made him look like a calm and self-respected person. His glance was mysterious, but at the same time thought-provoking. His face really was like Greg Lake—one of my favorite guitar players—and his style was practically the same: slim jeans, wasted denim shirt. The jeans were worn, labeled, and interestingly cut. I quickly realized that they weren't homemade, as Voldemar's were.

That day we didn't see his collection. The conversation took place on the staircase and it was about things that were far from my vocabulary. I really preferred the vinyl collection over the financial schemes Voldemar and he were concocting. After all, Voldemar only presented me as a music lover, and Andrey smiled thickly and shook my hand.

Finally, after I stole polyethylene for covering disks for him, Andrey allowed me to go inside to look at the collection. In his room there were giant speakers 35 AS—the largest speakers at the time. There were also power Odissey (the best Soviet amplifiers) and a reel-to-reel Maiak (wildly prestigious in those years).

Chicago, Blood, Sweat and Tears, Kansas, Bachman-Turner Overdrive, Iggy Pop, Sex Pistols, Rush, Genesis, Creedence Clearwater Revival, Black Sabbath, and God knows what else. At first glance it seemed like a completely random set of records, it was difficult to identify any single genre, although in fact the answer was simple: he liked to listen to good music.

Andrey immediately assembled a huge collection of punk rock vinyl. In less than a year his collection became probably the best in the country. He listened to music that even music lovers and collectors had no idea about.

We always went to the tolchok together, but Andrey always saw the disks that we didn't see—Iggy Pop, Public Image Limited, The Clash, XTC, Patti Smith, The Ramones—all of these records I heard first on the expensive Panov stereo system.[14]

Svin (center) and Friends, 1979, Yufit Collection

14 This is a condensed version of a response in Stogoff, *Anarkhia v RF*, 10–18.

Yevgeny Titov: The first Sex Pistols record appeared at Svin's almost immediately, as it was released at the end of 1978. Before that he already had an early Iggy Pop record, and one from Public Image Limited. These groups and performers had a very big impact, but he considered Iggy Pop the best performer.

Olga Korol-Borodiuk: Andrey created a group, and to paraphrase the Sex Pistols he named it Avtomaticheskie Udovletvoriteli, in other words, he named it the same thing. But he had no goal; he did it just for fun. He said that everyone wants to be the best, the coolest, and that he would create a group that will be the worst of the worst.

The uniqueness of the group lies in the fact that it passed through a huge number of musicians, including those who have become rock superstars in our country. For example, Viktor Tsoi started with Svin, playing bass.[15]

Aleksey "Ryba" Rybin: The composition of the first Russian punk band looked strange. The main participants were three: Svin, Cook, and Poster. On the road they were joined by Tsoi, Oleg Valinsky, Pinochet, Punker (who at this point was already trying to be a serious producer), and Andrey "Malenky Diusha" Mikhaylov, later the lead guitarist of Obyekt Nasmeshek.[16]

Igor "Pinochet" Pokrovsky: I don't have any relation to the group Avtomaticheskie Udovletvoriteli, neither does Rybin or Tsoi. Panov spread those lies for publicity when Kino was at the height of its popularity.[17] That's just not how it was. Only that different people gathered at Svin's to drink and listen to music, but that doesn't mean they were all members of Avtomaticheskie Udovletvoriteli.

Andrey "Svin" Panov: Tsoi began rehearsing with my little project Avtomaticheskie Udovletvoriteli. Mike Naumenko recorded *Duraki i Gastroli* with us.[18] Mike played, Rybin, and Tsoi, although Mike denies it now. All the songs were mine, only one was Mike's and one was Rybin's.

With great confidence Mike and us went to Moscow. Artemy Troitsky organized it all. He asked us whether it was true

---

15 Viktor Tsoi was one of late Soviet Russia's most popular singer/songwriters. He founded the band Kino which acquired international fame in the 1980s. He died tragically in a car collision in 1990.

16 *Obyekt Nasmeshek*—Object of Ridicule.

17 In the mid '80s Viktor Tsoi and Aleksey Rybin started their own New Wave band, Kino, which became one of the first and biggest iconic rock bands in Soviet and then Russian culture. Tsoi is still remembered as a national hero and rock icon.

18 Mike Naumenko was the frontman of famous rock band *Zoopark* (Zoo); *Duraki i Gastroli*—Fools and Tours.

that in Leningrad someone was already playing punk, and Mike said it was true and handed the phone to me.

Aleksey "Ryba" Rybin: Troitsky led his own perestroika in the late 1970s. Before, rock and roll was the music of the lower class. Artemy also led an attack on the upper strata of Soviet society—the so-called intellectuals, the press, TASS, the Union of Journalists, the radio, and television.[19] He organized small underground concerts at home and brought the music recordings to representatives of Moscow's elite, who could have caused him trouble.

Andrey "Svin" Panov: The winter of 1979 we went to Moscow with a large company to play gigs. But Moscow is a small city—by the time we were there people already heard about us. New people! New music! And we gave a concert in some apartment, and then in some club. When we returned to Leningrad people started to treat us differently. Until that point everyone regarded us as idiots. Now it became clear that people were talking about us in Moscow.[20]

Artemy Troitsky: [Svin] had appeared without warning at our apartment one night in December around midnight. He was dressed like a character from a Sex Pistols poster, except that his outfit was a Russian-winterized version. I remember a mass of safety pins and a loud tie hanging out of a grimy coat. He said he was a punk (that much was evident) and produced for inspection a reel of tape wrapped in cellophane. "This is our bullet," he said. To be more precise, it was an apartment tape of the group Avtomaticheskie Udovletvoriteli, in which Svin was vocalist and songwriter. Again the mid-tempo, heavy fuzzbox guitar sound, plus a vocal fighting its way through an over-abundance of saliva in the oral cavity. Their keynote number went like this:

---

19 TASS—Telegraph Agency of the Soviet Union—had a monopoly on the collection and distribution of domestic and international news for all radio, television, and newspapers.
20 Stogoff, *Anarkhia v RF*, 70–71. Svin almost certainly made a mistake on the year of this trip. According to Troitsky and other who accompanied him, the initial visit occurred in 1980.

Punks have appeared in Leningrad,
I don't know whether they're people or monsters,
They dance the twist and the pogo,
Show us the road to Rotten!

Like other Soviet "punks," Svin had no ties to the working class and hardly qualified as a street kid—his father was a choreographer, his mother a ballerina. He had grown up, in his own words, "surrounded by half-naked women." I liked him more than his songs; he was an odd figure, not without a certain twisted charm and not too bad a singer. After hearing my critique of his tape, Svin said that his music was a hundred times heavier "live" and that I had to come to one of their concerts. Thus came about my invitation to his birthday celebration, which promised to be a punk rock happening.

The party took place in a dingy restaurant called the Bow, or the Stern, or something like that.[21] The entire Leningrad punk commonwealth was in attendance—about 20 citizens, alongside an equal number of curious travelers. Avtomaticheskie Udovletvoriteli quickly proved that they couldn't play at all. What's worse, they were equally short on energy. Their sluggish anarchy on stage made an incongruous combination with the aggressiveness they showed toward the audience by spitting from all sides and smashing all tableware at hand. Svin was an able and improvising showman (from the School of Utter Repulsiveness).

The restaurant manager, properly appalled by such a rowdy crowd, hurried to close up, and so the happening continued in a brightly lit café somewhere nearby.[22]

Aleksey "Ryba" Rybin: The talks ended, and Svin and company gained an invitation to play in Moscow. Where it would be, how it would happen, and whether it would even happen at all was up in the

21 All other participants remember the event as Andrey Tropillo's birthday party at the café Trum, where Viktor Tsoi was recognized by Akvarium's frontman Boris Grebenshchikov as a talented musician.
22 Artemy Troitsky, *Back in the USSR: The True Story of Rock in Russia* (Winchester, MA: Faber and Faber, 1988), 68–70.

air. This wasn't also about payment. It was absolutely a promotional tour, touting the first punks in the country—advertising was needed. The trip was organized for Saturday and Sunday because everyone was afraid of skipping work, and after it was all decided everyone began to think, "Who will go, and who will play what?" Definitely those who considered themselves the Avtomaticheskie Udovletvoriteli: Svin, Cook, and Poster. The others had no title, but many wanted to go. As a result, Svin said that he would resolve the problem of the overnight stop on his own and invited everyone who was willing to keep him company.

Early Friday morning I hit the road to the Moscow railway station for tickets. To defend our place on the trip, I bought them for myself, Tsoi, and Punker. Avtomaticheskie Udovletvoriteli told us not to worry about them; they would figure it out themselves.

We had a free day that Friday. We went to do a dress rehearsal, bought dry wine, and began to figure out what our repertoire would be. Then we bought more dry wine. Back then the wine costs only 1 ruble and 7 kopeks… In extreme cases 1 ruble and 17 kopeks, and if you wanted the expensive stuff it was 1 ruble and 37 kopeks.

Then we decided who would play what. There were many musicians and everyone wanted to show off. Somehow we resolved the issue, and at this point Punker came with a whole case of beer. We decided to relax a bit and listen to music, and spend some time gaining strength before the trip.[23]

Artemy Troitsky: [After the birthday party] Boris Grebenshchikov (in whose flat I was staying) handed me two documents to read entitled "Proposal For a Rock Club" and "Charter Of The Rock Club." [24] There, in the most official language imaginable, I read a point-by-point outline of goals, tasks, rights and obligations, privileges and violations, hierarchy, and functions for the newly-proposed

23 Stogoff, *Anarkhia v RF*, 71–72.
24 Known as the "Grandfather of Russian Rock" Boris Grebenshchikov led the classic Russian rock band Akvarium from 1972 to the present.

organization. The word "rock" appeared infrequently and seemed preposterous in such a context. Take this phrase, for instance: "The Rock Club sets itself the goal of attracting youth to a wide range of amateur creative activities, of raising the cultural level of visual presentation and ideological artistic content in such performances, and likewise of portraying and propagandizing the best examples of national and international music in a given genre." These documents indicated that yet another attempt (the sixth to date) was being made in Leningrad to form an official organization for the unofficial groups.

A couple of years later the president of the Rock Club, Nikolay Mikhaylov, would explain the motives in this way: "At the beginning of 1981 the number of concerts in the city had sharply decreased, since the groups had no permission for official performances, while the city administration had become fairly effective at restraining the informal sessions. But there were over 50 known bands in Leningrad and a colossal, unfulfilled craving for concerts and socializing…"

Leningrad is only half the size of Moscow, and despite its refinement it is somehow provincial. Leningrad is more unitary; everything there is in plain view. The end result is that in Leningrad a single artistic community of rock musicians and other bohemians developed.[25]

Andrey "Malenky Diusha" Mikhaylov: We all jumped on the night train to Moscow without tickets. We really went there with a sense of adventure, and eventually the carriage supervisors figured out that we didn't pay for our tickets, and they were chasing us all around the train. Poster and I got so drunk that we managed to lock ourselves in one of the carriage toilets, where we slept and stayed until the end of the journey. When we woke up and opened the door, a bunch of angry people with their toothbrushes and towels in hand were standing and waiting for us to get out.

Yevgeny Titov: Punk rock in the early '80s in Leningrad was a subculture of togetherness. It was a fairly large company of people who liked spending time together, liked having fun. Everyone did not understand this "fun," and the music was generally not the principle aspect—some of our friends did not even listen to it at all. In our company, in addition to musicians, included some avant-garde artists and political thinkers. We were lovers of film and photography. We all went around town fooling around beating each other with sticks, and we had friends who filmed it all.

Svin and Avtomaticheskie Udovletvoriteli, 1988 Zinii Stadion 6th festival' of Leningrad Rock Club, photo by Valentina Baranovskii

1.2 The Leningrad Rock Club

Yevgeny Titov: The Rock Club was created under the attempt of the authorities to better control the underground rock scene. One of the most famous groups in Leningrad was Rossiyane, and they traveled across the country, where they garnered a wide audience despite official attempts to avoid that.[26] The government could not tolerate an independent band gaining such a following without official approval. The alternative was to seize everything, or bring it under control, which they could do under the pretext of "hooliganism" (if you walked down the street with abnormal clothes, they'd brand you a hooligan).

Anyway, bands like Rossiyane were getting bigger, and probably the central organ decided that it was easier to take control of the process. They allocated a concert hall, brought in acts, and imposed strict rules, all enforced by the Komsomol.[27]

Viktor Sologub: Two parallel musical lives used to exist. One involved official concert organizations (Lenkontsert, Moskontsert, etc), in which musicians drew a salary and played in the style of what is now called "pop music." The other treated music as a hobby. People worked somewhere (we were engineers, for example), and composed songs and played shows in our spare time. Usually for free.

Joanna Stingray: I had asked Boris [Grebenshchikov] on my first trip if there were any women rockers, and he said unfortunately not, that Russia was still old-fashioned. Toward the late 80's there was a singer in Moscow, Zhanna Arguzaria, who was very cool. I also think women didn't have any time. They had to have jobs, do all the shopping, and take care of the kids and their husbands. Underground rockers didn't get paid so there was no sense in

---

26 *Rossiyane*—(Ethnic) Russians.
27 *Komsomol*—A Communist Party youth organization.

women doing it. Of course, you had a few "official" singers like Alla Pugachova.

The Rock Club in Leningrad was the place where "unofficial bands" were allowed to play. It was run by this great guy, Nikolay Mikhaylov, who all the rockers liked, even though they all knew he had to report to the KGB. They understood that Nikolay walked a fine line in trying to help the rockers and keep them happy, as well as adhering to what the KGB wanted him to do. Many of the bands I was friends with (Boris from Akvarium, the guys from Kino, Strannye Igry, and Alisa) were contacted by the KGB.[28] Some of the guys would just hang up when they called, and some like Afrika got pulled from a concert and questioned when he had pink hair. I was grabbed by two men leaving a Rock Club concert and taken to a downstairs room and questioned. Foreigners were not supposed to be at these "unofficial" concerts and they wanted to know who brought me there.

Fedor "Begemot" Lavrov: Rubinstein Street 13, a narrow street in the old city, pretty close to Nevsky Prospekt and the legendary

Leningrad Rock Club crowd, 1986, Joanna Stingray

28 *Strannye Igry*—Strange Games.

Saigon Café, a corner down from the Prospekt.[29] The "theater of amateurs" (Leningrad Rock Club) was located in this old building with an entrance from the street with some back doors in the court. There were restroom windows looking out to the court and a comfortable fire safety metal ladder—or maybe it was a metal roof—some kind of construction underneath the windows. Anyway, the windows to the restroom were the main entrance for punks. Free of charge. When I went there the very first time, I didn't know about that. I went to the theater ticket booth, bought one, and went in.

Entering was not easy; people were crowding the street in front of the building, everywhere. The police were trying to make them move along. I felt excited and nervous when I entered the hall and saw old-fashioned decorations at the back of the stage. The club apparently had good sound equipment and the speakers were rather loud and clean. The entire hall was filled with rows of theater chairs—there was no dance floor at all. I don't remember what the gig was. Probably it was Rossiyane, and maybe some other hard rock bands like Pepel, Picnic, Strannye Igry.[30] The majority of the audience consisted of long haired hippies. Among them were seen Komsomoltsy dressed so casually, and informers dressed up in brand new jeans that looked so out of place on them, as if their clothes were just purchased from Berezka, the only shop that sold jeans[31] (It was a shop closed to common citizens. Only those who went abroad and had vouchers to buy foreign things and food could buy from there. Speculators would buy things there and then make money by selling to those who were not permitted to shop there, but could nevertheless afford buying expensive "deficit" things). Disguised agents were in line with the police and would go up and down the rows asking the audience not to jump, not to dance, and not to destroy the chairs. Those who were unable to control their emotions would be taken out under arrest. Usually by the end of

---

29 *Prospekt* simply means street or avenue here. Nevsky Prospekt is the main artery of St. Petersburg.
30 *Pepel*—Ash.
31 *Komsomoltsy* were boy members of the *Komsomol* (see footnote 26); *Berezka*—Birch.

the concert the crowd went crazy—the first rows jumped up on the chairs, and the police were unable to catch everyone so they would grab the most active. Wet and exhausted, but totally happy, attendees went out in the street where a police bus, already almost filled, waited with the arrested "hooligans." Bigger gigs required more buses and the police reaction was equal to the activity of the music lovers. The police sometimes even arrested musicians and "legal members of the Rock Club." Then their colleagues would go to "speak" with the officers or KGBists to help them get released.

Viktor Sologub: Before the Leningrad Rock Club there were Doma Kultury, where we could use instruments (usually German and Czech synths and guitars), which were bought for the youth.[32] To us it seemed like those instruments were terrible, because we knew about the existence of brands like Gibson and Fender. We dreamed of them.

Yevgeny Titov: In order to gain admittance to the club, you had to first register your group by becoming a "candidate for membership in the Rock Club." You had to provide a full list of members with full passport details—where you were born, where you are registered, where you work, education, and contact information. Then you had to bring six typewritten copies of your lyrics, so that they could be studied. This process typically took about a month. If they were consistent with and not contrary to official morality, then they would each get a "permitted" stamp, plus the date and signature of the person who authorized the lyrics. Not everyone was accepted. They could just say "you're not ready, come later, fix this."

Dmitry Levkovsky: I came to the club in 1984 as the manager of Strannye Igry. In order to play at the club you had to bring your entire group and lyrics. The censor was a woman, who ultimately approved the lyrics or not. For Narodnoe Opolchenie it was

32 *Doma Kultury*—Houses of Culture.

impossible.[33] We were one of the last bands to join the club. If we didn't get in, we would find somewhere else to play—apartments, the street, festivals, other cities.

Tatyana Motovilova: I, frankly, do not remember there being a lot of girls—just punks, and punk musicians, I don't know. I don't think that the Komsomol in any way influenced the sex of punk rock. In fact, I believe the Rock Club would not have refused women, if there had been any. It seems to me that even if we consider the state of World Rock or World Punk Rock at the time, then there were not so many women's groups. Apparently, rock is for the stronger sex.

I'm sure if there was a worthy women's band (moreover if they played punk) Nikolay Mikhaylov certainly would have accepted them. Maybe he would have refused them only if the lyrics were too political or anti-Soviet. But in terms of punk rock music, I don't think the Rock Club necessarily scared anyone; you only had to play well.

Norodnoe Opolchenie, 1988 Leningrad Rock Club advertisement

---

33 *Narodnoe Opulchenie*—People's Militia.

For example, my husband played in Narodnoe Opolchenie, and they entered the Rock Club under Brezhnev's regime. They had a lyric that went, "There will be no more Brezhnev!" Nikolay said, "Well, that's weird," so a recommended variant was: "Brezhnev will be coming soon!" And even though he admitted this change was not interesting, the club took them anyway.

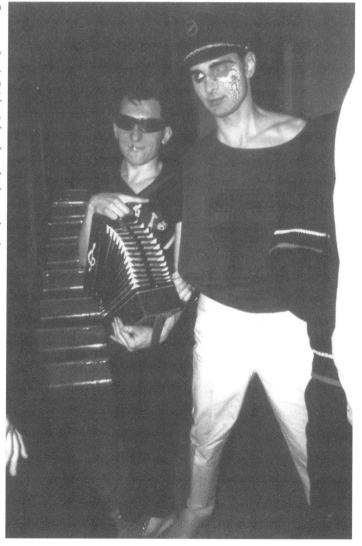

Strannye Igry's Grisha Solugub and Viktor Solugub, 1986, Joanna Stingray

Dmitry Buchin: Fans in the '80s were practically identical: hippies, rockers, children from disadvantageous families, artists and creative people, many drinkers and consumers of various things. There were KGB informers and everybody knew it, and they knew that everybody knew about them.

Yury Sobolev: I have a complicated attitude toward the Leningrad Rock Club. There were rumors that it was created by special services in order to establish control over independent musicians. Management had to write periodic reports on their work, and they created difficulties for unwanted bands. And I also thought that those administrators, who had been approved for those positions and were really enthusiastic about the unofficial music community, were akin to double agents.

Artemy Troitsky: The Rock Club's organizational structure was a three-tiered hierarchy. The base of the pyramid was the general membership, whose ranks included a few hundred musicians, plus artists, photographers, collectors, organizers, and others. Once each year the members's general meeting elected a council, made up of seven of the more esteemed and active club members, headed by a president.

Concerts began in the spring of 1981 and were a great success, but this didn't mean that the Rock Club has solved all the problems for everyone. For one thing, groups could not receive a fee for their performances; such was the official doctrine of the "amateurs" until the mid-eighties. Secondly, the Rock Club had no equipment and no space of its very own. The DST hall at 13 Rubinstein Street had to be shared with a theater group and other amateur cultural organizations, and these rather underprivileged conditions forced the Rock Club to walk the fine line between pure enthusiasm and traditional machinations employed previously for arranging "sessions."

Thirdly, the liberalism of the club's curators didn't extend to the more extreme bands in town. Svin and company were left out, as was Bugle Call, a boring group that sang banal songs on evangelical themes and enjoyed special favor with the BBC and Voice of America. As for Avtomaticheskie Udovletvoriteli, the opinion of the Rock Club's council was that they simply couldn't play, and in fact many weak bands (not just "punks") were denied a place in the Rock Club on the same grounds.[34]

Oleg Garkusha: You heard about a show from word-of-mouth mostly. There were no posters, and concerts initially took place in the [Leningrad] Rock Club, sometimes in culture centers like Dvorets Kultury Krupskoy, Dvorets Kultury Gorkogo, etc.[35] All of these concerts were like a celebration for us; we made arrangements, met at metro stations, and so on. I still remember a concert of Strannye Igry. There was a strange guy, Igor "Pinochet" Pokrovsky, and for that concert he bought a tailcoat, but he never made it to the concert because he was arrested somewhere at the railway station.

Fedor "Begemot" Lavrov: I saw Rossiyane in the Leningrad Rock Club in the 1983. But gig after gig they became less cool for me. They played the same songs that would have been cool at the end of the '70s. But by 1983 I had started my own band and recorded our first punk rock tracks. Rossiyane left—the old hippie farts. And then Ordanovsky disappeared.[36] I still think he was the best, the coolest of the Leningrad Rock Club members, the most dangerous for the system during the late '70s and early '80s. This is why it's possible that he could have been killed, or paid well and allowed to leave the country with no way to show his face anymore. But he disappeared for real and no one knows where he went.

34 Troitsky, *Back in the USSR*, 74–75.
35 *Dvorets Kultury Krupskoy*—Krupskaia Palace of Culture; *Dvorets Kultury Gorkogo*—Gorky Palace of Culture.
36 Georgy Ordanovsky was the leader of Rossiyane.

Dmitry Buchin: With punk groups it was mostly studio work, no concerts or tours, as concert activities were strictly supervised by the KGB. If some venue made a punk gig, then the organizers of the event, those responsible for the premises and equipment, faced a series of problems.

Valery Morozov: Concerts were perceived as rallies, not as shows. Unlike in the West, what we did was not perceived as a concert. Hence, we garnered a lot of attention from the authorities (the Leningrad Rock Club was overseen by Department 11 of the KGB).[37] To them, punk rock represented something unpredictable and uncontrollable.

Artemy Troitsky: Of course for such a great man, great artist who naturally has an uncompromising attitude, like Svin, it was wrong to be part of the Leningrad Rock Club... But he did want to join.[38]

Yevgeny Titov: Svin never wore underwear—just pants over his naked body. He wore things until there were holes in them. For example, when his asshole showed through his pants, he repaired them with a sewing machine. He loved to take his clothes off at concerts; he would undo the belt and a pair of buttons on his pants, making it look as if they accidentally slipped down.

Nikolay Mikhaylov: Neither Avtomaticheskie Udovletvoriteli or Narodnoe Opolchenie could join the club because of ideological reasons. The lyrics were too depressing or aggressive. It was impossible to soften their lyrics.[39]

Vadim Kurylev: Soviet propaganda tried to portray Western-style punk rock as a social and musical distortion, and they portrayed

---

37 Department 11 was the Advisor's Department (Informants).
38 "Svin 50" YouTube video, 5:55, Posted by Sergey Shutov, October 27, 2012, https://www.youtube.com/watch?v=olk6FvrRAbk
39 "Svin 50", 6:10.

punks as socially dangerous psychopaths. The fact that there were left-wing punk bands like the Clash, few people knew or heard about. But everyone knew that punk star Sid Vicious sported a swastika.

It seems like the leaders of the Leningrad Rock Club objectively understood the real point of punk rock, but they had to maintain some sort of balance to avoid KGB agitation. After all, the authorities could at any time ban a concert or festival, or even completely close the Rock Club.

Fedor "Begemot" Lavrov: I knew the Rock Club was just another Soviet organ, just like a Komsomol organization—the same means to control. I tried to enter the club in early 1983. I brought lyrics that Aleks Ogoltely and I made to their censor, and she told me that we were "not yet ready to enter." She said that my writing had a Maiakovsky-esque style, and yeah, I sincerely did like futurist writers, but they were considered a wrongful means of artistic expression, or so we were taught at school. She said, "You have to improve," "Still much work to do," and "Come back when you're ready." Then Aleks persuaded me to go to a solicitor, Boris Grebenshchikov.[40] I took a couple of records, among which there was a cover of one of his songs called "600 Prekrasnykh Dam" (600 instead of the original 10, because the word for 600 [*shestsot*] was a Leningrad punk slang word, meaning everything from "cool" to "nonsense").[41] The cover was rude and Boris didn't like it, as I guessed. What made me feel sick was that he almost completely repeated the same words that the censor told me, "You need to improve," "Still much work to do," and "Come back..." with the same manner and voice.

---

40 Boris Grebenshchikov was the frontman of Akvarium, but for the LRC he was like a consultant. He was one of the people that aspiring musicians needed to get approval from. With his approval, Boris would "lobby" the club to allow admittance.
41 *600 Prekrasnykh Dam*—600 Pretty Women.

Timothy W. Ryback: Providing a refreshing alternative to the mundane concerts of the professional vocal instrumental ensembles, Leningrad's Rock Club became the most popular concert venue in the city. On some evenings, as many as twelve hundred rock fans gathered outside the door at 13 Rubinstein Street in the hope of seeing bands like Akvarium, Kino, Televizor, and Zoopark. The newspaper *Trud*, in a deprecating review of a concert by Akvarium, Kino, Zoopark, and Mify, provides some insight into the reasons for the Rock Club's popularity.[42] "The ensembles sang songs with obviously depressing texts, played on wailing guitars, and pounded away on drums," Trud reported with obvious distaste on January 31, 1985, "while the young people threw themselves about like wild men." Despite the relatively tolerant atmosphere that prevailed at Leningrad's Rock Club, songs were still subject to censorship, and the concerts were patrolled by hefty babushkas wearing red armbands.[43]

Joanna Stingray: I did interview and see Narodnoe Opolchenie, and I was amazed at how similar they were to punk bands in the West. They were wild, and while I was filming them they broke glass, cut themselves, and just smeared blood all over and continued playing.

Jim Gallagher of the Chicago Tribune: The ideological watchdogs have been barking up a storm about how soft and self-centered Soviet youth have become, and they're putting much of the blame on the growing popularity of rock music.

The most menacing note was sounded by Sergei Tsvigun, the No. 2 man in the secret police, "The passion for pop music and Western way of life threatens to alienate Soviet youth from the communist ethos," the KGB official contended recently in this country's principal ideological journal, *Kommunist*.

---

42 *Trud*—The Work; *Mify*—The Myths.
43 Timothy W. Ryback, *Rock Around the Bloc: A History of Rock Music in Eastern Europe and the Soviet Union* (New York: Oxford University Press, 1990), 213.

That same week an article in *Izvestia*, the government daily, described rock and disco music as "bourgeois propaganda" imposed on vulnerable Soviet youth.

"What lies behind these musical stereotypes?" the article asked. "Nothing less than bourgeois mass culture which is aiming at the spiritual devastation of our youth and the assertion of an alien ideology."[44]

Andrey Mashnin: After moving from Taimyr to Leningrad I started studying at the Hydro-Meteorological Institute. There were eight of us living in one dorm, and we always listened to tapes there. In Leningrad, one could attend concerts, unlike in Siberia. I studied at the institute for two years, and that's when the Leningrad Rock Club appeared. I started going to rock gigs—it was a breakthrough for me, and in the meantime I was taught how to play the guitar with several chords, which helped a lot later.

Over seven to eight years of listening to the Leningrad Rock Club bands, I understood that I would never be as they were. All the niches of Russian rock were occupied, and every style already had its stars. I didn't want to repeat someone, and suddenly I heard this totally different music. It was knocking on my head as heavily as hard rock once did, but it was very different. I fell in love with it instantly, and there rose a wave of people like me in St. Petersburg. I thought this style was exactly what was needed to replace the old boring and dry sounds of Russian rock. The naïvety and stupid smugness.

Fedor "Begemot" Lavrov: The Rock Club did not inspire me to do anything else but create my own studio at home and never seek assistance or support.

Some friends and I just gathered in my small room where I lived and jammed. There was no audience there. Our first band,

44 Gallagher was the *Tribune's* Moscow Correspondent. Jim Gallagher, "Soviets blame hard rock for 'soft' youth," *Chicago Tribune*, November 1, 1981. Sec. 3, p. 1, accessed September 6, 2015, http://archives.chicagotribune.com/1981/11/01/page/39

Rezinovy Rikoshet, recorded four songs maybe, and we didn't even practice.[45] We would just get together and decide to have two verses, three choruses, and one solo, and somehow we would stop the song. It took us one day to record an album, and the next day we would bring the record copies to our friends and ask them if it was okay.

I think Otdel Samoiskorenenia released only two albums and one compilation, and meanwhile there were two or three albums from Narodnoe Opolchenie.[46]

When I created an Otdel Samoiskorenenia record, I showed it to the last drummer I played with. He played with Narodnoe Opolchenie and Otdel Samoiskorenenia, and he had some hippies taking drugs in his apartment; there was a lot of sketchy shit going on there. So when the KGB got ahold of the Otdel Samoiskorenenia record, he was more scared than all of us. He said someone stole this record from him—there were always people coming and going—many things could have been stolen.

For the KGB, this self-recording punk was an activity that was not allowed at all—making records at home, and then delivering them to different people. They heard anti-Soviet lyrics and some other things on the records. We even had some artwork on the tapes, and there were a lot of things on that as well. We were not the only band to be brought in for investigation, though. Most of the Leningrad Rock Club, like Akvarium (at least the leaders from the band) were invited there as well.

Timothy W. Ryback: In 1983, conservatives in the Kremlin, weary of excesses of rock bands and their fans, decided to clean up the Soviet rock scene, which had run rampant under the lax ideological controls of Brezhnev's waning years. On January 25, 1982, Mikhail Suslov, Brezhnev's ideological spokesman, died. Eight months later, on November 10, 1982, Brezhnev himself passed away. As Yuri Andropov advanced to the party head and Konstantin Chernenko

---

45 *Rezinovy Rikoshet*—The Rubber Ricochet.
46 *Otdel Samoiskorenenia*—Department of Self Eradication.

emerged as the moving force on ideological issues, anti-rock forces rallied. At the party plenum on June 14, 1983, the seventy-one-year-old Chernenko warned against laxness on the ideological front. Chernenko observed that the West was "launching increasingly massive attacks" in an attempt to "poison the minds of the Soviet people."[47]

Aleks "Ogoltely" Strogachev: They were ready to put me in jail for hooliganism, for the rude words in our songs. They said, "We're gonna tell the prisoners about you, so that you will get fucked up your ass, in a year you will straighten up."

I said, "Forgive me guys, can I bend my knees and kiss your boots?" They were shocked. "I can stand on my hands and knees and you can fuck me right here, never mind in jail!" Shortly after saying this they kicked me out! Hahaha!

Down the street Feddy [Begemot] was waiting for me, dressed in underpants and a t-shirt with the red star painted on it, a swastika on top of the star, and a saying "no law for fools" on the back. We went away and immediately got caught by the police again. They took us to an office on Fontanka embankment, let me go, and said, "Go fuck yourself, but the fool is staying!"

After that, Feddy stopped writing songs. It was real shitty.[48]

Fedor "Begemot" Lavrov: At the interrogation, they had a box of my things, which they slammed on the table and asked, "What the hell is this?" They had one guy walking behind me with a heavy book—trying to scare me—the other was playing the good cop.

As punishment, I was forced to sign an agreement that I would never have a band of that kind, or write lyrics of that kind anymore. I would never shake the basic establishment of the country. I signed it, of course—what else could I do? I was facing jail time.

47 Timothy W. Ryback, *Rock Around the Bloc,* 218.
48 "Otdel Samoiskorenenia/Department of Self eradication/Interview" Youtube video, Posted by "Begemotion Records" March 17, 2015, https://www.youtube.com/watch?v=MiG0DDO2Brg.

A celebration is coming—the city is pretty
People happily hurry to rallies.
Standing still, setting a good example
Voting for peace and responses.

Reagan and Andropov
Fucked the whole of Europe
Reagan and Andropov
From behind.

For what reason
Why the fuck
Do we have
This military monarchy?[49]

Dmitry Buchin: One day I went to Mike Naumenko's work (he worked as a janitor at a furniture factory), and we drank wine and talked. I was careless enough to call Feddy Begemot, I think this was in 1985. In the conversation I said something like "Aleks and the Militia [Opolchenie]," and Mike grabbed me and took me to the street where he sternly asked me to never mention "Aleks and the Militia" and to never call Begemot on the telephone. I admit that Mike could have been wiretapped…

Dmitry Levkovsky: Aleks Ogoltely and Svin were just about making punk a fun twist on reality. Of course the message was anarchy and disorder, and they succeeded at testing the order and mocking personal freedom (or lack thereof). It was a sharp social satire, and that's why the cops hated the group.

---

49 "Responses" is translated from the Russian *Otvetnye mery*, which was a term used to describe the deployment of Russian rockets. This is from the 1983 version of "Voennaia Monarkhia" (Military Monarchy) by Otdel Samoiskorenenia. Lyrics written by Fedor "Begemot" Lavrov.

Fedor "Begemot" Lavrov, 1984, after returning from the army, Alexandra Lavrov

Oleg Garkusha: Well, it was fun. They were arresting us all the time. In Maiakovskaia station there was a room with a sign on the door that said "Militia," and I remember after having arrested me the officers started bragging, "And right before you we had Grebenshchikov here." If a person didn't look like a normal Soviet person, if he was wearing short trousers, pointed shoes, a black tie, black glasses, he was always arrested. We used to make excuses by saying that these were our mother's glasses, uncle's tie, etc. In their opinion we were a disgrace to Soviet society.

1.3 *"Perestroika Punk"*

Grazhdanskaia Oborona, Moscow House of Culture 1988-89, Lev Goncharov

Bill Keller of the *New York Times*: "The Young Communist League, increasingly maligned by officials for losing the interest of young citizens, seized on rock concerts and discotheques as a way to revive attendance.

   The result has been a proliferation of rock on radio and television, and in concerts and films. Rock concerts—ranging from mainstream pop to screaming heavy metal—are available almost any night in Moscow. Amateur groups have begun to tour, and have been invited to audition for Melodiya, the state record monopoly.[50]

   The freedom is not complete, however.

   Bands are usually required to submit their lyrics for approval before major concerts. Overtly political material and sexual innuendo are generally forbidden, and rarely tried."[51]

---

50 State owned record company Melodia held a monopoly on the record industry in the Soviet Union from 1964-1989. It was primarily used to print and distribute classical music and other state-approved singers/songwriters. A few rock bands managed to release from *Melodia* Records, including *Mashina Vremeni* (Time Machine) and *Avtograf* (Autograph). The label also re-released many Western musicians.
51 Bill Keller, "For Soviet Rock Musicians, Glasnost is Angst," *The New York Times*, April 9, 1987.

47

Viktor Sologub: After 1986 the scene exploded with both good and bad bands. It's referred to as "perestroika rock."

Natalya Terekhova: [During and after perestroika] there arose girls playing and in bands. [For perestroika] I cannot speak for Zhenskaia Bolezn, only Lamia.[52] Women musicians were just not liked by men, who thought that such a woman was not suitable for family, and male musicians (from wild jealousy or envy for rock, maybe) didn't like musical women. Women in rock were given a maximum role as a vocalist. All the other women were not registered by men.

For example, they thought that a women's place was with children, in the kitchen. "Have you ever seen a woman playing the guitar?" Well, as a result men didn't want such women. Neither in groups, nor in marriage.

[I formed Lamia] not just because—I wanted to play guitar. Nobody wanted to take me as a guitarist, so I assembled my own group. We didn't seek to prove anything, did not play music or rock. We did our favorite thing simply for ourselves.

Artemy Troitsky: The spring of perestroika blossomed slowly but steadily. The most visible changes occurred in the fields of economy, public relations, and the political and government line-up. The experiments and reforms of industry, trade, and agriculture started to happen; the papers became far more interesting and informative. There was the new trend of glasnost, dozens of officials and ministers were replaced by younger ones. The whole style of relations between the people and the establishment was now more open and democratic.

Not only social criticism, but also such economic values as profit now became highly regarded, and the commercial potential of rock was obvious. Rock could help the cultural institutions survive under the new profit-conscious economic policy.

---

52 *Zhenskaia Bolezn*—Women's Disease. Natalya didn't join *Zhenskaia Bolezn* until the mid 1990s.

The monumental anti-alcohol campaign meant not only prohibition and various restrictions, but also advocating some "sober" alternatives for the drinking youngsters, like clubs, discos, concerts, and fan associations, etc. Here again, rock was the inevitable alternative.[53]

Obyekt Nasmeshek's Zhenya Fedorov, Rikoshet, 1986, Joanna Stingray

Vadim Kurylev: With the advent of perestroika, bands from the Rock Club could play paid gigs, and many moved from amateur to professional. Now formally underground bands could work legally with their own group—this was a fundamental change that occurred in rock music. Now every band could go on tour to other cities and abroad.

Joanna Stingray: The glasnost years were great. I didn't notice too many new bands except for Televizor, DDT, and a few others. But I did notice there were more places these "unofficial" bands could play. All these bands seemed optimistic. As long as they could write

53 Troitsky, *Back in the USSR*, 115–116.

songs and perform the way they always did, but on a bigger level and with monetary gain. All was good.

Zhenskaia Bolezn's Irina Lokteva (vocals), Olga Suvorkina (guitar), perform in 1986 for a film documenting perestroika. Used with permission from Irina Lokteva

Irina Lokteva: Zhenskaia Bolezn's first concert was in 1987, at Gorbunov House of Culture. Vopli Vidopliasova, Kollezhsky Asessor, *EST* and us.[54] One day there were two concerts in the afternoon and evening. One of the first commercial concerts of Perestroika. When we played there was a decent audience of music lovers, bohemian party-goers, journalists, photographers, and in the evening a screaming crowd of punks, metalheads, and bikers.

I'm not a concert person. I'm a home girl. Just everything I do, music, poetry, ends up being punk.

Andrey Burlaka: After one and a half years under Gorbachev's administration, first Akvarium and then other top bands got an

54 *Vopli Vidopliasova*—Vidopliasov's Yelling; *Kollezhsky Asessor*—Collegiate Assessor.

opportunity to play legal concerts and tour the entire Soviet Union. Melodia Records printed underground records that Andrey Tropillo recorded in the mid 1980s.[55]

For a couple of years the Rock Club was popular, but close to the end of the '80s it lost importance because bands got the opportunity to arrange gigs themselves or through promoters, who also received the rights to do it legally.

We changed our mask
We changed our clothes
We forgot about the fairy tale
And filled a new cargo hold.
The whirlwind—perestroika
Is our element.
Each of us, a destroyer
Of public anesthesia.

It's a new age and we've come just in time
It's a time for those who are still burning
We want it right here, and tomorrow—right now
We've come just in time
This is an era for us.

The road signs
Are tired of rotting in the rain
Those who put them up before us
Spit at our backs as we pass

It's a new age and we've come just in time
It's a time for those who are still burning
We want it right here, and tomorrow—right now
We've come just in time
This is an era for us.[56]

Aleksandr "Rikoshet" Aksenov: [Perestroika] gives us the possibility to express struggle and affirm our views. I think it depends on whether people believe in the possibility of solving the

---

55 Andrey Tropillo was a sound producer who ran a recording studio in the *Dvorets Pionerov* (Palace of Pioneers) and legally recorded amateur artists and bands that he either liked or was allowed to produce. He is frequently mentioned by some of the interviewees.
56 "Epokha dlia Nas" (Epoch For Us), by *Obyekt Nasmeshek*. Accessible lyrics here: http://obekt-rikoshet.narod.ru/disk/glasnost/index.html#2. Translated by the author.

problems in our country… I do believe that people can live better than they do. They can understand each other. In general, I believe in a better future. The central idea of punk is that there is no future, but I don't share those views.[57]

Obyekt Nasmeshek's Rikoshet, 1986, Joanna Stingray

Characters in the order they appear:

Aleksey "Ryba" Rybin—Most notable for his role as lead guitarist for Russia's premier rock group, Kino, with Viktor Tsoi. Aleksey also enjoyed the company of Svin and other early Leningrad punk rockers.

Yevgeny "Yufa" Yufit (1961–2016)—Artistic persona and director of many necro-realist independent films. He is the founding member of Russia's Parallel Cinema movement, and a member of Leningrad's earliest punk scene.

Yevgeny Titov—Musician and later member of Avtomaticheskie Udovletvoriteli from 1985-1989. Friends with the members before formally joining the group.

Fedor (Feddy) "Begemot" Lavrov—Musician and arguably one of Russia's first anarcho-punks. Feddy operated his own recording studio, Begemotion Records, where he recorded many early Leningrad acts, including his own bands Otdel Samoiskorenenia and Narodnoe Opolchenie.

Olga Korol-Borodiuk—Wife of the late Andrey "Svin" Panov.

Leah Panova—Mother of the late Andrey "Svin" Panov.

57 Taken from an interview. "*Obyekt Nasmeshek* – Epokha dlya nas + Interv'iu na angliyskom", Youtube video, Posted by "pengvin86," January 7, 2009, https://www.youtube.com/watch?v=Csh4PLX22d4. Translation provided by the video.

Andrey "Svin" Panov (1960-1998)—Arguably Leningrad's first punk provocateur. Svin started Leningrad's first punk act, Avtomaticheskie Udovletvoriteli, and various side projects. For more information on Svin, read Tommy Dean and Alex Herbert's article in *Maximum Rocknroll* #375, August 2014, "Andrey 'Svin' Panov: Leningrad Punk Progenitor."

Igor "Pinochet" Pokrovsky—Fan, musician, band manager, and follower of early Leningrad rock scene. Friend of Svin, Tsoi, Rybin, and others.

Artemy Troitsky—Notable music critic and long time journalist of Russian rock music, broadly speaking. Author of *Back in the USSR*, a major English-language source of the Soviet Union's earliest Rock culture.

Andrey "Malenky Diusha" Mikhaylov—Member and co-founder with Aleksandr "Rikoshet" Aksenov of Obyekt Nasmeshek, frontman for Klimaks Skandalnogo Krizisa, guitarist for Avtomaticheskie Udovletvoriteli.[58]

Viktor Sologub—Founder of Strannye Igry, vocalist and bass-guitarist.

Joanna Stingray—American musician from Los Angeles who went to the Soviet Union in the mid 1980s with her sister. There she fell in love with the city and made an effort to export Soviet music to the West. Without her unique perspective of the Leningrad Rock Club, many of the documentary sources would not exist. She made friends with members of Akvarium, Kino, and others in 1984. She sent music home many times and helped release the compilation "Red Wave," which introduced four Soviet bands to the West in 1986.

Dmitry Levkovsky—Tour manager for Narodnoe Opolchenie.

Tatyana Motovilova—Fan of punk music during the Leningrad Rock Club days. Wife of Igor Motovilov of Narodnoe Opulchenie.

Dmitry Buchin—Drummer for the bands Narodnoe Opolchenie, Otdel Samoiskorenenia, and Nate![59]

Yury Sobolev—Guitarist for Brigandy Podriad.

Oleg Garkusha—Showman and lyricist for Auktsyon.[60]

Natalya Terekhova—Founder and guitarist for Lamia (1989-1995) (Alma-Ata, Kazakhstan) and guitarist for Zhenskaia Bolezn (1995-1997) (Moscow).

Valery Morozov—Drummer for Avtomaticheskie Udovletvoriteli from 1987-1989.

Nikolay Mikhaylov—Leading coordinator of the Leningrad Rock Club.

Vadim Kurylev—Frontman for Elektricheskie Partisany.

Andrey Mashnin—Frontman for the band Mashinband, and temporarily with Bondzinsky.

Aleks "Ogoltely" Strogachev (1962-2005)—Frontman for Narodnoe Opolchenie.

---

58 *Klimaks Skandalnogo Krizisa*—Climax of Scandalous Crisis.
59 *Nate!*—Take it!
60 *Auktsyon*—Auction.

Irina Lokteva—Frontwoman for Zhenskaia Bolezn (Moscow, 1987, 1996-1997).

Andrey Burlaka—Rock music journalist, coordinator of the Leningrad Rock Club.

Aleksandr "Rikoshet" Aksenov (1964-2007)—Frontman for Obyekt Nasmeshek.

AN ORAL HISTORY OF SIBERIAN PUNK 1984-1991

Composed and Translated by Vladimir Kozlov[61]

Roman Neumoev: There weren't as many punk bands as in Siberia, for instance in Novosibirsk or Omsk, even in Moscow or St. Petersburg [at that time].

Vladimir Bogomiakov: Life in Siberia was apparently different from life, say, in Moscow, St. Petersburg, or even Yekaterinburg. It was harder and somewhat rootless.

Aleksandr Kushnir: Suddenly, a very sincere, very honest kind of rock emerged in the USSR. It was really like a religion of death, like a knife in your pocket. And compared to 90% of Moscow, St. Petersburg, and Yekaterinburg rock—which rock critics were so proud of—it looked phony and worthless. For me, it was probably the quintessential primeval rock.

Sergey Letov: For Russian culture, pressure from the authorities was always crucial. While in the Urals or in St. Petersburg it wasn't too bad, in Siberia it was very hard.

Sergey Firsov: If you live in Siberia, you create a lot.

Artur Strukov: Because it's cold—and for most of the year—you sit at home, you read and reflect.

Nataliya "Kometa" Komarova: [Russian] punks, and especially Siberian punks, were very intellectual people.

---

61 This chapter is based on interviews filmed by Vladimir Kozlov for the documentary *Sledy na Snegu* (*Traces in the Snow*) in the Fall and Winter of 2013. Interviews with Igor Plotnikov and Yevgeny Kuznetsov were filmed by Igor Plotnikov.

Sergey Guryev: In the world of punk, there are two opposing poles, probably: Californian punk and Siberian punk.

Oleg Sudakov: We denied punk aesthetics, like, say, a Mohawk, or a leather jacket, or a certain style of playing guitar. What was important was rebellion—opposition.

Roman Neumoev: We weren't interested in appearances; we were interested in the essence [of punk], in its avant-garde essence and its intellectual roots. On the surface, it was impossible to see that we were punks. We didn't wear mohawks or riveted jackets. When we came to the Baltics later, we saw "real" punks—in leather jackets, with chains, rivets, mohawks, and dyed hair. But in Siberia, if you looked like that you wouldn't be able to walk more than 100 meters. After that, someone would just take you around the corner and beat the shit out of you.

Artur Strukov: After the alternative fest... We were approached by *Komsomol* officials from Sverdlovsk, probably the same ones who organized tours for [the rock band] Nautilus.[62] And they offered to work with us. Later, I sometimes regretted that I refused, but we just couldn't do it because we had a totally different approach to music. It killed us that we would have to play the same program three times a day. For us, it was totally unacceptable because repeating your songs, which you consider as something personal, three times a day for a week in one city and then in another was something... I refused to do.

Nikolay "Nick Rock 'n' Roll" Kuntsevich: It was genuine in Siberia... Not only an I-don't-give-a-fuck attitude—it's something else—some Siberian laziness. This is their characteristic. In a good way! They didn't work to promote themselves. Fuck, they didn't.

---

62 For a definition of *Komsomol*, see footnote 26, Part 1.1.

Siberian punks reacted to the advent of commerce and showbiz in various ways.

Grazhdanskaia Oborona performs at SyRock[63] festival in 1988, Yuri Chashkin

Omsk: Grazhdanskaia Oborona and GrOb Records

Konstantin "Kuzia UO" Riabinov: I once saw a magazine photo, there wasn't even a punk in it, but some conceptual artist. He wore a white robe and a dog collar with a piece of raw meat. And the caption said he was a "punk." Someone related to music that's honest and totally crazy. It was just what we wanted. I had been childhood friends with a guy named Sasha. He was actually called Ivan Morg. But not anymore because he's dead now. I came to Sasha's every night after work, and one night he introduced me to someone. A long-haired guy sat in his room, writing something in small handwriting. He was filling in a questionnaire—kid stuff—basically. It turned out to be [Yegor] Letov. And the three of us decided to play together. We began to hang out, but because both

---

he and Sasha wanted to be leaders, they didn't get along. So I began to spend more time making music with [Letov].

Yegor Letov: From the birth of Grazhdanskaia Oborona, me and Kuzia UO focused on recording and distribution of tape albums, having reasonably decided that we wouldn't be able to perform live anytime soon.[64]

Konstantin "Kuzia UO" Riabinov: There were the three of us, me, Letov, and "Boss" Andrey Babenko. And once Letov said, 'Let's call ourselves Grazhdanskaia Oborona.' It's a good title. It's a bit long, but still very good. Andrey soon distanced himself from us, and in 1985 just the two of us were making homespun records. But the "official" birthdate of Grazhdanskaia Oborona is December 8, 1984. We used reel-to-reels to record. We had a bass guitar and a totally crazy guitar, which I don't remember where it came from. We also used homemade guitar pedals. We knew guys who soldered them together from parts.

Yegor Letov: In late fall of 1985, our heretical activities came to a fucking end. After a series of conversations [with KGB officials], Kuzia was conscripted to the army and sent to the closed area of Baykonur cosmodrome, and I was sent to the mental institution.

Konstantin "Kuzia UO" Riabinov: Everyone gave whatever statements, even me, trying to save my silly personal life. But it didn't save me and I was eventually conscripted.

Sergey Letov: All participants of my brother's first lineups cooperated with the law enforcers. They betrayed him, and he was under immense pressure. He spent three months in a mental institution in Omsk.

---

64 Yegor Letov's quotes are taken from the underground magazine *Kontr Kult URa* #3, 1991.

Yegor Letov: In March [1986] I was discharged and decided to record by myself as, sadly, there was a total lack of understanding people—not to mention collaborators like Kuzia UO—and there were KGB informers all around. In early summer 1987, I recorded material that accumulated in the previous hapless years, which amounted to as many as five 30-minute albums. Recording each of which took me about two days of non-stop, 12-hour recording.

Konstantin "Kuzia UO" Riabinov: I was discharged from the army in 1987, when about one half of what became Grazhdanskaia Oborona's iconic albums were already recorded by Letov alone. I didn't immediately rejoin the band, because it was already doing well. I began to play in Grazhdanskaia Oborona again in May 1989, when the entire band moved to St. Petersburg and joined the Leningrad Rock Club. The club welcomed us because by that time, the popularity of Grazhdanskaia Oborona was already huge.

Oleg Sudakov: Letov's contribution is that he believed that everyone had to make records, not put it off until some other time, some other year. You have to come, sit down, play, record, and release the record. The process of recording was very fast compared with these days. There was no special focus on quality. Some quality was there, and that was enough. In rock 'n' roll, the idea is to play dirty, hard, fast, and energetically. You make a record in two nights.

Igor "Jeff" Zhevtun: The idea not to drag out the recording. That was the band's attitude and Yegor's. He, for instance, recorded three albums over one month—all by himself. And we always had the same approach. You adjust the sound by yourself, looking for what you want to achieve; you are the producer, the director, the musician, and the creator.

Sergey Letov: Records were made on reels, and those reels, 270 meters or longer, were distributed illegally through distribution networks. A high-quality master was sent from Moscow or, say, Ufa, to other cities, and then copies were made for the end user.

Roman Neumoev: Maybe in the 19th century, poems by [Russian poet Mikhail] Lermontov were distributed by copying them in handwriting on paper. And we were doing just about the same, but on magnetic tape. Letov just sent his albums all over the country, to people he knew. And they made further copies. And, of course, a user who got a fourth or fifth copy had everything wheezing and crackling in their speakers. However, despite that, people still could perceive the music.

Oleg Tarasov: Yegor's productivity at that time was huge. For instance, he would come and bring four new Grazhdanskaia Oborona albums, like in 1989, plus, records by Communism, Anarkhia and Armia Vlasova.[65]

Sergey Guryev: Even though the lyrics [at Grazhdanskaia Oborona's first ever Moscow performance at SyRock festival in December 1988] weren't understandable, and the sound quality was mediocre, there was a feeling of powerful energy. It just came as more proof that the most important component of rock was not music. Music is the most important in classical. You don't go to a rock concert for music—for that you go to a classical concert—but energy, a powerful energy blow.

Nataliya "Kometa" Komarova: I think [Yegor] wasn't totally aware of what was going on because he already had some managers at that time, some people hanging around him. When Grazhdanskaia Oborona was supposed to enter the stage, some guy was yelling at me, saying in a very categorical way, "Until I collect the fee upfront right now, the band won't perform." We paid, and Grazhdanskaia Oborona entered the stage.

---

65 *Anarkhia*—Anarchy; *Armia Vlasova*—Army of Vlasov.

Yegor Letov: On April 13 [1990] in Tallinn, Grazhdanskaia Oborona played its last gig, after which the band with that name definitively ceased to exist.[66]

Konstantin "Kuzia UO" Riabinov: He must have had enough of it. It was too... It was too much, and he probably saw that it couldn't go on like that.

Oleg Tarasov: There were shitheads [showing up at gigs], some stupid teenagers, who only wanted the brutal element of punk rock and probably the idea that "everything is shit and I am shit." After [a 1989 show at Moscow's] DK MAI, three first rows were just missing.[67] They turned them into slivers, into dust. It was some savagery.

Oleg Sudakov: When 900 or 1000 people are going crazy, destroying the seats to pieces, you need to be absolutely... narcissistic and like it because it is happening for you. Or, on the contrary, to hate all that because you sing songs. And Grazhdanskaia Oborona never wanted to translate just bare energy. If you want to, you can get drunk, or fall in love with a beautiful woman, or drive a car into the wall. You'll get the same kind of adrenalin as at a rock concert.

Oleg Tarasov: [Letov] decided to change his story and told me, "Tell everyone that I'm dead, if anyone asks."

Sergey Firsov: I believe it was the wrong move, because it was a period of a surge in interest—there were shows, there were records. At that time, many became massively popular, performed at large venues, and Yegor just retreated to Omsk and sat there.

---

66 Yegor Letov relaunched *Grazhdanskaia Oborona* in 1992, and the band performed and recorded until his death in February 2008.
67 DK MAI –The Palace of Culture and Technics of Moscow Aviation Institute.

Sergey Letov: My brother understood a rock musician as primarily a rebel, revolutionary, and intellectual, not a showbiz employee or a waiter. And at that time rock, as I see it, turned to a large extent, into pure entertainment.

Instruksia po Vyzhivaniu performs at Tyumen festival in 1988, from Artur Strukov's archives

Instruktsia po Vyzhivaniu and the Tiumen scene

Miroslav Nemirov: I believe that my main achievement in Siberian punk is the creation of an environment, atmosphere, and ground. Tiumen was basically an ice-covered ground; there was no life there, and I created it. In 1985, I organized a rock club in Tiumen. We began to have meetings. And we drank a lot. We drank the cheapest wine available in Tiumen at the time— Bulgarian dry red wine. At some point, musicians began to show up.

Igor Plotnikov: Nemirov had a mad idea to form a band and stir up shit. And he did it. At the initial stage, he was the lyricist and singer. Unfortunately, Nemirov had neither an ear for music, nor a sense of rhythm. Well, he had a sense of rhythm, but it was inside of him and no one was able to catch it. The first performance of Instruktsia po Vyzhivaniu was at Tiumen University. It was just one song: "Prednovogodnie Dni."[68] Nemirov was a creative personality who did not want to conform to the norms of Soviet society. He just lived by his own rules. In 1986 he was "Enemy No. 1." Articles about him came out in regional papers, calling for "stopping" him. In fact, he posed no threat, but it was very unusual by the standards of the time.

Yevgeny "Jack" Kuznetsov: [The] Siberian punk movement owes Nemirov a lot because he instigated the whole thing. He knew what to do. There were people who liked punk and wanted to make music. But he showed everyone how to write and perform songs. He streamlined our tastes.

Miroslav Nemirov: [Yury Shapovalov] asked me, "Can I bring a guy from the industrial institute? He's in the oil and gas department and he knows the music we like and he plays a little." So he brought him. It was [Igor] Zhevtun, "Jeff", who went on to become the guitar player for many bands, including Grazhdanskaia Oborona. He soon began to write songs. The first two that became known are "Ne Ostalos Nikogo" and "My Vse v Kontse."[69] He got inspiration for those songs from the Stranglers' album *No More Heroes*. Apart from Zhevtun, Arkady Kuznetsov showed up. He was a final-year high school student at the time. And a year before, I did an internship at his school. I worked as a teacher there. So I came across him, and he asked me about the rock club and asked if he could come. He shows up and tells me that he'd like to play music but he's not yet sure what kind. He said he'd like to play something similar to Genesis, Jethro Tull or King Crimson. I tell him, "Are you out of your mind? Play punk rock instead!" Next day he says "I listened to the tapes you gave me and wrote a song in the same vein." And he sang:

68 *Prednovogodnie Dni*—Days Before New Year's.
69 *"Ne Ostalos Nikogo"* (No One Is Still There); *"My Vse v Kontse"* (We Are All Screwed).

I'm agile like a cook
and I'm very smart!
You're fuckers!
My parents are fuckers,
the rulers are fuckers!
Fuckers!

Okay, now we've got a second musician. So we hooked him up with Zhevtun. I called [the band] Instruktsia po Vyzhivaniu, after my poem.

Igor Plotnikov: So there was Zhevtun and there was Arkady, but the band had no bass player and no drummer. And I tell [Yevgeny Kuznetsov], "You know how to play drums, and you know Zhevtun, why don't you join?"

Miroslav Nemirov: When I organized the band, Roman Neumoev bought a guitar and began to learn how to play—to compete with me.

Roman Neumoev: It was actually me who organized Instruktsia po Vyzhivaniu. And the rock club in Tiumen was formed by three people: Miroslav Nemirov as the main initiator (and let's say, ideologue), the late Yura Shapovalov, and me. The first stuff we played was, of course, copycat to a large extent. We basically lifted entire riffs and arrangements from the bands we liked most. Our most favorite band was, of course, the Sex Pistols.

Yevgeny "Jack" Kuznetsov: On April 12, 1986, we played a grandiose, powerful, and strong show. The shit hit the fan, and there was a lot of controversy. KGB launched an investigation. The rock club was dispersed. Many were expelled from Komsomol and from the university. Some people were conscripted to the army. Nemirov left town.

Miroslav Nemirov: What is strange is that they acted so late. We were daring and behaved badly from the very beginning.

Yevgeny "Jack" Kuznetsov: Authorities's arsenal of tools for dealing with people like us was limited. They could either praise or punish. Just like they didn't know then what to do with Instruktsia po Vyzhivaniu, now Putin doesn't know what to do with all this fucking shit.

Igor Plotnikov: In the summer of 1986, [Roman Neumoev] took the reins of Instruktsia po Vyzhivaniu. The band's second gig was in Sverdlovsk in August 1986. The reception was mixed, because

Instriktsia po Vyzhivaniu's Roman Neumoyev, 1988, photographer Yuri Chashkin

at the time Sverdlovsk was a city of metal heads, and they didn't understand any music other than heavy metal and hard rock. And here a band enters the stage, which is set to play their second show ever and the first one in this lineup. The sound was awful and they played sloppily, but it was very punk. There was a lot of energy. And there were people in the audience who wanted to get on stage and beat up the musicians.

Yevgeny "Jack" Kuznetsov: There was a difference between reception in Tiumen and Sverdlovsk. In Tiumen, audiences received us very warmly, but we were harassed by KGB, Komsomol, and Communist officials. In Sverdlovsk, officials allowed us to do anything on stage—we could take a shit there. But the audiences were hostile.

Roman Neumoev: The desire to be free was very acute. Soviet society wasn't free; it was totalitarian. Everything was regulated, everything was controlled.

Yevgeny "Jack" Kuznetsov: In the summer of 1988, the festival of alternative and left radical music was held in Tiumen. [Bands] from all over showed up. Putti played, Grazhdanskaia Oborona played, and, of course, Instruktsia po Vyzhivaniu. Yanka was there, too. Kulturnaia Revolutsia performed and won the first prize.[70] It was cool.

Nikolay "Nick Rock 'n' Roll" Kuntsevich: It had an atmosphere of brotherhood, absolutely. Audiences saved the artists from the cops, really. They would just come to the dressing room. They saved me, for instance. Before me, Letov cursed on stage and no one cared. And as soon as I entered the stage, they grabbed me.

Igor Plotnikov: [At the festival], contacts were established. Musicians from Instruktsia po Vyzhivaniu joined Grazhdanskaia Oborona, like Zhevtun—he was Instruktsia po Vyzhivaniu's first guitarist.

70 *Kulturnaia Revolutsia*—Cultural Revolution.

Kulturnaia Revolutsia performs at Tyumen festival in 1988, from Artur Strukov's archives

Roman Neumoev: We had an informal community. It was between Novosibirsk, Omsk, and Tiumen. An unofficial, self-organized community. We played gigs together at absolutely underground venues, like in Akademgorodok.[71] We played in apartment kitchens with an acoustic guitar.

Yevgeny "Jackson" Kokorin: Kulturnaia Revolutsia, Kooperativ Nishtiak, and Instruktsia po Vyzhivaniu were close friends, like a family, like a sect.[72] We had two self-made guitars between all these bands, and they were really made on a lathe.

Nikolay "Nick Rock 'n' Roll" Kuntsevich: In Tiumen, they had neither Saigon, a cafe in St. Petersburg, nor *Aromat*, a cafe in Moscow.[73] They didn't have a specific place to hang out. However, I witnessed such great stuff in people's apartments, such gigs! The show was eternal, or more precise, it was endless. There, I heard Roma Neumoev play Tovarishch Gorbachev for the first time.[74] I was baffled, just baffled. I was just overwhelmed because I felt how cool it all was.

71 *Akademgorodok* is a scientific center outside Novosibirsk. It literally means "Academic City"
72 *Kooperativ Nishtiak*—Cooperative Goodie.
73 *Aromat*—Fragnance.
74 *Tovarishch Gorbachev*—Comrade Gorbachev.

Putti, photographer Yuri Chashkin

Novosibirsk: Putti, BOMZH and Pishchevye Otkhody[75]

Nikolay "Nick Rock 'n' Roll" Kuntsevich: Everything happened in Akademgorodok. That was the epicenter of everything. Not Novosibirsk, but Akademgorodok.

---

75 *Pishchevye Othody*—Food Waste.

Aleksandr Rozhkov: [In the '80s,] Akademgorodok was some sort of an oasis, a zone of free thinking. Nowhere else in the country, even in Moscow and St. Petersburg, were conditions like here.

Valery Murzin: Akademgorodok is very unique. And only there, a band like, for instance, BOMZH could emerge, which may not have been that different from Moscow-based bands, but it was fronted by Dzhonik [Yevgeny Solovyov].

Vladimir Ziubin: Originally, there was a band called Chetyre Tankista i Sobaka, in which Yevgeny Solovyov played on drums.[76] He was the only one left in a new lineup, which was renamed BOMZH—an abbreviation for "without a permanent place of residence," meaning that the band did not want to stick to any specific genre. It was 1985. I had just been discharged from the army, and I joined on bass. We began to rehearse and in the fall of that year, we played our first show at student dormitory No. 5. It was at some sort of rock festival. The quality of play was impressive in the way that it was almost non-existent. The guitars were out of tune, the drummer was out of rhythm. But there was energy. There was a recording of the show, and it was curious to later listen to all that chaos. It turned out to be distributed quite widely in underground distribution, and professional musicians from the conservatory tried to analyze that terrible stuff, trying to figure out to what degree the guitars were out of tune.

Aleksandr Chirkin: At the early stages, we just covered songs by Russian rock bands. Then we began to play our own stuff. And we thought that we were playing hard rock, something heavy. But then Koka and Nikolay Katkov listened to our stuff and said, "Hey guys, this is jazz punk." So, we were punks? Okay, we're punks, whatever! We had heard The Sex Pistols and The Clash back in 1984. And we thought we could try something similar, too. Unlike other bands, we didn't go too much into politics. We wanted to be entertaining above all. We played our first show in Akademgorodok in 1985. No

76 *Chetyre Tankista i Sobaka*—Four Tankers and a Dog.

Putti, 1988, Yuri Chashkin (2)

one really knew how to play. In fact, no one knew how to play at all. But we looked at old magazine photos and gave ourselves mohawks and painted our faces, so we looked like Kiss. We entered the stage, they looked at us and immediately cut the sound. Then [Dmitry] Selivanov grabbed some pipe and began to play. And I was on the drums, drumming something crazy. Within one month after that gig, I was conscripted to the army. But they made one big mistake because they sent me to a military unit in Omsk. There I met Letov, and members of Pik Klakson.[77] I would go AWOL to rehearse with Letov—we had a project named Kayf. We also had an underground Putti show. I can boast that Letov played bass in my band.

Valery Murzin: I published *Tusovka*, an underground zine.[78] *Tusovka* survived only because I always… honestly took the first copy to my KGB curator. As my job was developing rockets, I had to go to the KGB every month or every other month to report on my activities. I said "Guys I am publishing an illegal zine, and here's the first copy for you." That is the reason why they didn't arrest me.

---

77 *Klakson*—Claxon.
78 *Tusovka*—Coterie.

Aleksandr Chirkin: Our records at the time were homespun. We would take a reel-to-reel and put two mics in the opposite corners of the room. Instead of reverb we would use a metal bath tub. I would put my head into it and yell. We invented whatever we could. Guitars were homemade. There were even guitars made out of plywood.

Vladimir Ziubin: Before the set at Podolsk rock festival [outside Moscow in 1987], we played a number of gigs. So we were more or less prepared, and the audience received us well. There was a plan to have Letov and Nick Rock 'n' Roll join us on stage after a few songs, but it didn't work out. We were onstage, so we didn't know who exactly didn't allow them to perform.

Fedor Fomin: It all started when some air of freedom began to shift to the Soviet Union in the '80s. There were records. We listened to The Clash, Ramones, Iggy Pop, Exploited, Crass. And then we figured that at some point all those bands switched to playing some crap. So we thought "Why don't we play ourselves?" Yegor Letov helped me to pick the name for the band. I showed him a bunch of options, but he said that band with English equivalents of those names already exist. But we wanted to say that we were the very worst. And Letov suggested Pishchevye Otkhody. I was totally against deriving any profits from music. We just did what we liked to do. We played shows that were close to our home. We did shows in Novosibirsk, went to Tiumen a couple times, also to Barnaul.

Guzel Nemirova: I stopped by [Neumoev's] apartment and saw him trying to put up a tent in the middle of the only room. I said, "Roman, why are you doing that?" And he said, "Letov is coming with his wife." We didn't yet know Yanka, and he said, "They're staying at my apartment, and I only got one room, so I'm setting up a tent for them."

Artur Strukov: Yanka came with a tent and put it up right in [Neumoev's] one-room apartment.

BOMZh's Yevgeny Solovyov, 1988, Yuri Chashkin

Guzel Nemirova: I'm sitting on a bench on a sunny day and I see Letov approach—a skinny guy dressed in black, with long-hair and glasses. And I see something walking next to him. What is it? First I see just black clothes and a lot of red hair. She was laughing like a countryside woman. I fell in love with Yanka immediately.

Yanka Diagileva, 1988, Yuri Chashkin

Roman Neumoev: It was immediately clear that Yanka… Yanka would be a big artist.

Oleg Sudakov: It's always difficult for a girl to be in male company for a number of reasons, whoever she was. So she had to put up with young ambitious guys around her, and someone could offend her unintentionally.

Roman Neumoev: She had problems of organizational nature. For instance, she was unable to form a band. She never had her own band. And her electric recordings were either made on GrOb Records by Yegor Letov or they were made in Tiumen.

Nataliya "Kometa" Komarova: When I entered that apartment and… spent a few days there, with these guys and Yanka, they didn't look like healthy people to me. That upset me so much that I… I never organized gigs for Yanka.

Oleg Sudakov: Yanka was probably… an embodiment of "God's fool" because the girl had to bear a burden at just 22 or 23 years old.

She was exposed to the world's literature and the world's music and entire layers of human ideas, discoveries, and even follies.

Artur Strukov: She was a comrade, a friend, a sister, and a brother. She always used masculine gender forms when she spoke about herself. She suffered from depression. But she was such a positive person. She could make you laugh even when she was depressed.

Yevgeny "Jackson" Kokorin: Some people say: she was always frowning, always in her thoughts. I never saw her like that. She was always funny, always kidding. She had a lot of irony and self-irony.

Nikolay "Nick Rock 'n' Roll" Kuntsevich: I knew two different persons. There was one Yanka—a redhead crazy friend, real fucking crazy girl in a men's trousers. And there was another Yanka, whom I unfortunately met when we came to Novosibirsk when Cherny Lukich had a project there, Muzhskoy Tanets.[79] Me and Bert came to see her, and she wouldn't even talk to us. I think that was anhedonia. I myself had experienced something like that, a lack of joy in life.

Yanka Diagileva, Moscow House of Culture 1988-89, Lev Goncharov

---

79 *Cherny Lukich*—Black Lukich; *Muzhskoi Tanets*—Male Dance.

Characters in the order they appear:

Roman Neumoev—Musician, frontman for Instruktsia po Vyzhivaniu (Tiumen).

Vladimir Bogomiakov—Poet, fan, observer of the Siberian punk scene.

Aleksandr Kushnir—Journalist, editor of the iconic underground magazine *Kontr Kult URa* in the '80s and early '90s.

Sergey Letov—Musician, elder brother of Yegor Letov.

Sergey Firsov—Manager of Grazhdanskaia Oborona (Omsk) in the '80s.

Artur Strukov—Musician, founder, and frontman for Kulturnaia Revolutsia (Tiumen).

Nataliya "Kometa" Komarova—Organizer of the rock festival *SyRock*, held in Moscow in the late '80s, featuring bands from the Soviet Union's other regions, which didn't yet perform in Moscow.

Sergey Guryev—Music critic and journalist, vocalist for Chistaia Lubov (Moscow).

Oleg Sudakov—Musician, participant of Yegor Letov's projects, frontman for Rodina (Novosibirsk).[80]

Nikolay "Nick Rock 'n' Roll" Kuntsevich—Musician, poet, front man of many projects.

Konstantin "Kuzia UO" Riabinov—Musician, founding member of Grazhdanskaia Oborona.

Yegor Letov (1964–2008)—Musician, founder and frontman for Grazhdanskaia Oborona.

Igor "Jeff" Zhevtun—Musician for Instruktsia po Vyzhivaniu, Grazhdanskaia Oborona, and other Siberian punk bands.

Oleg Tarasov—Fan, observer of the underground music scene, founder of the label Solnze Records.

Miroslav Nemirov (1961–2016)—Poet, founder and ideologue of Tiumen Rock Club and the band Instruktsia po Vyzhivaniu.

Igor Plotnikov—Fan, musician, observer of the Tiumen punk scene.

Yevgeny "Jack" Kuznetsov (1968–2016)—Drummer for Instruktsia po Vyzhivaniu in the '80s and '90s.

Yevgeny "Jackson" Kokorin—Musician for Instruktsia po Vyzhivaniu and other Siberian punk bands.

Aleksandr Rozhkov—Musician, observer of the Siberian punk scene.

Valery Murzin—Founder and chairman of the Novosibirsk Rock Club in the late 1980s.

Vladimir Ziubin—Musician, member of Putti (Novosibirsk).

Aleksandr Chirkin—Musician, frontman for Putti.

Fedor Fomin—Musician, frontman for Pishchevye Otkhody (Novosibirsk).

---

80 *Rodina*—Motherland.

Guzel Nemirova—Organizer of the festival of alternative and left radical music in Tiumen in 1988, widow of the late poet Miroslav Nemirov.

PART TWO:
BECOMING POST-SOVIET PUNKS 1989-1999
2.1: Generation TaMtAm

Seva Gakkel: In New York I was surprised by the harmony I saw. In this city there were many levels of being; next to the supergroups and Madison Square Garden, there were a huge number of clubs—alternative, experimental, jazz, blues, anything. That is the life I wanted to live when I was young, and I saw it now in an older age. Nothing was similar here. I was infected with the idea, and when everything with the club went really easy, my priority was to keep young people from temptations of a giant audience and money. I formulated a definition of the underground—this is something that exists independently from formality. In Soviet times, it was believed that the underground was contrary to the system, the vast ideas. But it turns out that all those people who were in the Soviet underground quietly said goodbye and went to earn money as the barriers were taken away. That is, the underground was divided for purely economic reasons. It was totally unacceptable to me, and the construction of a new underground in the '90s was an attempt to restore a cultural layer, so that people could feel the joy of the game for a small audience of their own kind. At least those who understand the rules of the game. Because in this case, this game becomes a mutually enriching experience, a natural exchange of ideas and energy.[81]

Andrey Aliakrinsky: There were no houses of culture at that time. Seva Gakkel went to New York and London, saw how things were there, went to CBGB, and made friends with the group Sonic Youth and others.

---

81 Translated from *Furfur*, "Kak zhil russky muzykalny andergraund 1990-h" ("How Russian music underground lived in the 1990s") December 3, 2014. Accessible here: http://www.furfur.me/furfur/culture/culture/178623-pesni-v-pustotu.

Seva Gakkel, 1977, Andrey Usov

Vadim Kurylev: Soviet man in the street, who often believed what he read in the newspapers, considered punks in principle as socially dangerous psychopaths.

By the end of the '80s, there appeared in St. Petersburg the club TaMtAm—and most St. Petersburg punks rushed there, considering the old Leningrad Rock Club too conservative. The Rock Club was a "temple of classic rock" and, in principle, could not become Petersburg's CBGB. The punk revolution needed new spaces to appear…

Seva Gakkel: I still had permission to go abroad from my passport. One of my friends asked me to do some business for him in Budapest, with him covering the cost of a three-day trip. It was stupid to refuse, so I accepted the offer.

We had an agreement that within a week of my return we would have a punk-rock group named Pupsy and a German group Hordy-Tordy playing in the club.[82] TaMtAm was starting to form.

The beauty of Budapest impressed me. The color of the Danube however didn't seem to be blue at all—it was muddy just like coffee from a Soviet coffee machine. The train that was taking

82 *Pupsy*—Kewpie Dolls.

me back to St. Petersburg stopped in the middle of a field several kilometers from the city for three hours. I had a bad feeling about it, and as soon as I got home, I found out that I was right; on the 19th of August, 1991 the military coup [of ideologically conservative communists] took place.[83]

It happened very untimely. I didn't want to end something [the club] I'd barely started. But luckily everything went fine. We had to shift the upcoming concert due to the official day for mourning. In a week's time we already had the band Vostochny Sindrom playing in front of a huge audience.[84]

Oleg Gitarkin: The first time we did a concert as Nozh dlia Frau Müller was in 1991.[85] Ilya Bortniuk was in charge of the organization of the country's first punk-rock festival in the Leningrad Palace of Youth. Everyone enjoyed our concert, but we didn't know what to do next.

By that time Leningrad Rock Club ceased to exist. Playing concerts was difficult. Right now there are many clubs in the city and someone plays a concert every day. Fifteen years ago, information about these concert sessions was spread via rumor. People would call their friends and gather for the concert from every corner of the city.

Lesha Miksher told me that Seva Gakkel found a new place on Vasilyevsky Island.[86] He said, "Let's go! We can do a show in there!"

The first time we went, there was no club at all. It looked like a provincial philharmonic hall: the scene, the orchestra, and the red chairs—that meant that people came here to enjoy music while seated. There was no sound either: practically unplugged.

---

83 This refers to the August Coup, in which conservative members of the Communist Party tried to seize power from Gorbachev and his reformers. More on that below.
84 *Vostochny Sindrom*—Eastern Syndrome; Seva Gakkel in *Greshniki*, Ilya Stogoff (Saint Petersburg: Amfora, 2006), 52–53.
85 *Nozh dlia Frau Müller*—A Knife for Frau Müller.
86 Lesha Miksher—drummer for Narodnoe Opolchenie and now a member of the band Leningrad; Vasilyevsky Island in the Neva's delta, right in the center of the old town. It is an expensive area with some low-income side parts with broken houses, closer to the open bay water. Today the bay embankment is built over with new houses.

The first show at TaMtAm was sold-out. They wanted us to play again. The second time we came, there were no chairs—only a couple of couches near the walls. The middle of the hall was cleared for dancing. Although the couches didn't stay there for too long either.

Six months later TaMtAm hosted psychobilly parties and punk concerts.[87] The interior was getting wilder. It ended up as an empty room with charred walls, separated from the crowd with a metal beam at breast height to stop people from jumping on the stage.[88]

Seva Gakkel: For the first three months the concerts were free. The audience consisted of pretty much anyone. I was really bothered by random people who were drinking on the first floor and then went upstairs to get into a fight with someone. This one time in the late evening, a big group of people entered the club and knocked out a tooth of our bouncer. The guy was stressed out and he left.

After that I went to the dorm upstairs and asked a random cop if he could be our security for a reasonable wage. By that time we already had a couple of gopniki asking us who we were paying for the protection of the club.[89] People in uniform created an illusion of a protection racket. Security guards were fine with everything we were doing, and when outside police forces came they would just leave through the back door. Three years later one of them almost lost his job because of this, and the second one quit on his own and started own business. He saved his uniform and still came to work for us.

The concerts in TaMtAm took place three times a week. On a concert day, my friends would come around four o'clock and we would get on our bicycles to go to the club. Going there together gave us an incredible sense of unity. I realized one weird thing:

87 The early rockabilly and psychobilly scene is a phenomena well documented in Kirill Yermichev, *Russkaia psikhataka: zapiski v stile psychobilly* (St. Petersburg: Amfora, 2007).
88 Stogoff, *Greshniki*, 28–29.
89 *Gopniki*, see footnote 4, Introduction.

I didn't care where my activities would lead me, as long as I was happily communicating with people around me. I was absolutely happy.

Rockabilly concerts were the most popular. Bikers would attend them and make bike shows. Half of the audience would be hanging out outside. The windows were open; it was really loud and the bottles were flying out to the street. This didn't just happen in front of me, I was actually the one taking active part in it with my own hands… It was hard to believe.

There were many rockabilly groups. Some of them were fighting each other, but at first I couldn't distinguish between them. Sometimes we made mistakes and invited groups from different gangs. The first show of the group Meantraitors was particularly dreadful because the fight broke out no sooner than they had started playing.[90]

Artemy Troitsky: I can say with certainty that there has never been a place like TaMtAm in Russia, and never will be. It was something—hell, hell is real. With a narrow minded point of view. The noise, heat, zero comfort, a lot of people, a very aggressive atmosphere. In general, it was hard to stay there. It was a hyperintense place. Unbelievable. It was the type of club where you were just compressed and pulled apart. However, it was very nice. The people there were full of feverish enthusiasm. I fear that the drugs here played a role in that, although I know that Gakkel was their absolute opponent. In general, it is difficult to imagine a "TaMtAm" without Gakkel. The place combined incongruous things. On the one hand the infernal underground of [St.] Petersburg] and its coarse grinding. On the other hand, Alesha Karamazov—he's Seva Gakkel, a real saint, who in this hell made heavenly orders.[91] How this place could exist at all, I don't know. But these two principles combined there absolutely

90 Stogoff, *Greshniki*, 74–75.
91 Alesha Karamazov is the name of the protagonist in Fedor Dostoievsky's novel "The Brothers Karamazov".

organically. This is one of the most amazing places I've ever been in my life.[92]

Seva Gakkel: The next concert almost became the last one. We had Pupsy playing. There was a crowd of people. For TaMtAm this was the first real punk concert.

Previously, Russian punk rock had no origins; musicians were underground. Punk rock started to make sense only when the giants of Russian rock were born. It contained protest against whatever the [Leningrad] Rock Club turned into. With a decade-long delay, Russian musicians walked the same path their Western counterparts did. By the beginning of the '90s there was a whole generation of people who considered the language of Akvarium to be obsolete.

I was shocked by the audience at the Pupsy concert because it was very peculiar. I'd never seen so many punks in one place. Nothing could hold them back. For them, every concert in a new place served as the last one. I was freaked out and excited about this fact at the same time. I felt like if I had been 20 at that time, I'd most likely have acted the same way.

Whatever we prepared for the concert was destroyed immediately. There were so many people that chairs were redundant. The pillows that we put on the floor were shredded. The bathroom sink was torn away. Everything was clattered up with bottles and shattered glass. I saw people destroying my newborn club, but I felt that they brought this new appealing vigor with them.

I was concerned that the owner of the place, Sasha Kostrikin, would have a problem and that the club would be closed (having barely started). But Sasha kept it cool and said that we could continue as soon as we fixed the sink.[93]

92 *Furfur*, "Kak zhil russky muzykalny andergraund 1990-h".
93 Stogoff, *Greshniki*, 55–56.

Andrey Chernov: Put it this way: when club TaMtAm existed, then punk rock existed. There are no clubs like that anymore. I've never seen anything like it again, neither in Russia nor outside of it. TaMtAm was unique with a unique atmosphere and people who worked there.

Ilya Chert: The first time I went to TaMtAm was a few months after its opening. The place surprised me. Musicians were sitting on the stage right on the floor. I could barely hear the music. Whoever it was addressed to were the only ones who could hear it. It was like the Lord's Supper. The outside world could die, but life was preserved here. I was eighteen and this was the most beautiful thing I had ever seen.

During my childhood years I argued a lot with my mom. When I was a schoolboy I hated the district where I was born. Later I understood that it was not about the district— it was about the whole world that was badly suited for life. It was impossible to go on like this. You cannot go on hating everything in the world. There must be a place out there for someone like me. That night, I thought that TaMtAm was just the place.

Korol i Shut, September 7, 1995 A. Nastalskaia

The most vivid childhood memory is my mother screaming at me for whatever reason. She divorced my dad when I was four. My dad had always been my friend. I could share anything with him, but at that time he started living in a separate apartment and I was left with my mother.

I still don't understand what it was like to be loved. Life has never shown me what it feels like to be the most precious thing on the earth. Being a little boy, I couldn't understand what I was punished for. My mother is an old lady now. We see each other once every two months or so, and I've forgiven her for many things… But when I was a kid I only felt hatred.

Having barely graduated from high school I abandoned the house. I realized that I was old enough to stand up for myself. At first I threw a stool at her several times. Then I told her to stay away from me… The next time we had a normal conversation I was already thirty.

Parents, school friends, neighbors—I didn't want them anymore. The '90s started and my life had to change.[94]

Daniil Liapin: Yeah, sure there were fights at our concerts at TaMtAm; we were very radical. I remember when I used to be very attracted to those dangerous concerts when I was a part of the audience. I was scared, but it didn't stop me—on the contrary, it motivated me. Same thing happened at our concerts. People were all excited and energetic and this energy had to go somewhere, so there were fights.

Dmitry Buchin: I never played at TaMtAm, but I went as a fan to listen to other bands. I was there because I liked the surprisingly cozy atmosphere created by Seva Gakkel.

Yury Sobolev: I visited the club a few times, but I cannot say that the coziness and comfort pleased me, although such were the

94 Stogoff, *Greshniki*, 57–58.

times. Maybe I was already too old to be fascinated by such an underground. Another cult club, Moloko, was more to my liking.[95]

Maria Zalnova: I think it was unusual that we were were treated as equals in this male world. At the same time we were not "tomboyish;" we were women.

Andrey Mashnin: The public [at TaMtAm] could devour you, but we managed to fit in. Those were our first concerts, and we always had a lot of people. I liked it there, the stage was good, as well as the green room with a box of Baltika No.3 beer from Seva Gakkel as part of the payment.[96]

Ilya Nikitin: Musicians only brought their guitars to concerts, and drummers brought their own sticks. Everything else was already there to use—amps and a complete drum set. On the stage there was a stand for guitarists. In general, of course, mostly men were at the shows. Bands were always paid with a box of 20 beers.

Seva Gakkel: Having no license to sell alcohol, having no rights to commercial activity at all, we bought several crates of beer at our own risk and went into business. The musicians played for free, but every group got a crate of beer, not in payment for their performance, but as refreshments. We gradually switched to working twice a week, Fridays and Saturdays. There were more and more people coming, and in order to limit their numbers we asked for a cover charge, although we tried to keep it as low as possible. This allowed us to keep out those people who would get drunk in the cafe [below] and come upstairs, not out of love of for music but just to fight. We had to think about maintaining order.[97]

---

95 *Moloko*—Milk.
96 *Baltika*—popular variety of beer produced in Russia, equivalent to most generic brands in the United States.
97 Vsevolod Gakkel, "TaMtAm without Illusions,"*A Rock and a Hard Place: Petersburg Civil Society from the Pages of Pchela (The Bee)* (1998), 84.

(Left to right) Unknown, Ilya Nikitin, Roma Voinkov, Evgenii Kopeikin, TaMtAm, A. Nastalskaia, 1994

Andrey Aliakrinsky: One often encounters the memories of some obscure people who write what TaMtAm was to them. For me it was not like that—for me TaMtAm meant home, as well as for all those who worked there. It was a place with very bright ideological objectives; it was freedom. To me TaMtAm never seemed to be a particularly brutal or vicious place, and I saw it all from the inside.[98]

Ilya Chert: Back then there was no law that prevented you from taking drugs. There were loads of mind-expanding substances in TaMtAm. Besides, they were very cheap. PCP cost like three or six times less than vodka. And vodka gave you a headache in the morning, unlike this thing that turned you into an alien for several days. Everybody was saying that PCP was not bad for your health.

By 1994 TaMtAm turned into a spaceport. The place was crowded with aliens. A bunch of ideas, funny faces, absolute freedom, incredible diversity. There were no adequate individuals in the club at all. Security only let in the aliens and told normal people that this was not the right place for them.

---

98 Translated from Aleksandr Gorbachev and Ilya Zinin, *Pesni v pustotu. Poteriannoe pokolenie russkogo roka 90-h* (Moscow: Corpus, 2014), 52.

On the outside the country was in trouble—but we didn't give a shit. The world was agonizing and changing several times a day, but our world was changing even faster. One has to give TaMtAm credit for the fact that it showed a whole generation of people that you can live without the rest of the world. If you want to play music, screw show business, go ahead and play! You want to be free—come be free with us. Musicians from the Leningrad Rock Club generation were trying to achieve something, find their niche, and prove something. In TaMtAm we felt self-sufficient. We had our club and that was all we needed.

I started playing in the group when I was seventeen. We played trash-metal. Our audience consisted of rough gloomy people: aggressive look, black leather, pins and skulls. I should say that behind those skulls were hidden probably the most sincere relationships in my entire life.[99]

Daniil Liapin: When I became actively involved in punk, political motives were not there anymore. We could do anything in TaMtAm. The first problem we caused led to more, which eventually led to

Vibrator's Daniil Liapin, TaMtAm, 1993, Permission from their archive

99 Stogoff, *Greshniki*, 65–66.

the closure of TaMtAm. It was during our concert on Yegor Letov's birthday on either the 10th or 11th of September, 1993.[100] Korol i Shut, Vibrator—everyone was there.[101] We were the third ones to play, and right after our set cops got into the place. Since then they came like every month and bust the shows.

Today I got paid
Everyone calls! Blowout!
Party!
Today "Royale" will pour like a river
Today, the cops will not rest!
Party!
We will be on the streets shouting obscenities
Shitting everywhere, vomiting
Party!
Drunken women, taking it from behind
Will choke on sperm
Party![102]

Ilya Bortniuk: The situation with drugs was exactly the same as everywhere, in all music gatherings. No more, no less. That is, it was not mayhem. The group Nirvana did drugs, no? But nobody wrote about that—they were such an exceptional group using drugs. I don't think there was more drug usage in TaMtAm than anywhere else. There were just a couple scenes in the show "600 Seconds," and after that everyone began to talk about it. But I wouldn't say it took some extreme forms. Yeah, there were always several people stoned. But there are such people in any club… You see, I believe the myth of drugs in TaMtAm was created by the counter-narcotics department—they had to do something. Where would they go? Moscow railway station? Probably not. Mariinsky or the cinema?[103]

---

100 Frontman of the Siberian punk band *Grazhdanskaia Oborona* (Civil Defense). Refer to the section on *Grazhdanaksaia Oborona* in Part 1.4.
101 *Korol i shut*—King and Jester.
102 "Gulbon" (Party) by *Vibrator*..
103 Mariinsky theatre.

Hardly. There's not much chance of finding something there. And then there is TaMtAm. Even if they found a couple bags of marijuana, for them it was the path to a career in crime detection.[104]

Ribson: I was born in TaMtAm from the beginning. It wasn't violent… of course, it was violent times in general. The system was broke, a new one just started, we had a lot of criminals on the streets, thieves, and even the cops were corrupt and selling drugs. It was a mess. The first time I saw Daniil [Liapin] he was sitting on a windowsill with a huge Mohawk, and I was like wow! So we started being friends.

Denis Kuptsov (D.J. Messer): In the '90s the police were busy looking for drug dealers and trafficking by beating up kids. We used to call "mask shows" shows when heavily armored police guys wearing masks would break into the club and construct a human wall with their hands. They were searching for drugs and would beat the shit out of you if you said anything. Not even something about them, but just something… Crazy times. Some of them ended with fatal injuries. There were even some stories when some crazy punks and skins beat the shit out of policemen…

We won't stay face down
We won't lay faced in the dirt
We won't listen to those
Who are crushed under our feet
Hindering our walking
We will break the deadlock in our way
If we have enough money for a couple of beers
We stand on the threshold of sound that will fall on ears of those who are
Chewing snot.
Cry in a secluded location
So as not to encounter pity.

---

104 *Furfur*, "Kak zhil russky muzykalny andergraund 1990-h."

Do not cause sympathy
Broken hearts and muzzles
Became a habit.
Stop waiting for protection
Time to attack
Until the jaw drops
Exit the will from the nerve sells
Already—there handing out slingshots[105]

Andrey Mashnin: Concerts were attended by different youth groups, but I didn't care. I wasn't friends with them, I wasn't representing anybody's views. But it was funny when people found secret messages in my lyrics all of a sudden. For example, I sing, "There were no negroes in the white army," and then rumors spread "Have you heard? Mashnin doesn't like negroes." Or there is a song where I sing, "Lonely as Stalin," and then again the news spread, "Mashnin sings about Stalin!"

Ilya Bortniuk: Everything (or almost everything) significant in today's Russian music scene was born in TaMtAm. Some of my musician friends brought me there for the first time. I remember it was a concert for the group Swindlers. Their drummer was Koshchey, who is now playing in the band Leningrad. The place seemed excellent. People were listening to music, drinking beer, and everyone was fine with both things. They were jumping, screaming, fighting, and dancing. In the middle of sad and barely floating St. Petersburg, I found a small island of Europe.

Musicians who were cultivating the image of TaMtAm were very different. From insane rockabillies coming to the club with knives and one meter long chains, to fiddlers with classical education playing experimental jazz, industrial noise artists, and Rastafarians. People were different, but they became part of the whole and the club kept going.

---

105 "Skazat Net" (To Say No) by *Mashninband.*

Mashninband, TaMtAm, 1996, Permission from Andrey Mashnin

In the early '90s I lived 10 minutes from TaMtAm. It was very convenient to go there. At first I went there as part of the audience. Every week I would make this or that music discovery for myself. Then I made a radio program about TaMtAm musicians. A couple of months later I started working there. Although "working" in TaMtAm is a very vague notion. Nobody hired you officially. There was no salary, no schedule, no working hours either. People just went there to help the club any way they could. It was a clique; a crew in the first place. I met Seva Gakkel there and made friends with other guys, too. That's how I started taking part in it.[106]

Kirill "George" Mikhailov: My first punk show was in 1993 at club TaMtAm. I met Avtomaticheskie Udovletvoriteli, Chudo-Yudo, and the local band Slang.[107] There was a lot of dancing, but there was no cultural dancing... People just did it the way they felt. It was violent—a lot of fights between punks and skins. Because in the '90s it was a hard time, people did every crazy thing they could at the time. Now it's funny to remember it. There were a lot of nazis of course, but it didn't matter in those times. There was a lot of

106 Stogoff, *Greshniki*, 68–69.
107 *Chudo-Yudo*—Whangdoodle.

motivation to fight each other in the subculture, not just the street life, but in the subculture.

In the '90s there were no politics in music, because old punk rock in Leningrad was antisocial, absolutely; they didn't want politics.

Il-78: I would say my perception of the music in the '90s in the underground clubs was, like, everyone was trying lots of styles. The most favorite bands of ours during the TaMtAm period were Khimera, The Pauki, and Spitfire.[108] They combined lots of styles like oi, punk, hardcore, metal, and ska. It could be danceable, heavy, aggressive, dreamy, acoustic. And Khimera played an unbelievable acoustic set—like aggressive music in an acoustic setting, which used to be associated with Russian/Soviet rock only. In fact, most of the bands of '90s hated that Soviet rock tradition, as did I. Soviet rock in its classical form turned out to be the essence of the Leningrad Rock Club (classical examples are bands Kino and Akvarium).

In the '90s I witnessed some of these bands, and while talking to the art director of Moloko Rock Club he said, "You haven't seen many of them, but there was a huge wave of bands copying the standards of Russian rock but in even worse form." And these TaMtAm guys wanted to do anything but be like these bands. According to Seva Gakkel, all bands playing TaMtAm must have nothing to do with the old Leningrad Rock Club. So discovering Khimera in acoustic, they really sounded different—it was my realization that you could play anything. It was different, you can try anything vivid, aggressive, funny, you can make fun of it all. For example, when Marradery had musical fragments in their songs poking fun of the band Kirpichi and other bands, thinking they were hardcore.[109] And it was a joke on them. For one of Ankylym's first songs, we made a song that was a joke against Marradery—if they can laugh at someone, we can laugh at them. We thought it was quite an atmosphere; you could try anything.

108 *Khimera*—Chimera; *Pauki*—Spiders.
109 *Marradery*—Garbled form of the word "Marrauders"; *Kirpichi*—Bricks.

Also I remember, coming back to childhood, I was really interested in theoretical parts related to rock music. The information from *Radio Katiusha* and articles in *Rock Fuzz* magazine, mostly from Kurbanovsky (a professor in the Russian museum) were really interesting. [They were] talking about Grazhdanskaia Oborona, Nozh dlia Frau Müller, and Yegor Letov, and he had articles about underground culture. Sometimes it was difficult to understand, but when you tried to feel what he was talking about—philosophy, modern culture of the 20th century—I discovered that rock is not just a music for fun, not to waste time; it's all very serious, and that you can put and find real meaning in it. That's why I was really interested in finding the background for all the bands. While collecting articles, I remember there was one English language article from the newspaper *St. Petersburg Times* about TaMtAm. It was an interview with Ed Starkov from Khimera, and he noted a term "TaMtAm generation," describing the bands associated with the club. They were really avant-garde in extreme music—Yugendshtil, The Pauki, Nozh dlia Frau Müller, Khimera, and some other bands. The explanation was that all of them sounded different, but our perception of music was similar. I was really thinking about this— you could really sound different, but all capture the same vibes. It was an experiment.

Ribson: You know in TaMtAm the director, Seva Gakkel, he was a big democrat. Really. He gave your group a lot of freedom, no matter what opinion. He only cared about the underground, not politics. But he wanted to give bands a place to express their opinion and defend their views freely.

I don't feel pity for you
I, I, I, I'll shoot you
I, I, I, I'll shoot you
I, I, I, I'll shoot you
I don't give a fuck if you're not guilty

I have an AK-47
I, I, I, I'll shoot you
I, I, I, I'll shoot you
I, I, I, I'll shoot you
Have to get his attention
Have to pique his interest
So she bought herself a new dress

And I cut myself a mohawk[110]

Chertovy Kukly's Masha and Alina, 1998, Den Kamenskii

110 "Liubov" (Love) by *Chertovy Kukly*—Fucking Dolls, (1999).

Maria Zalnova: I don't consider ["Liubov"] to be feminist lyrics. I never shared feminist ideas. Feminist ideas are stupid. This is not a popular idea in Russia; our women have worked a hundred years shoulder to shoulder with men. If a man does not open the door at the supermarket for me, and will not let me go ahead, I find him rude and very upsetting. I'm used to being protected and giving way. I'm not a feminist. I negatively regard their "ideas."

Why do you think a woman would get a mohawk? A girl who doesn't look pretty with a mohawk would never do it. The "weapon" is a different thing. It has a double meaning. But of course, mohawks are cool. We were cool.

Andrey Kniazev: TaMtAm was a wild place. Everything was allowed there. But the first concerts of Korol i Shut were too wild even for TaMtAm.

Gorshok and I went to the same art school. We were both studying to become fine art restorers. I was bald and dressed in quite an extravagant jacket. I instantly knew that Gorshok was a military man's son. He was dressed in trousers with creases and a buttoned up shirt right up to his neck. He didn't look particularly nice, but we still found common ground.

I showed him my poems and drawings. He told me that he and his schoolmates had formed a band that was based out of his apartment in Rzhevka.[111] This one time we went there for a band practice. Before that I thought about becoming an artist. But of course, playing punk rock was a lot more fun.

At first Seva didn't want us to play in TaMtAm. Now I perfectly understand why. The group was only one year old, nobody could really play an instrument, skinheads were among our audience, and Gorshok always went to TaMtAm totally wasted—besides, he was missing his front teeth. How could one let these people on stage?

---

111 Industrial region north of St. Petersburg.

We did our first public concert at Rubinstein 13, the place where the Leningrad Rock Club used to be. And after a year, in spring of 1993, Seva tolerated us.

The preparation for the first concert didn't take much time. I was dressed in striped pajamas and had a leather-like biker jacket on top.

Doing a show sober was unacceptable in TaMtAm. I had to drink, but I only had enough money for a beer bottle.

I went to the store, and in the waiting line I got acquainted with a guy who liked my outfit and bought a whole box of Baltika. We went to the club together. It was one hell of a night.[112]

In 1993 I joined the military, and when I got back I immediately went to TaMtAm. I met some people I hadn't seen for two years. We got really drunk, were beaten by special police forces. I got a taste of *Cheremukha* tear gas and spent the whole night at a police station. I was assured that things didn't change at all since my military deployment.

Every concert in TaMtAm would end at a police station for me. After the concert punks would split into interest groups: some wanted to fight, others wanted to buy drugs. But the cops thought they knew a better place for us. Masked *OMON* agents would seize crowds of people and put them into buses.[113]

Please don't think that I liked it all. The army made me look at a lot of things differently. When I came back, I had a chance to give this whole thing a fresh look. I didn't like what I saw. The guys were living in a rented apartment, and instead of band practices they would drink around the clock. The band was rolling into the abyss.[114]

Aleksandr "Balu" Balunov: We first came up with the idea to start a band in high school. It was back in 1987, we were 14 to 15 years

---

112 Stogoff, *Greshniki*, 79–80.
113 At that time called *Otriad militsii osobogo naznachenia*, nowadays renamed as *Otriad mobilny osobogo naznachenia (Special Purpose Mobility Unit, OMON)*—a Federal Police special-forces unit.
114 Stogoff, *Greshniki*, 83–84.

old, seventh graders, and the idea was to start a band, a community of like-minded individuals, not just the "let's play guitars together" kind of thing. It was the common way of thinking, a quest for freedom and search for a true name of god, so to say. Initially, it wasn't really that much about music. Well, we didn't even have guitars. But we quickly found them. One of the instruments was broken and required constant repairing. When we started playing, it was punk rock from the get-go. Although we had no clue it was punk rock. It wasn't until 1989 that we heard Sex Pistols—before that we'd listen to Russian rock: Alisa, Kino, DDT. Well, it's kind of

Korol i Shut's Gorshok, TaMtAm, September 7, 1995. A. Nastalskaia

a stretch to say we'd been listening to those bands, 'cause none of us owned a tape player. Gorshok had a very poor quality cheap mono model, though. However, he wasn't allowed to listen to the music at home because his dad worked for the KGB. We wore ripped pants with orange patches, acted punk, and shocked people. It was really fun. We had no idea how to play music, but still wanted to play it and do theatre. That's why we weren't bothered by any boundaries or rules to music; we weren't aware of any.

We couldn't care less about the opinions of the people around us. And we wanted to shock people to the maximum extent. Simultaneously. Fortunately, we had access to punk zines or images of punk outfits, and we weren't limited by anything other than our imagination.

Seva Gakkel: TaMtAm is no longer the only club in town [1996]: the scene has spread out. Clubs have now divided according to genre. In TaMtAm's first years all the coolest and, in many senses, most okay young people came here. Now some very conveniently located places have opened downtown, with bars and cafes. True, with higher cover charges, but with a certain amount of comfort, which a lot of people need. In some clubs it's become possible to play for money, to which musicians have quickly grown accustomed. Sometimes, when negotiating to play concerts here, musicians start talking about pay, which we aren't ready for yet. In addition, the constant threat of [drug enforcement] searches in our club isn't a draw. Obeying some unknown law, the skinheads have become active; their appearance in the club is always reason for anxiety. Thus we've gradually lost a significant part of our audience, and now only the most devoted come. True, sometimes during the performance of some group that's already become well known (but is willing to play for free), a rather large number of people show up, reminding us of the days gone by when that was routine.[115]

---

115 Gakkel, "TaMtAm without Illusions," article written in March 1996, published in *A Rock and a Hard Place: Petersburg Civil Society from the Pages of Pchela (The Bee)* (1998), 90.

2.2 Intelligent Punk[116]

Artemy Troitsky: In Moscow at that time there were two clubs. Sexton—punk/metal, where the music and audience were absolutely dumb. There were guys in black leather, some kind of bikers, showing off their motorcycles. I never liked them. There was never anything interesting there. It was very aggressive—Sexton was known for the fact that there were several murders committed there. One of the musicians was finished off there, some common visitors, and I think even one of the owners. But the place was just unpleasant itself, It was a black spot for bikers and rednecks playing any music like AC/DC or Motorhead, only the Russian version of it. The second club, I think formed a little later than Sexton, was Bunker, which started the whole "B2" and "B1" empire. It was at Trifonovskaya Street near the metro station Rizhskaya. It was much more civilized and pleasant, where groups played a variety of styles.[117]

Svetlana Yelchaninova: When I graduated school, I had a dream with a few friends to start a rock club, because there simply was no rock club in Moscow. There was the Moscow Rock Laboratory [see section 4.4], which under the auspices of the Komsomol had a festival once a year. It had a small place to play, but there was no place to party.[118] We wanted to create that. The idea was in the air— but our Jerry Rubin Club was the first. There were no rock clubs in Moscow—at least called rock clubs. There were two or three night discos, where pop stars performed. Therefore, we were all friends with each other, helped each other out, and shared music. And we were always hanging out because there was nothing else to do.

---

116 Many of the interviews from this section are translated from Russian publications, due to the present condition of the interviewees or their inaccessibility. The source is cited at the end of each paragraph.

117 Gorbachev and Zinin, *Pesni v pustotu*, 34.

118 For a definition of *Komsomol*, see footnote 26, Part One.1. The Moscow Rock Laboratory was a civic organization which controlled the activities of rockers in the '80s in Moscow. For more on that, read Max Kotchetkov's article below.

There was no need to advertise concerts, because everyone you already knew. You would come to Pushka, where every day there would be punks, and you would say "Tomorrow at Jerry so and so are playing."[119] That's all. In general it was all underground. It was only later when some money appeared that some bandits realized it was possible to invest moula to sell alcohol and get a real profit. And then it began to appear at other places.[120]

Sergey Guryev: In Moscow in the beginning of the '90s, music was a failure. The *Kontr Kult URa* at the time came from the fact that we had the support of Siberian punks like Letov, Nick Rock 'n' Roll, Yanka, and Komitet Okhrany Tepla.[121] Even Matrosskaia Tishina had no interest, not to mention the rest of Moscow rock— nevertheless, if you ever came across something as massive and spiritual, you will not agree to anything less. And Rezervatsia Zdes set themselves the goal to fill these lacunas.[122] Santim was a music lover who realized in time that if he wanted to hear a certain group in Moscow, then he had to create it himself.[123] It turned into some kind of punk-alternative with an ear toward Siberia, but with a very Moscow feel—both in lyrics and sound. At the festival *Indiuki* they shocked Valera Murzin, president of the Novosibirsk Rock Club.[124] He came to me and asked, "What do they sing about? 'Moscow for Muscovites?' hey want me to get out of here?"[125]

Konstantin Mishin: Punk rock in Moscow started to spread from the studio Kolokol, known by everyone. I was not far from there—I wrote for *Strit* magazine, connected to the Rock Laboratory, and spent time near local activists.[126] The rock movement in those times

---

119 Pushkinskaia square.
120 Gorbachev and Zinin, *Pesni v pustotu*, 33.
121 *Komitet Okhrany Tepla*—Committee for the Protection of Heat.
122 *Rezervatsia Zdes*—Reservation Here.
123 *Rezervatsia Zdes*, along with *Banda Chetyrekh* (*Band of Four*), were the projects of Ilya "Santim" Malashenkov. These can easily be considered some of Moscow's first punk or post-punk underground bands.
124 *Indiuki*—Turkeys.
125 Feliks Sandalov, *Formation. Istoria odnoy stseny* (*Formation. The History of One Scene*) (Moscow: Common Place, 2016), 77.
126 *Kolokol*—Bell, was the studio owned and operated under the auspices of the Moscow Rock

came from stadiums and concert halls, but I thought that there must be some alternative and decided to make *kvartirniki* (without the Rock Laboratory's help), starting with Zhenia Morozov, vocalist of DK, and it continued.[127] Finally Olia Baraboshkina suggested that I make a concert for Nick Rock 'n' Roll. She said, "Look, his manager Boris Usov will call you," and added with adoration, "a very talented boy."

A week and a half before the concert we made a call to Usov and Rudkin, and we met to discuss how to attract people. "If we invite people by phone, 30-35 people will come. We don't know anything, and I just started organizing concerts," I said.

"Let's put an ad or flyer in Kolokol studio a week before," suggested Usov. "Then 100 or 120 people will come together and destroy the flat, and even not everyone will fit."

"So what? Who cares?" said Boris, with a tone of Karlsson—jauntily, like "It's a small matter."[128]

"Why don't you make a concert at your own home?" I asked angrily. "I can't, and my parents are at home," said Boris, "I am also not an orphan, you know. My old mother would not survive if they destroyed everything."

We decided to put up posters three days before the kvartirnik. Usov did a cool drawing—some freaky, animalistic thing. Then we started agreeing upon the conditions: "You take one third (you make the posters, you gather the audience, you deliver the 'performers'), I take one third (I provide an apartment and deal with the neighbors), and Nick takes one third." That was my suggestion.

"I'm gonna give my money to Nick Rock 'n' Roll", Usov said proudly.

"That's cool, way to go, but I wouldn't do it. It's gonna be a good addition to my study allowance." Usov gave me a grim look

Laboratory.

127 *Kvartirniki* (apartment concerts) were more common in Moscow than St. Petersburg; rock-band *DK* formed in Moscow in 1980.

128 Lazy and spontaneous Karlsson is the lead character of Astrid Lindgren's fairy tales that were very popular in the Soviet Union.

under his glasses, but didn't say anything this time. Rudkin snorted. We shook hands and got down to business.

I was a smart kid. I read *Kontr Kult URa* magazine and I knew what to expect from Nick and his group Koba, so I hid my colognes, money, and valuables. There were loads of people at the meeting point in the middle of the Beliaevo metro station hall. I took the crowd to the trash hole near my house, explained the rules in my apartment, and started taking small groups of people inside. I let about 70 people in with three ruble "tickets." The last four people didn't fit in the apartment, so I gave them stools to watch the concert from behind the door, cramming their necks (I charged them one ruble). Then we started counting the pot and Usov made a scene. "You stole from the musicians! Take two more rubles from those in the corridor or throw them out!!!" "It would be easier for me to throw you out, drama queen. Don't forget that you are at my place…"

The star of *samizdat* rock-journalism attacked me with his fists.[129] I socked him back. Guryev, Baraboshkina, and Rudkin pulled us apart, stopping the fight. The concert started. Tolik Pogodaev

Solomenye Enoty, Kvartirnik (apartment show), March 8, 1995, Oleg Panaryin

---

129 *Samizdat*: Literature banned by the Soviet State, which was clandestinely copied and passed from reader to reader.

and Sania Zlatozub were sitting on the windowsill with acoustic guitars and their legs against the radiator. Nick was standing on the windowsill embracing the frame; he was technically outside the apartment on the other side.[130]

Aleksey "Ekzich" Slezov: Kvartirniki could be either electric or acoustic, but most importantly everything happened very chaotically. Especially with alcohol, which was almost always there. Kolia Grigoryev was sponsoring us back then. There was this one time when he brought a whole cart of alcohol with very expensive drinks: whiskey, gin, rum. At that time these were unaffordable, so everyone got fucked-up beyond recognition. I didn't, because I took the concert seriously. Although it turned into a booze night—I can't say that I liked it. Unfortunately, this happened very often, but it didn't bother people much.[131]

Ilya "Santim" Malashenkov: The '90s were the time of absolute freedom. Now it's hard to believe it, but back in 1993 we were running our own business—we had a big sales outlet where we were selling porn magazines right near the KGB office at Lubianka Street. We were hiding porn under erotic magazines and didn't even bribe anyone—neither cops, nor bandits. I assume both parties were thinking that the other one was giving us protection. Then we opened five more sales outlets. We were making really big money, but were spending everything on booze. Later, Daun was pressed by the cops about his magazines and was taken to court.[132] As a result, he got a fine and was granted amnesty in 1993. I sold all of his magazines by wholesale and made enough money to not work for a very long time. This is what it used to be like everywhere. As a libertarian, I appreciated it very much. The times were not destructive, rather constructive. Now I understood the disappointment of the people of the '60s, who thought that freedom was to be forever. That's what

130 Sandalov, *Formation*, 85–86.
131 Sandalov, *Formation*, 87.
132 Daun—one of the musicians.

happened to us. The '90s were too fun and roaring for us to gauge that time. We were swimming along the non-conformist tide, and got out of it only by the 2000s.[133]

Everyday is a funeral, everyday someone is buried.
A place of survival—urban zone.
Here dirty snow falls on the asphalt under your feet.
But this day—it's normal, just a little scarier.
A normal day, here it is.
Who's to blame for the reservation?
Everyday there are fireworks, everyday there are parades.
Veterans are teaching to build barricades.
And what about the kids? Study. And how? You bet.
But this day—it's normal, just a little scary.
Everyday there is drinking, everyday there are parties
Those who survived are wounded birds.
Everything is clear, everything is important.
But this day—it's normal, that's why it's terrible.
A normal day, here it is.
Who's to blame for the reservation here?

I'm not to blame for the reservation here.[134]

Boris Usov: Existential punk is a label that was created by Guryev and *Kontr Kult URa* magazine. The only existential thing that I felt was loneliness, even when surrounded by a crowd of people. But there was a decisive moment in my life, it happened when I was a student of the Institute of Asian and African Countries. My path to the subway was through the house where Rudkin lived. The group *Bresh Bezopasnosti* did rehearsals there.[135] Kulganek and Rudkin were mixing vodka with hot tea, singing songs. I used to visit them and stay, instead of going to classes about the history of the party. This was probably that existential moment that I wasn't really aware of.[136]

133 Sandalov, *Formation*, 93.
134 "Rezervatsia Zdes" by *Banda Chetyrekh*, written by and also performed by the band named after the song.
135 *Bresh Bezopasnosti*—Security Flaw.
136 Sandalov, *Formation*, 109-110.

Aleksandr Kushnir: At some point the St. Petersburg magazine *Roxi* stated that Moscow groups were different in a way; they could hardly accumulate legends and myths around them. There were two exceptions: Zvuki Mu and Solomennye Yenoty.[137] We can say that they created their own sect, but we should admit it with a certain level of warmth—because I favor this type of sect.[138]

Solomenye Enoty, Kvartirnik (apartment show), March 8, 1995, Oleg Panaryin

Arina Stroganova: Borian was the only one who was tied to Solomennye Yenoty longer than I. When I came, he was already playing in Yenoty. He was also playing in the last rendition of Solomennye Yenoty, and basically organized the recording of their last album. In between these periods he didn't communicate much with Boris Usov and didn't play in the group, but all the same. How did I manage to stay close to Usov for so long? We had a special connection, some unexplainable attachment united us. That's why I could forgive this poorly communicative person in situations where other people would hold grudges, either for years or maybe even forever. Usov, in turn, could cope with my drawbacks. He infected me with his ideas and interests; it was exciting and enlightening to

137 *Zvuki Mu*—Sounds 'Mu'; *Solomennye Yenoty*—Straw Racoons.
138 Sandalov, *Formation*, 126.

be close to such an extraordinary person. Although from the moral and ethical standpoint, some of his views turned my world upside down and I used to lose ground when I couldn't map my values to some of his views. On the whole he had a very big impact on me in many ways. Not only through his works, but also through real-life communication. He had a major influence on many of his other friends too.[139]

Viktor Kulganek: We were all young and stupid, but at the same time energetic and passionate. The revolutionary-anarchist ideas, obviously, haunted us. However, they were not dominant in our works; it was more of a beautiful romantic position. When things had gotten more serious, I started to get involved less. With that being said, I still like the National Bolshevik Party and their head Limonov—I have a number of his books in my library. Besides, I have many NBP-related friends, like Sasha Aronov who was a prominent representative of the movement. But back in 1994–1995 it was a boring mixture of concepts like Communist ideas and "Russian breakthroughs." People were into everything from Eurasianism to half-fascism. In reality, we just had to take things less seriously. Later the movement started to break up into formations, like *konkovsky* formation, *liublinsky,* and others.[140] During one of our last conversations Boris was passionately telling me that Zakhar Mukhin, Borian, and "Liskhleb" were "our people." I agreed that they were awesome people, but what I didn't understand was the whole concept of "our people." It was just another group of people friendly to you, so you don't have to consider them spiritual brothers or anything, because you will be disappointed to find out that they are still very different from you. This happened all the time, and every time Boris would take it very personally.[141]

139 Sandalov, *Formation*, 154.
140 Konkovo and Liublino are districts of Moscow.
141 Sandalov, *Formation*, 154–155.

Boris Usov: We went to visit Nemirov once and he was showing off so much, just like Neumoev, with whom we never got along because of his megalomania that knew no limits.[142] Roma had that period where he turned into Nemirov the businessman. He was wearing a suit; he had a fountain pen and looked quite decent. We asked him to give us *Sibirskaia Yazva* magazine to make a copy, and he tried to charge an arm and a leg for it.[143] "Money, money, money, fellas." We were shocked. What kind of Rock 'n' Roll brotherhood is that?...We tried to convince him by saying that the magazine was dedicated to Tiumen and the second wave of Tiumen punk. "What second wave? After Instruktsia punk ended!" This made us really mad. Later our relationship only worsened.[144]

Aleksandr "Leshy" Ionov: We were a group of intellectuals, not *intelligentsia*. It's important to separate the two terms. We read a lot, heard a lot, watched a lot, but it didn't make us delicate or soft. We were outrageous, rude, and wild. We all loved postpunk. Post-punk had its thing where you had to look ordinary, wear ordinary stuff on stage and in daily life, like we were normal guys without mohawks and stuff. When we went on tour in the '90s, our audience was different. They were wearing leather biker jackets, had fancy hairstyles, and were bedecking themselves with all kinds of things. That's why they were surprised to see us, because we looked like nerds to them. Their skeptical looks faded away, once we started to rock.[145]

A sunny day over the country of Muravia
Confused in the wires,
People bustle about like an ant army
In the stone cities

---

142 Miroslav Nemirov was writer for the band *Instruktsia po Vyzhivaniu (Survival Instruction)*, a New Wave band that formed in the mid '80s, and based its name off of a *Grazhdanskaia Oborona* song; Roman Neumoev is the vocalist, guitarist, harmonist, and writer for *Instruktsia po Vyzhivaniu*. For more on *Instruktsia*, read Vladimir Kozlov's oral history of punk in Siberia, Part 1.4.
143 *Sibirskaia Yazva*—Siberian plague.
144 Sandalov, *Formation*, 207.
145 Sandalov, *Formation*, 207.

And they run along the paths sprinkled with salt,
And they are proud of their social responsibility
But I have another interest in this life
I'm from the Russian intelligentsia!!!

Sometimes I write poems and articles at leisure,
In short, I'm from the Russian intelligentsia,
Do not stand in my way!

In the evenings I go to restaurants,
To dispel my sorrow
I get drunk with one glass—I am drunk,
And I sermonize,

To make people forget their despair
So they begin to fight evil,
And what if there is spirituality in Russia?
Then it's only in me!

I have many familiar chicks
Because I'm famous.
The chicks do not understand anything at all,
But it does not even make me angry.

I communicate with them through gestures
And I do not listen to their stupid words.
 This was taught to me by Leo Shestov,
Berdiaev and Smirnoff vodka!

I'm a proud descendant of the White Guards,
Workers, bourgeois and Red Army men
Yeah, what do you care where I'm from?
I just want to snatch a piece of your happiness

And if I manage to take it away,
I'll deal with you!
And you will pray with me for the St. Khavronya Rus!
I'm from the intelligentsia![146]

---

146 "Intelligent" by *Solomennye Yenoty*, from the album *Razvilka* (Fork). Lyrics by Boris Usov, translated by Alexander Herbert. The song is obviously meant to be a satire on the traditional Russian "intelligentsia."

Characters in the order they appear:

Seva Gakkel—Violinist for rock band Akvarium (St. Petersburg) and founder of club TaMtAm.

Andrey Aliakrinsky—Sound engineer.

Vadim Kurylev—Frontman for Elektricheskie Partisany (St. Petersburg).

Oleg Gitarkin—Guitarist and founder of bands Nozh dlia Frau Müller and Messer Chups (St. Petersburg).

Artemy Troitsky—Notable music critic and long time journalist of Russian rock music, broadly speaking. Author of "Back in the USSR," a major English-language source of the Soviet Union's earliest Rock culture.

Andrey Chernov—Guitarist for Avtomaticheskie Udovletvoriteli (St. Petersburg), longtime fan of Russian punk.

Ilya Chert—Frontman for Pilot (St. Petersburg).

Daniil Liapin—Frontman for Vibrator (St. Petersburg).

Dmitry Buchin—Drum player in the bands Narodnoe Opolchenie, Otdel Samoiskorenenia and Nate! (St. Petersburg).

Maria Zalnova—Frontwoman of Chertovy Kukly (St. Petersburg)

Yury Sobolev— Guitarist for Brigandy Podriad (St. Petersburg).

Andrey Mashnin—Frontman for Mashinband, and temporarily with Bondzinsky (St. Petersburg).

Ilya Nikitin—Frontman and guitarist for Marradery and Port (812) (St. Petersburg).

Ilya Bortniuk—Founder of Stereoleto festival, producer of (some albums) by Kirpichi, Nozh dlia Frau Müller and Spitfire (St. Petersburg).

Ribson—Co-frontman in the '90s for Piat Uglov, frontman for Next Round (St. Petersburg).[147]

Denis Kuptsov (D.J. Messer)—Drummer for The Swindlers, Spitfire, The Pikes, Leningrad, and Tequilajazzz (St. Petersburg).

Kirill "George" Mikhailov—Guitarist for the bands Svinokop, 01 band, Cut'n'Run, Dottie Danger, and vocalist for Upor Lezha (St. Petersburg).[148] Founder of Karma Mira and NotLG tapes record labels.[149]

Ilya "Il-78" Alekseev—Frontman and songwriter for Ankylym (St. Petersburg), academically trained observer of the scene.

Andrey Kniazev—One of two frontman for Korol i Shut (St. Petersburg).

Aleksandr "Balu" Balunov—Bass player for Korol i Shut.

Svetlana Yelchaninova—Founder of Moscow's Jerry Rubin Club.

Sergey Guryev—Music critic and journalist, vocalist of Chistaia Lubov (Moscow).[150]

---

147 *Piat Uglov*—Five Corners.
148 *Upor Lezha*—Prone Position.
149 *Karma Mira*—Karma of the World.
150 *Chistaia Lubov*—Pure Love.

Konstantin Mishin—Guitarist for Banda Chetyrekh, frontman and guitarist for Ozhog (Moscow).[151]

Aleksey "Ekzich" Slezov—Guitarist and bassist for Banda Chetyrekh, Ozhog, Solomennye Yenoty, Zateriannye v Kosmose, and Region-77 (Moscow).[152]

Ilya "Santim" Malashenkov—Frontman for the bands Guliay-Pole, Rezervatsia Zdes and Banda Chetyrekh (Moscow).[153]

Boris Belokurov (originally Usov)—Frontman and songwriter for Solomennye Yenoty.

Aleksandr Kushnir—Journalist, editor of the iconic underground magazine *Kontr Kult URa* in the '80s and early '90s.

Arina Stroganova—Vocalist and *guitarist for Solomennye Yenoty.*

Viktor Kulganek—Frontman for Bresh Bezopasnosti (Moscow).

Aleksandr "Leshy" Ionov—Frontman for Ogon and Region-77 (Moscow).[154]

---

151 *Ozhog*—Burn.
152 *Zateriannye v Kosmose*—Lost in Cosmos.
153 *Guliay-Pole*—Up for Grabs.
154 *Ogon*—Fire.

2.3: "THE MOSCOW ROCK LABORATORY" REVISITED

By Max Kochetkov (Naive)

Edited and Translated by Alexander Herbert[155]

*I*n many ways this is a historical article that merits reproduction in full. Originally published in Maximum Rocknroll # 96 (1991, the "Special Soviet Punk Issue"), it really represented one of the first opportunities for Western punks to peer into the world of underground Moscow rock culture. While Max's primary objective was to invite exchange between Russia and the West, the article in context demonstrates the comparative wealth of Moscow in the late '80s and early '90s. Compared to Leningrad and St. Petersburg, the resources of Moscow permitted an organization like the Moscow Rock Laboratory to flourish for some time, paving the way for the emergence not only of commercial punk, but multiple styles of punk rock. While Max seems particularly pessimistic about certain aspects of the Rock Laboratory's manufacturing abilities, it makes Leningrad and St. Petersburg look desolate. Better than any other source, this article helps draw a bridge between the early years of punk in Leningrad and the emergence of "The Moscow Giants."

I have edited the grammar and wording in some places for clarity, but the structure and points remain the same. At the end, I asked Max, who is now a professional translator and writer, to reflect on his time working for the Moscow Rock Laboratory and its eventual demise.

1991:

*T*he Moscow Rock Laboratory was founded in 1985 as an umbrella organization for Moscow's various unofficial rock bands. Since 1986, it operated as an independent concert promoting entity. In 1986 it acquired an official

---

155 The first half of this article appeared in Maximum Rocknroll #96, 1991, under the title "The Moscow Rock Laboratory." That part has only been edited, while the second half—Max's reflection on the Rock Laboratory's demise—was written by Max in 2018 and translated by Alexander Herbert.

stamp of approval, with the objective of identifying young bands playing non-commercial rock and giving them the opportunity to become known to the public—promoting their creative growth and giving them administrative support.

The Moscow Rock Laboratory provides training facilities, free apparatuses, and covers the cost of video and sound recordings. It also organizes concert tours and takes care of public relations and commercial presentations.

The Rock Laboratory brings together over 600 performers, artists, photographers, journalists, engineers, technicians, and managers. It caters to more than 60 bands, has a technical center, artistic workshops, studio, and sound recording facilities. It also has a concert office and an editorial board.

The Moscow Rock Laboratory builds its membership on the basis of collective recommendations of its artistic council. It is a cost-accounting organization, with revenues coming primarily from concert activities, publications, and technical services. The following examines some of the areas of the music industry of Moscow that we cover.

When it comes to the topic of touring in Russia, I would like to note that as a rule, the Rock Laboratory organizes concerts for Western bands within Moscow city limits, though we have had other experiences in that area. In general, our touring organization activities lie in bands that are of a considerable creative and professional interest to us.

The Rock Laboratory has two concert halls in the so-called Houses of Culture (one more note—there's no club-scene in the Soviet Union). The capacity of the first hall is 200 people and the other holds 1,500 people. There is a 2 kilowatt-rated power, Czechoslovakian made P.A., and a 60-source stage light installed in the smaller hall. The P.A. power for the second one is unlimited. We've got a 36-track mixing stand by "Soundcraft," a set of treatment and processing apparatuses, "Fender" and "Marshall" guitar amplifiers and monitors, a 300-source stage light, and two kinds of stage-smoke.

Transportation matters are easily settled, for we use our own buses and cars. No trucks, though (we lease them).

The Rock Laboratory also owns a hotel big enough for 50 people with low comfort standards. Yet, still, it's a very cozy place and if someone is interested in seriously "conquering" Russia, we'd be very happy to have you, as it would benefit both parties.

There are some obstacles, though. The first is that there is no possibility for us to buy traveling tickets for touring bands, because there is a law forbidding Soviets from doing it. That's why bands that want to play in Russia should pay for their own fare from one country to another, and vice versa.

The second problem is that in order to draw a crowd for an unknown band, say about 100 people, it takes about 400 rubles to cover the costs of month-long commercial advertisements. The maximum price for such a concert should be no more than three rubles. The income from ticket sales most often does not cover the expenses for the P.A. and hall lease. Losses from such concerts total up to 7,000 or 8,000 rubles, usually. Hence, "pure" touring is not suitable for groups playing non-commercial music. Nevertheless, the Moscow Rock Laboratory has other opportunities to offer Western-bands in the USSR. Generally, the Rock Laboratory is ready to discuss any ideas and make out a suitable project for both sides. Our *Sdvig* magazine, as well as "Sdvig-Afisha" newspaper, are open for band ads, for example.[156]

The Rock Laboratory is also ready to place at your disposal more than 35 bands. The groups operating under our auspices are winners of many festivals and contests held in the Soviet Union and abroad. Some bands have had their records issued in Great Britain, France, West Germany, and Finland. The Rock Laboratory's performers tour Denmark, Sweden, Finland, Belgium, France, UK, Germany, Italy, the USA, and Norway. According to press accounts

156 *Sdvig*—Shift, Move.

and judging by the increasing number of invitations, the Rock Laboratory musicians fully represent "underground" Soviet rock outside the country, ranging from ethnographical jazz to outrageous punk.

Since 1988 we've been publishing our magazine *Sdvig*, covering topical information in the music scene and problems of the "musical underground" in Russia. The zine has a circulation of more than 10,000 copies and has a subscription all over the USSR. In the autumn of 1990, we started printing an English supplement with authorized translations. In addition to that, twice a month we publish "Sdvig-Afisha," a newspaper which is also an independent publication. Part of the "Sdvig-Afisha" circulation is distributed retail.

There is still a totalitarian monopoly on record issuing in the USSR. That is of the State record company, Melodia.[157] That is why it is still a big problem to release records from independent bands. In the five years of the Moscow Rock Laboratory's existence, we've released only six records on Melodia. There is no other choice—that record label is the only one in the country. But we've tried to cooperate with foreigners, and as a result, the Laboratory has more than fifteen records released in the West.

Furthermore, the problem with Melodia is that it is only interested in huge circulations that bring in "big" returns. So, the basis of the company's repertoire is (no doubt!) popular commercial music. Besides that, Melodia doesn't pay for tape masters used for pressing and doesn't pay any percentage to the musicians either. A band having its record released through Melodia receives only about 100 rubles for an LP. That is a rip off, that's for sure. Long publishing periods scare off bands also, as it takes about a year or two to print a record. Things being that way on Melodia make any record release a terrible headache and a charitable action of the band and the Rock Laboratory.

---

157 See footnote 48, Part 1.1.

The principle form of non-commercial music distribution in the USSR is through cassettes. There is a big network of sound recording studios that quickly distribute new releases. It's a pity, though, that the majority of such studios are, again, oriented toward commercial music. Still, there are a certain number of studios that supply the whole independent music scene in the country with non-commercial music by post. The Rock Laboratory has one like that called Kolokol, possessing a unique collection of Soviet Rock 'n' Roll recordings made in the past 15 years (since 1975).[158] Kolokol's catalog is sent by mail on request. If you're interested in something, the studio will send it to you.

We do not have our own recording studio, though some groups pay for their recordings on favorable terms if they are rich enough. Sometimes we will cover part of the sum. Still, the most serious problem of recording in the USSR is a lack of professional producers, the lack of studio tapes, and the fact that we are unable to distribute our music even inside the country, each press being rather small. The tapes are distributed through retail-trade spots. The Rock Laboratory has three of them in the city.

Now the good news. The CD manufacturing section has stirred up its activities. Because of the new economic policy, they showed interest not long ago in collaborating with us. At the moment, preliminary negotiations are in the works. Besides that, some cooperative companies livened up their efforts also, though we haven't seen any results yet.

We are seeking contacts with foreign publishing firms, record companies, and distributors. The Laboratory has some experience in that area and we'd be glad to find new partners. The Rock Laboratory can offer different kinds of mutual collaboration in the process of issuing records and tapes.

In addition, I dare say that Moscow Rock Laboratory's collection of recordings (practically a history-manual of the 20-year

158 *Kolokol*—Bell.

development of Russian Rock 'n' Roll) is a rarity in the Soviet Union and can be of a great interest to anyone.

Promotion is impossible on TV. It's a pity to state the fact that Rock Laboratory's relations with the State-owned TV company resembles that of Melodia and are quite "polarized." The administration of this organization even made lists forbidding the TV appearance of bands of the Moscow Rock Laboratory. It might seem crazy, but the bands have never been shown, nor will they be.

Things being that way made us search for alternative ways to promote. In 1989, the Moscow Rock Laboratory shot its first 150 minute long video-film called "Sdvig-Rock 'n' Roll," presenting 18 bands to mass audiences. By now we've sold more than 2,000 copies of that film inside the country and abroad (part of the circulation being sold to Japan, France, and Holland).

Another aspect of our daily work is photography. There are several photographers among the Laboratory's personnel who take photos of the bands on and off stage.

Airplay and radio promotion in the USSR also pose a whole lot of difficulties and one can hardly regard it as possible, for the radio network is, again, owned by the State. All radio stations in the USSR play pop-commercial music and occasional spins of our bands do not change the situation on the whole.

Thus, mass media, as long as it is owned by the State, cannot be used for independent music promotion.

Other Rock Laboratory activities include production and distribution of music-related advertising goods. We manufacture and sell t-shirts, buttons, stickers, patches, and other stuff. Now we are thinking of opening up our own rock-shop specializing in everything connected with music.

The Moscow Rock Laboratory's annual festivals significantly influence any band's popularity, and that is not a lie. Every year we stage two festivals. One of them is called Festival Nadezhd, that takes place in spring or late winter.[159] The event

159 *Festival Nadezhd*—The Festival of New Hopefuls.

requires considerable preparation. The Rock Laboratory collects auditioning demos of the new bands that want to join in. After Christmas every weekend, we organize live auditions for bands that are considered to be potential participants after their demos have been listened to. The bands with hope are then given a chance to show their worth during the festival. A big number of people dealing with independent music from all around the country come to see fresh bands live. As a rule, all of the festivals are professionally recorded on video and cassette.

This year (1991) we had our annual spring Festival Nadezhd for the 6th time. About 80 bands, nowadays enjoying great popularity in the scene, were presented to the audience for the first time during the festival. The second festival staged by the Moscow Rock Laboratory in the autumn represents the most popular bands, and is a kind of "concluding" gig. Last year, it was on the 15th and 16th of December (more than 20 bands took part in it) and it was dedicated to our 5th anniversary.

2018:

When I took office as the Head of the International Department of the Moscow City Creative Rock Music Laboratory under the auspices of the Moscow City Committee of the All-Union Leninist Young Communist League, I inherited the Rock Laboratory in a very different, modified format. As TASS later put it: "When the Freedom of Speech and the Freedom of the Song had sprouted from under the Soviet asphalt."[160] Indeed, the Rock Laboratory had existed already for seven years, from 1985 to 1992, and I came in 1990. Already it was missing Artem Troitsky, Vasia Shumov (Tsentr), Zhanna Aguzarova (Bravo), Petr Mamonov and Aleksandr Lipnitsky (Zvuki Mu), no Garik Sukachev (Brigada S), no Hank and Mamont (Chudo-Yudo), no Pauk, Borov, or Kostyl from

---

160 TASS—See footnote 18, Part 1.

Korrozia Metalla.[161] There was practically no E.S.T., no Va-Bank, and no Pogo.[162]

Already the Kurchatov House of Culture was closed, but the Gorbunov House of Culture operated. Already there were no Rock Laboratory lyric censors. And then many scenesters claim, "The Laboratory tried to put the underground under the control of the KGB and to place concert activity under their umbrella." The director of the Rock Laboratory was Olga Opriatnaia, with security at concerts presided over by the "Night Wolves" biker gang. The Rock Laboratory competed, made friends, and fought all the new players in the musical market: Feelee, UrLait, Kontr Kult URa, Indiuki, SyRock, the Moscow State University Rock Club, and many, many others.

Sleeping on the couch at Olga Opriatnaia's house was not Viktor Tsoi of Kino, but Max Kochetkov of Naive. Some bikers often came by like Kim Ir Sen from the motorcycle club "Russian Cossacks," competing with the "Night Wolves," roping the Rock Laboratory's activities into the criminal world. People stopped talking about rubles, and started talking dollars.

Yet Olga persevered. The first circulation of the Moscow Rock Laboratory's fanzine *Sdvig* was confiscated due to articles by Sergey Zharikov from DK, who wrote with a strong right wing influence. There was the totalitarian art of DK, and a cult of Grazhdanskaia Oborona.

In the army, I gleaned a lot of leftist and anarchist ideas from fanzines like *Maximum Rocknroll* and brought them back to the Rock Laboratory. A lot of my New York punk ideas also trickled in. So MRR and CBGB seeds fell on prepared soil. With my joining, the Rock Laboratory organization turned its assets in a new direction, focusing on Soviet proto-punk, with groups like Nogu Svelo!, Mongol Shuudan, Matrosskaia Tishina, Naive, Klinika, Zhenskaia Bolezn, Rukasty Perets, Chetyre Tarakana, ANCh, A-Y, Tupye, T-34,

161 *Brigada C*—Brigade C; *Borov*—Boar; *Kostyl*—Crutch; *Korrozia Metalla*—Metal Corrosion.
162 *Va-Bank*—All-In.

and Distemper.[163] Under my leadership, the Rock Laboratory (or the Belch Lab, as some called it) started steering away from ethno-jazz toward straightforward punk and straightforward messages.

Olga was a strong character with lots of balls. I didn't know a lot about this, but she was closely connected with the Ministry of Culture of the USSR, and she did a lot through them. I also knew that her friends traded cars and other scarce junk. She decided on the questions to ask the bands with the KGB and the City Communist Party Committee, and she assured me that there were people there who understood the new direction of the Rock Laboratory. As for me, I was outside of the Soviet system and didn't believe in it—the logo of my band Naive even had the anarchist symbol inside of it. After serving in the army from 1987 to 1989, and having seen the lawlessness of the Red Army firsthand, I knew the country would soon collapse. The Soviet Union imploded and anarchy filled the void—nobody recognized what stood in the place of the old regime.

Olga and I became close, and we spent a lot of time together. She filled me in on a lot that she was unable to tell others. She knew that only I could move our common business further. There was already a lot she couldn't do—she couldn't speak English, and she had no connections to the West. By the time I started working at the Rock Laboratory, the organization had accumulated a bunch of letters from different countries, and they all required an answer, but nobody was capable of the task. I took the responsibility of translations and built additional contacts with Westerners. I continued to reach out to anyone that had a punk attitude and cast aside anyone that expressed opinions contrary to punk (racism, nazism, fascism, homophobia, sexism, etc.). I must have been the only punk among the Laboratory leadership.

But the Rock Laboratory was a Soviet organization, and its activity was curbed after the events of 1991—the August Putsch.[164] The Soviet Union, as a country, started to swiftly fall

163 *Nogu Svelo!*—A Camp in a Foot!; *Rukasty Peretz*—Handy Pepper; *Chetyre Tarakana*—The Four Cockroaches—was the first name of the band Tarakany!; *Tupye*—Stupid.
164 For the August Coup, refer to footnote 81, Part 2.1. See also *Naïve's* concert activities during

apart. It was a serious test for musicians and for those who tried to work with us. The administrators of the Rock Laboratory, as well as residents throughout the Soviet Bloc, found new interests—in particular, money. The point is that nobody wanted to build Communism anymore. Capitalism won; greed and accumulation prevailed. The Rock Laboratory stopped being able to trade with state-owned companies. *Maximum Rocknroll* tried to help at one point, transferring $500.00 to Moscow. I knew that such an amount wouldn't save the Rock Laboratory, and after much contemplation, I used the money to purchase my ticket to San Francisco. So for me, the Rock Laboratory ceased to exist. Key representatives in the upper echelons of the organization—Ageev, Opriatnaia, Yevdokimova—followed close behind me to California. Where all these characters are now, I don't know.

The Rock Laboratory closed in connection with the initiation of predatory exploitation of musicians. I recall that some Frenchman arrived in Moscow and asked to buy all audio recordings of the Rock Laboratory's studio. A huge deal ensured, and I tried to insist that each group should get paid at least twenty dollars, but my initiative was forfeited. This was the first crack, and then my relationship with Olga split. Later on in 2007, I heard that she dumped all the documents from that time. I don't know if this is true. I presume that they were all just burned.

In sum, the Rock Lab's extinction was inevitable. Whether participants wanted it or not, the institution that freely promoted punk shows under the hand of the Komsomol disappeared. The atmosphere of the scene changed: freebies disappeared, all came under the lure of the ruble and domestic punk producers. The collapse of the Rock Laboratory had a positive influence on developing the "Moscow Giants." It is likely that if a band like NOFX and Fat Wreck Chords appeared in Russia in early-mid '90s, things would have developed quite differently. Moscow punk is not missing anything without the Rock Laboratory.

the coup in the next chapter.

PART THREE:
THE (TRANS)FORMATION OF A SCENE 1990-2008

3.1: The Moscow Giants

Sasha "Chacha" Ivanov: In August 1991, some guy who I think was connected to politics, called our management and said there was a coup d'état in the city, and Russia, your motherland, needs your help. You need to go and bring your equipment and play in front of the White House, to support democracy and not allow the Soviet fucks to take power back.[165] We said, "Yeah sure!" We hated the Soviets; they were fucking assholes. They didn't let us play punk rock, drink coca cola, chew bubblegum. We didn't have jeans—things we really needed.

I realize that sounds stupid, but imagine a reality in which you don't have these things. You see them in movies, but you can't buy it, because nobody is selling it. We didn't like Soviets and Bolsheviks. I started to get information that Bolsheviks were not the cool guys, as I was told in school books. They were not the good guys; they were fucking cruel. I was really critical of the Soviet system at the time. But everybody probably was. Everybody started to understand that it didn't work. The officials said publically one thing, but they were not doing what they were saying.

So we played at the White House to support democracy. At that time it wasn't clear who would be the leader. People started saying it would be Yeltsin, and we didn't like Yeltsin. I didn't like Yeltsin.

Yeah, he was an ex-Communist. It was obvious he was the same as the others, but he only started to sing a different tune. For me it was clear that this was not real change. People were angry

---

165 The White House in Moscow is the House of the Government of the Russian Federation, not to be confused with the American White House, where the president lives. For more on the August Coup, see footnote 81, Part 2.1.

at politicians, so we sang "Boris Yeltsin is an asshole!" and people were upset because they thought he was some kind of God. The organizers of the show said, "You need to evacuate, Naïve, safely." Somehow nobody killed us.

Naïve's Sasha "ChaCha" Ivanov and Ruslan Stupin, Kievskaia Bomb Shelter, Moscow 1991, Cammie Toloui

I used to be a bastard
An ugly snotty child
Now I am a Soviet Soldaten

I want to destroy the NATO bloc
We will destroy the bourgeois ANZUS
For Glorious Mother Russia!

Tanks, tanks, tanks, tanks,
In them sit the soldier-punks
Tanks, tanks, tanks, tanks,
Crushing their heads like cans

In the Soviet Army I enlisted as a tank man
So I don't have time to listen to the Sex Pistols[166]

166 "Tanki Panki" (Tanks Punks) by *Naïve*, from their first album *Switch-Blade Knaife*, released by Maximum Rocknroll in 1990.

Naïve in _Maximum Rocknroll_

Max: Let's destroy NATO bloc for our Russian motherland. Let's destroy that and that and that—you know all the small blocs like Malasla [sic] and other small countries—let's destroy all of that for our motherland. That's all the bullshit that they tell you in the army.

Chacha: Tell them about the punk…

Max: It's very interesting that I wrote that song ("Tanki Panki") and about a year later when we came back, we read a newspaper article that said that a guy who really was a punk escaped in a tank and we went around the city scaring all the people!

Chacha: He was in the army.

Max: The majority of people that go to the army, even the rednecks and the dumbheads, don't want to serve because the conditions are very awful and poor there. Everybody has to serve, but now if you are a student you don't have to go to the army. So, Mike (drummer) is staying in college only for that reason, because he doesn't want to be a psycho or go to jail. Two or three years ago when you didn't go to the army, you had to go to jail. You had two choices—you go to the psychiatric hospital and they say that you are crazy and they make some tests for you. Ruslan (guitarist), show them your hands. See. He did all this stuff.

Maximum Rocknroll: He slit his wrists.[167]

Dmitry Spirin: The first time I heard punk was about 1990-1991. I was about 16 years old, and it was "Never Mind the Bollocks, Here's the Sex Pistols." My first experience of punk was when the movie _Avaria—Doch Menta_ was released.[168] It was shot in '88 or '89. It's a dramatic movie about the life of a policeman whose daughter became a punk, and they had Chudo-Yudo in it. They shot a live concert and had it in the movie… So that was our first experience of punk, sitting in a cinema.

But we soon realized that Russian rock and punk, after long years of Communism, were not so great, and it looked much

167 Maximum Rocknroll #96, 1990. Interview conducted by Cammie Toloui.
168 _Avaria-Doch Menta_—Breakdown-Daughter of a Cop.

less convincing than the new Western stuff. Besides, Western rock was forbidden and records were really hard to find. We were told in schools "But you don't know English, so how do you know what they are singing about? What if they sing Lenin is a jerk, or 'lets bomb the USSR?' or something like that." But the real enemies of Russian teachers were not punk bands, but Kiss, and that's why punk was so appealing and fascinating for us—it had a drive. So that's when I got the idea to take all the best that exists in the West— Ramones, New York Dolls, Pistols—and make lyrics in Russian so people could understand it here.

Chetyre Tarkana, 1993 Drug Free Youth Cover, Used with permission of Dmitry Spirin

Anna Andreeva: [Senkevich's] first concert was in 1990 in a club called Otryzhka, around the Ortradnoye metro station.[169] Everybody played for free then, but sometimes they gave you beer. The indie scene was not big and everybody knew each other, everybody was friends.

We formed by accident. I was asked by a band to write texts in English because I was studying at the Linguistic University. I wrote a couple of texts, but the guys couldn't sing them, so I stayed as vocalist. The band already played punkish stuff, so I just added a female touch.

There were very few women in the indie scene then, you could count them literally on the fingers of one hand. So I felt kind of in priority, in the rock world with only men around; it was nice to be a woman. And as I already said, we were all friends.

Chetyre Tarakana! in *Maximum Rocknroll*

Dmitry Spirin: We got together in 1991, just like the majority of present day punk bands. Or better say, we were just like many other people who wanted to kick ass musically and were fixated on Western music, having inclinations for music and punk rudiments in their cuts and itching to do something about it. Or was it the itch to hang out and party all the time? I don't know… you know, we just wanted to be cool.

Vova Rodionov: We only played [at this time] in St. Petersburg. The musical scene there is very different from the Moscow scene. I think it's because Moscow is a more expensive city. Here there's more expensive clubs and life is more expensive, of course.

That's why people in St. Petersburg are more honest. There are a lot of clubs that are completely non-commercial. Where it is still a pleasure for us to play at. Moscow lacks these kinds of places these days. One of the clubs [in St. Petersburg] is called TaMtAm. It's probably the biggest and most "central" Rock 'n' Roll venue.

---

169 *Otryzhksa*—burp.

Absolutely non-commercial, they are tied by the lease contract too, which forbids them to sell alcohol. But the policy of the club is that every band there play for a box of beer, no matter who they are.[170]

Slavik Dacent: I heard heavy metal before punk, because metal was a popular commercial style of music. Many German groups like Accept and so on. After metal music, I accidently got to hear something similar. That's when I took interest in thrash metal, because its delivery was unlike the gloomy and diabolic subtexts of metal groups. Later I realized that this was trashcore. That's how I shifted from heavy metal to thrash metal. Then I went through thrash metal to get close to hardcore, and only after that I heard

Distemper Concert Poster, Jerry Rubin Club, 1992-1993, Sveta Yelchaninova

170 Maximum Rocknroll, #170, July 1997. Interview conducted by Max Kochetkov. *Chetyre Tarakana!*—See footnote 162, Part 2.3.

punk rock. I actually heard elements of ska in punk rock. So I found out what ska music was and tried to mix it with punk.

Concerts were like all metal concerts. We had long hair, we were trying to look like metal-heads at first. Of course, we were not particularly good at it because our energy was different, our message was positive. It was positive and had sarcasm in it and so on. We had nobody to play with except metal-heads, so we did it, but we looked different and played a different style of music. That's why we were noticed. Otherwise we probably wouldn't have been.

Masha Kinder: The first concert with Vosmaia Marta was in the club Treti Put in the very, very center of Moscow—across the river from Red Square.[171] I don't remember the exact date, but somewhere around the winter of 1998-1999. Before that, I played concerts with other bands, about twenty exactly.

Sasha "Chacha" Ivanov: Max carried a cassette with him. On one side was the Sex Pistols' "Never Mind the Bollocks," and on the other side was the Ramones' "Rocket to Russia." This was the first punk music I ever heard, and it was in the Soviet Army in 1988.

From the very first listen, I realized this was the music I had been searching for. There were a lot of metal bands around. I listened to them like, "That's nice, but the type of vocals and lyrics, especially the ideas of the songs were so stupid and lame." I never could accept them. On the other extreme, there was a huge culture of Russian rock music like Kino, Akvarium, and many, many other Russian bands. Which were cool in lyrics sometimes, but the music was not interesting.

There was Grazhdanskaia Oborona, Avtomaticheskie Udovletvoriteli, and Zvuki Mu. The older brothers were in a band called Va-Bank. They played punk music. The scene in the '90s was like the vanguard, kind of. Before that, not many people could understand the general idea. Like playing music for example—who

---

171 Vosmaia Marta—March 8th; *Treti Put*—Third Way

gave you permission to play music? In Soviet times you had to have permission for everything, so it was a kind of rebellion. Probably the most educated and people most interested in life were involved in this process. So it was a good time. But radical, because we were the minority and the majority were people who lost their country at the time. The Soviet Union was like a huge country with its own rules for 70 years, and one day the officials said "Oops, we realized after 70 years that we did the wrong thing. Now let's go back." It was culture shock for a huge population because people were not ready for the change. So it was a difficult time. It was hard to think about art, because you needed to eat. I couldn't play in my band and make enough money to live, so I had different jobs in advertising, banking, and all these new bourgeois institutions that started to appear in Russia.

Naïve in *Maximum Rocknroll*
Sasha "Chacha" Ivanov: Our label, S.O.S. Music, appeared in 1993. We had this idea floating around for a long time. We were always thinking that we should make our own, produce independently from other people. That we should not go and bow in front of somebody, but do it ourself and to risk with our own finances, and also to control the process completely, too.

Maximum Rocknroll: Is it the only label of its kind in Moscow, or are there others?

Sasha "Chacha" Ivanov: Yes, but they are not registered labels. They are not, as if to say, "official" in the eyes for the government. If you take a look at this St. Petersburg zine called *Rock Fuzz*, you'll find a bunch of record reviews and they would usually print the name of the label in there too. I think most of the labels in Russia exist illegally, like pirates, only because there's no legal fundations or institutions and there's no jurisdictional system that could regulate that kind of activity.

Maximum Rocknroll: So it's just the two of you responsible for S.O.S.?

Sasha "Chacha" Ivanov: No, not really. There is a good "helper" that suddenly appeared for us—Sid (Dmitry Spirin) the vocalist for Chetyre Tarakana. He's a type of guy with original peculiarity! He did some time in prison for half a year. For drug-dealing. It wasn't a big deal! He got arrested in St. Petersburg and they found half a kilogram of LSD in his pocket, which is a sizable amount.[172]

Dmitry Spirin: I always expected more artistic vividness from music, sound, energy—more rock 'n' roll, rather than philosophical meditations. What's why when I started getting into punk rock, there was already a very vast and powerful Russian rock scene from the USSR—bands like Akvarium, Kino, Alisa, Chaif.[173] That's what we hated, that's what we wanted to get rid of, and to make our punk

Naïve, Switch-Blade Knaife Cassette Jacket, Maximum Rocknroll, 1990, Used with permission from Max Kotchetkov

172 Maximum Rocknroll #177, 1998. Interview conducted by Max Kotchetkov.
173 Neologism *Chaif* was invented by a member of the band's original lineup, Vadim Kukushkin, by combining the words *chai* (tea) and *kaif*.

rock the leading genre. Like the Ramones opposed to Pink Floyd or Elton John, we wanted to be an alternative to Akvarium. The first bands I liked were Va-Bank, Pogo, and Naïve—all from Moscow.

We were a DIY band; we didn't have a contract, nobody was even dreaming of contracts back then, that's why we had to finance recordings ourselves. And in order to make it we came up with a method. Back then, Russia was transferring from a planned economy to private property, and it was done by means of a special check called Chubays' vouchers. They were given to everyone for free, so everybody could have a part of state property. These vouchers could be sold, bought, or exchanged, so we sold all our vouchers to get money for our first album. After selling the vouchers we got $200.00, and it was enough to rent a studio for 35 or 40 hours, which was almost nothing.

Distribution was also a funny story. There were tapes, and we copied them by means of a two-tape recorder and xeroxed the artwork. Don't forget that you had to have special permission to use a xerox machine at this time. We were lucky that the first place with a commercial xerox was opened in our neighborhood. So we distributed the album by tapes, played concerts, and sold them there. There were also two or three music shops in Moscow, so we had our tapes there. We sold about 500–1000 tapes this way before the commercial release.

Sasha "Chacha" Ivanov: For ex-Soviet kids, the sound was already political. This sound—distortion, drums, that was political. That was enough to understand that if someone listens to that kind of music, he's on the same side of the road as you. And it was so rare. It was really, really cool. It was more a time of feelings: frustration, knowing nothing about the future, and stuff like that. The same causes started punk in Britain and maybe the United States—kids were frustrated, their teachers didn't understand them, and their parents had a different type of culture that was not interesting to the kids. Kids just wanted to play stupid short songs with silly melodies just to protest the culture of grownups.

Nikolay "Nick Rock 'n' Roll" Kuntsevich, Jerry Rubin Club, 1998-1999, Ivan Savchenko

Masha Kinder: In my life, I played on a permanent basis in purely female groups in two different countries (in Russia and in Italy), in five different groups (there were much more mixed groups in my career), and I always observed a special attitude precisely because of gender. Another thing is that sexism in this way is more convenient: look at a women's group with everything equal [skills], and I guarantee it will be more appealing to the people—well, simply because beautiful girls with guitars are always attractive, and especially if they perform shows and play cool. However, in the '90s no one really expected that a women's group could be surprising in any way besides the gender peculiarity. For a very long time I was under the weight of such a complex problem of this kind: allegedly "male" drummers a priori play better than female. Only after playing a few years in clubs in conjunction with other groups (from two to ten groups per evening), I found that the percentage of well-playing guys was about the same as that of well-playing girls, just women then were numerically smaller for different reasons. These stupid stereotypes appeared because, on the one hand, there was still very little information on the Internet on the topic of women in music, and on the other because it's still easier for many guys to think that women are more defective, and they can be adamant about this opinion.

Dmitry Spirin: If there was any new club opening and it allowed rock music, all musicians and punk rockers knew right away. Everybody would rush there asking for a day when they could play. "Give me Thursday, give me Friday." There were long periods without concerts because there was really no place to play.

There wasn't such a thing as renting a gym, or playing at school or in church. In school, the administration always felt that rock was dangerous and didn't agree with it. Besides, we had always been poor and didn't have extra money or our own equipment. So if there was a place to play, the next question would be—with what? Rock music requires amplifiers and equipment, that's why we needed real clubs. So we had to settle for places where one day you would play, and the next day some fascist band would play. It violated punk ethics. But if you didn't want to do it, then you didn't have concerts.

Sasha "Chacha" Ivanov: The older generation of Russian musicians played in apartments, but our generation started to play in small venues. We started to create new places where we could play.

Because nobody wanted to play us on the radio, the only chance to deliver our music was through touring. We tried our best to do it. It was impossible to tour a lot. The regions of Russia were so poorly equipped, and there was no possibility of bringing our own equipment. There was only one company to rent equipment from, and they were connected with the government and didn't care about idiots like us. It was probably the hardest time to play music and get it out there. The new country that called itself "Free Russia" had no idea what was going on, and tried to create Capitalism without anyone knowing what it meant.

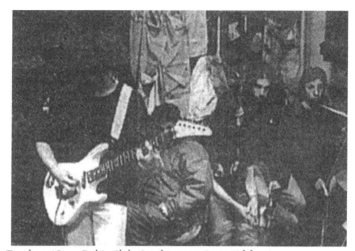

Tarakany! Jerry Rubin Club, October 1992, Sveta Yelchaninova

Slavik Dacent: We played other cities through friends. It was all based on friendships back then. The first time we went to St. Petersburg was only due to the fact that we had friends there. That's the way it used to be done in the DIY scene for amateur groups. Any young group (even today) needs to go through this process to become acquainted with the value of friendships. That's when you understand if a group is worth something. People use their advantages to the full. We were also invited to some DIY shows without any directors or concert organizers or promoters. They simply didn't exist, they only appeared in 2005 or later. So everything was based on friendship ties. We also had a friend in St. Petersburg who worked at [the radio station] Radio Baltika, and he invited us. So bit by bit, more and more, people started to recognize us.

Dmitry Khankin: I went to one of Naïve's first concerts in the club Sexton. It was like the very end of September 1990. There were huge bikers as bouncers—the Night Wolves. It was a kind of punk alternative club. I remember the show; I was back from New York and a friend of mine called and asked to go to Sexton because "there

is a punk rock show going on there." I laughed—it was unbelievable—
but I was so amazed by the equality of the band.

Slavik Dacent: We were fucking shocked during our first concert
in Stockholm, Sweden. We were amazed to get to Finland at first,
because coming from the Soviet Union and performing someplace
else was incredible. I don't remember the exact year; it was probably
around 2000. When we first went, the difference between the
Russian and foreign audiences was huge. They were rocking like
crazy in Europe. In Germany people were going nuts, I'd never seen
anything like that before. The atmosphere was so great that it got us
high, and I didn't want to go back to Russia because we didn't have
that type of scene. But as time passed the differences were erased,
so by 2005–2006 everything was pretty much the same. Right now,
the commercial scene and punk scene in Europe exist separately.
It's a lot messier in Russia because the punk scene can't exist here
on its own. Our government won't let it happen.

Sasha "Chacha" Ivanov: When we started to record our first album
we had a connection with Yesa Shirazia and Cammie Toloui from
Maximum Rocknroll. Somehow they came to Russia and met us,
and we gave them a copy of the first video we made for our first
song. It was called "Tanki-Panki." These guys went back to the
United States and Tim Yo (editor at the time) watched it and really
liked it. They asked us if we wanted to release a record in the United
States, so it was like that. We recorded it and he released it and we
got our first international attention.

      This release helped us organize our first European tour. In
1993 we went to Europe for the first time (at a time when Europe was
not yet united, so we had to acquire 11 visas for all the countries).
All the visa registrations and paperwork were new to us, because
before that "Soviet people, they shouldn't travel abroad." We couldn't
travel without permission, which you couldn't get unless you were a
special person. So for the majority there was absolutely, no fucking

way, you will never see a foreign country. Maybe if you were lucky Germany, but where else? It was impossible. So touring in Europe was super fucking cool.

Everything was our first experience. Our first city was Berlin by train. We were picked up by Adam P. Schwartz, our tour manager who was living in Denmark at the time. He was waiting for us in a minivan. I remember we went into a really big tunnel in Germany. I looked up and saw that the ceiling was covered with rows of lamps, and every fucking lamp was working. It wasn't broken or something. And that was really unbelievable for me, because nothing worked in the Soviet Union. My brain couldn't accept this truth.

In 1993 who could understand the expression DIY in Russia? Nobody. We only played in places like that in Europe— squats, anarchist basements, something like that. People connected with *Maximum Rocknroll* were genuinely interested in a new Russian punk band. But we realized that Russia was 50 years behind what was going on in the rest of the world. We realized we weren't ready to tour professionally. We started to rehearse more, and realized we had to write better songs. Not like we thought before: "We don't give a fuck and that is cool." I realized this was not actually cool. Cool is something interesting, or if the others can stand listening to you, then that's cool. If you are drunk and can't sing and can't stand, that's not cool.

Slavik Dacent: The difference between contemporary punk rock and punk in the '90s is the same as the difference between people living in this or that time. It's like a geometric progression to me. As the information appeared, instruments appeared, money appeared, and opportunity to play those instruments appeared. Studios appeared, the sound appeared. People started paying attention to sound, started to think in a more creative way, started writing interesting lyrics. Some things never changed through. Young groups start off trying to imitate their idols. They sing their lyrics in

English, although the text is made up of two or three words. They want to be a part of something bigger and it's absolutely normal, it's not a bad thing. In order to feel that you relate to something bigger, to feel that you are a part of the punk rock movement, hardcore movement, you have to do something similar. That's why many people copy things.

Masha Kinder: In the punk scene there were always brightly painted "toads," as the punks themselves called them. But, more often than not, these girls returned home after partying, changed their clothes, and washed off their cosmetics and everything. That is, their immersion in the culture of punk was role-playing, inconsistent. Such an outrageous carnival, nothing serious. Some of them were only interested in appearance, and they did not listen to punk in the form of music at all, except under the pressure of a punk boyfriend, and then, rather pretended, it seemed to me.

Distemper, Jerry Rubin Club, 1998, Photographer unknown, used with permission from Denis Gradov

Anna Andreeva—I wrote texts for Tarakany! They gave me a box of weed for it, and I thanked them very much for that. Other bands were not so generous.

Sasha "Chacha" Ivanov: In St. Petersburg they are more bohemian, they don't care about money. Moscow has always been more practical. More concerned with results. Moscow musicians are the most well-equipped, well-prepared, well-influenced musicians, because they are in the center of all that. All the money is here, all the producers, all the companies playing music. Everything is here in Moscow. In the eyes of the country, we are the merchants for music. Not my band, but in general…

Chetyre Tarakany! in *Maximum Rocknroll*

Dmitry Spirin: 80% of Moscow skinheads are into shit like "white power," they all have radical right wing ambitions. They do show up at our gigs, but I would never scream like crazy Naïve: "Skinheads! Fuck off!" only because I do not want to offend the other 20% of skinheads who are not nazis and racists. I always tell them, as I said before, that we are not nazis.

We say, "skinheads," and, "the rest of the audience." But instead of this you might call them "drunk, aggressive hooligans" and "peace-loving people" on the other hand. You know what I mean? It doesn't matter if it's a show; it can happen to you on a street, when you'd have to face four drunk rednecks that want to beat the shit out of you. So the only thing you can do is start kicking back or run away. Either you are afraid of them or face them. It doesn't matter if your head is shaved and you are wearing a t-shirt that says, "Oi!" It's just that the society is in this stage right now when you can smell violence in the air.[174]

Pavel: At underground hardcore shows there were no fascist people in the '90s, I can say that absolutely. On the big shows, when hardcore bands like Distemper played, there were some football

174 Maximum Rocknroll # 170, July 1997. Interview conducted by Max Kochetkov.

hooligans, but not a big crowd and most of them didn't flaunt this nazi bullshit.

Sasha "Chacha" Ivanov: We had some problems with local fascists, local right-wing guys. Not really wild. Ten years later people were killed. But in the '90s it was really offensive, it was really a big threat, but at least there was no killing as I remember.

Slavik Dacent: During the '90s we realized that people with swastikas at our concerts were an eyesore for us. They were not supposed to be there. As we got deeper into punk rock, we realized that there couldn't be a place for any right-wing movement at all. I'd say we were the first band to tell fascists to go fuck themselves. We even did it on that radio in St. Petersburg, I don't remember the exact year, I think 1995 or 1993. At that time nobody paid attention to that because it wasn't a huge issue, but when people started

(Left to right) Vovan Podina (Ulyi), Masha Kinder, Sid (Tarakany!), Maria Guguberidze, Vosma Marta, 1998, Treti Put, Unknown phorographer, used with permission from Masha Kinder

understanding certain things, roughly speaking when people started to get beaten up or even killed by right-wingers, it was already too late. Now protesting against Putin sounds funny, compared to what we had during the '90s. Back then we were protesting against government in general, not some crappy president. There was a real protest wave against any kind of system… That's why now we don't even protest against Putin, because it's trendy and every asshole out there is protesting against him just to fit in, to get their 10 seconds of fame. It's really quite funny.

Masha Kinder: I played alongside many different groups (not only in Vosmaia Marta), with Tarakany!, Naïve, and Distemper, on the same stage starting in 1997. I saw Distemper for the first time as a spectator in 1992—practically the day after my prom. We then made friends with them, because after the concert we all drank together; it was normal.

It was fun. During my first concert with Vosmaia Marta Sid from Tarakany! came. There is a completely killer photo from the dressing room where I sit in underwear with dripping cosmetics between him and Vovan from the group Ulyi, and Vovan gives Sid money, as if buying me.[175] Naïve and Tarakany! treated us very warmly, fraternally, and in every way supported and helped us. We were even recognized in some works of Tarakany! Marina modeled for the cover of *Posadki Net* (1998), and the song "Pank-Rok Zvezda" is dedicated to Galia.[176]

---

175 *Ulyi*—Hives.
176 *Posadki Net!*—No Boarding!, *Pank-Rok Zvezda*—Punk Rock Star.

3.2: The Anti-Fascist Movement[177]

Il-78: In the 2000s there was something different because of the new politics and the new national style. You know before Hitler came to power there was a huge depression, and on this basis the government promoted national traditions—operas, theater, old German history—and the German aristocracy tended more to support nationalism. Their population was suffering, so they had to support a new identity that blamed others; it's a well-known sociological principle that in order to reinforce the community you need to find an enemy. And it's easier to blame someone else for your problems in order to become stronger. It happened with Germany, and the same thing happened in the early 2000s in Russia. Even while being a student of sociology, I saw it. Russian people had no social security, no confidence in tomorrow, their younger generation did nothing except drugs and clubbing, and it seemed that nobody was taking care of the younger generation of Russians. They saw that nationalists would take care of them and give them a platform to blame foreigners for their problems, watch their health, and get them a job. It was very easy to predict. So these traditions, movies, and pseudo-national folk bands formed. People were looking for their identity in a post-Soviet world. And we had a joke that you can compare punk bands and nazi bands—they're doing the same music, and they're blaming each other. They can't play, but punks can play. They did manage to steal lots of ideas and musical treatments, so there was a very strong right-wing straight edge scene, hip hop scene, etc., and so they produced and played quite well.

In the '90s, it was the whole feeling of fresh air and freedom. Only later on people became involved with politics. Those

---

177 Many of the personages in this section are intentionally obscured for their own protection. Pjtor, as you will see, is the leading narrator, and for good reason. Any Russian involved in the scene back then will know automatically who "Pjtor" is. Many people involved in the early movement are unwilling to talk about their history, or are excessively vague about it. Pjtor not only was the center of this movement for a long time, but he is also well positioned at the moment to explicate his story in full.

people who were punks and skins in the '90s had a Soviet education; they read humanistic cartoons and films, they were not going to beat someone to death. They just wanted to behave aggressively. The 2000s generation were the children of the '90s, when nobody cared about them, no relatives, no relations, so all they had was cheap alcohol. You had to survive how you could. So following the strong leader was their way. This was the same situation with the guys beating people in the '90s for fun, sure, but the new nazis had a greater idea. These nazis were fighting for the "freedom of their nation." Quite an excuse; they perceived they were knights or something like that.

Ankylym Band Practice, Velikii Novgorod, 2005, Used with permission from the band

Masha Kinder: I hung out with metal groups often (thrash, doom, and death metal), and after concerts like this there were clashes with *liubera* and other shaved, pumped-up boys from provincial Russian cities that came to Moscow in such a way—cornering metal people in subway cars and electric trains and beating them and even cutting their hair violently.[178] It was not uncommon. I will explain

178 *Liubera*—Youth clique from Moscow suburb Liubertsky, active at the end of the '80s.

that these were not skinheads. With skinheads, the most paradoxical way, the relationship was good. I even had friends that partied with them. Nevertheless, everything that happened occurred after the concerts. At concerts, I do not remember anything like that.

Ivan WWF: The roots of today's neo-Nazi scene are also in the punk scene. Many people who are active today in the neo-Nazi movement—as musicians or in the audience—were at one point associated with the punk scene. We had a common scene with the nazis. It was perfectly normal that there were nazis at punk, hardcore, and ska concerts. This was simply part of reality. There were no attacks at the time; we tolerated each other. But then there were attacks and they lasted several years and it began a war in the street. It was a kind of punk and hardcore resistance against nazi pressure, and we joined it.

Kristina Doga: Well, before the Internet in Russia, not many people knew that punk was supposed to be anti-fascist. When I was around 13, I was literally living on the street and hanging with skinheads and punks. I didn't even know that anti-fascist skinheads were a thing. It was like "I'm not nazi, but you are, it's okay, let's drink"— you know. Then my friend shows me a book by Craig O'Hara, *The Philosophy of Punk*, and it was saying a lot of fucking enlightening things about punk, and it changed my life. I was reading about skinheads. And I remember when the guy that showed us this book left, many around were saying stuff like, "What do you think of him? He said skinheads started with black people. What a fool he is." I was the only one thinking, 'Wow, that's crazy.'

So then he took me a few times to a DIY hardcore show, and I saw for the first time other skinheads. Well, I mean, like two of them, but also vegetarians and other DIY people, and I never saw this before in my life. They had the ideology of "fuck the world." I didn't even know punk could be that deep. It was a Cut'n'Run, Engage at Will, Next Round, and Distress show.

Kristina Doga, Winter 2005-2006 (before stabbing), used with her permission

Kirill "George" Mikhailov: St. Petersburg had an anti-fascist movement. They were looking for fights, but generally we had a cozier situation compared to Moscow. There were nazis in the '90s, but it was mostly about fashion, not like neo-nazi skinheads in Europe, but a culture of violence. At the end of the '90s they finished that shit, and by the early 2000s there was a new generation more about style and ideology. They were on their own too, and we had no common points. They were developing their own scene, and the big problem was that when that generation came into being, they believed only in ideology. They looked like regular teenagers or hooligans and they were real neo-Nazis. They started attacking everyone; they were dangerous, sometimes very young. These young guys had no brains and no fear. In the scene, we needed each other at these times.

Aleksey "Shkobar" Olesinov: It was like white power skinheads were the majority in the city, and they were against us at every punk rock gig. And the hardcore scene was very small at the time, so they brought violence into our world. For me, it wasn't simply about racism or fascism, it was like the majority versus the minority that was the real reason. So the early antifa movement was like ten or fifteen people who, in the end of the '90s, tried to change the situation.

Ribson: Next Round started in 2005. You know the questions of left and right, fascist and anti-fascist was more relevant for Piat Uglov when the '90s finished. In the 2000s the situation was easier for Next Round. In St. Petersburg, of course, there were problems with people thinking they could change the world, and many, many fucking politics—of course there's a problem when people are dying. I was an old punk rocker though, and when we had shows we controlled it. The fascists didn't come. They were afraid of us; they understood who I was and my friends, and that we could scrap with them. Many of my friends worked with me as security guards at nightclubs—big guys, and the fascists understood that. Many times in Moscow they threatened to come, but never came.

Il-78: So I read an article on how nazis were to kill enemies, and it said that "for sure we admit that this idea was invented by our enemies with them in mind—punk and hardcore, but to make our struggle effective we should use the force of our enemy, and their weapon. We must consider straight edge effective, and let's put it

Moscow, 2006, Used with Permission from Pjtor's personal archive

against punk, not those who are sniffing glue, and we should take care of our health, our generation, nation, etc., So let's do nazi straight edge." And so it was quite strong. A couple of years before I noticed in Moscow there was a big festival BadyukFest. It caught a lot of attention on Facebook, and there was pressure to cancel it due to impending danger. There were all styles—hip hop, rap, punk—some I never heard. I listened and I was like "Well, alright, they sound interesting." Youngsters like school children might be into rap, hardcore, and there were nazi versions of all of it. It was quite professional, and for me there was something systemic with it. There was a guy from Argentina maybe, and he made the line *"ne bukhai sieg heil!"*[179] It was such an innovative rhyme and it's catchy. They were totally using the same mechanism of music to get notoriety. Shit, what's happening.

Aleksey "Shkobar" Olesinov: The fascists listened to the same kind of music, so they were only into music fashion—not the ideas

179 *"Ne bukhai"*—"Don't drink up."

behind it or anything. They didn't give a fuck about what the bands were singing. They just drank and fought and loved violence… No positive ideas.

Pjtor: I got involved in whatever scene really late in my life—I first visited a hardcore show when I was 18, or something. I had never been interested in subcultures or music at all; I was more about literature, history, sociology. Eventually, I entered the university to study "comparative religions" and social-anthropology a year before. Twelve years later, I still know shit about the music and that doesn't really bother me.

I despised the musical subcultures, because they were predominantly middle-classy in Moscow at the time. I was both older and poorer than all those kids in skater clothes with walkmans—totally not my company. Football hooligans were a different story. That was the time of the rise of the new wave of hooliganism in Russia. The movement has been really huge for decades before the scene first started to adopt the tactics and new approach developed by hooligans in Britain—proper urban warfare, instead of chaotic drunk clashes. That involved a sophisticated system of scouting, discreet maneuvering in the city, renewed tactics of engagement, communication, fundraising—all that stuff. And socially the guys who got involved in it were more understandable for me—lower middle class intelligentsia or working class kids. Not to mention, the main action—organized clashes in the center of the city—looked beautiful.

Youth nazism was a big thing for all ex-Eastern bloc countries during the '90s, and the roots are obvious: the new neoliberal authorities in all the countries heavily exploited the idea of national superiority as part of their political agenda opposed to the socialist past. Religion and nationalism were promoted as the new spiritual core in Russia, Ukraine, Bulgaria, Rumania, Hungary, ex-Yugoslavia, Poland, the Baltic countries, Georgia, and so on. So taking one step forward and becoming a nazi in all those countries was both an exciting challenge, and a safe choice. Nazism gave the hooligans what football was lacking—a wholesome narrative.

My ex-classmate Shkobar had been involved in hooliganism since the 10th grade. He had just moved to Moscow from Siberia, and was really energetic and ambitious. He was also irritated that the majority of hooligans were nazis—it was the time of expanding Internet access in Russia (2000–2001), so he quickly discovered that a huge anti-fascist hooligan and skinhead scene had developed in the UK, Germany, and Southern Europe. Nothing like that ever existed in the ex-USSR before. But Shkobar was not the only one in Moscow who made that discovery at that time. Russian Internet space was still very narrow, so finally those people could contact each other and form the first gang of anti-fascist skinheads in the country. I participated in a couple of their meetings moved by pure curiosity—they were very interesting guys but the pattern of their actions was unclear. Mostly they would gather somewhere in the center, all seven to 10 of them, have a beer, and walk through the city encountering random nazi gangs and fighting them. The way Moscow functions is that it has an enormous center, surrounded by circular highways, and all the population (at least the active part of it) sees the center as the meeting point—an area to hang out or have a drink or for any other activity after work. So at that time the center was really swarming with hooligans or skinhead gangs hanging out everywhere; finding an opponent was not a problem.

I tried to get involved with the tiny straight edge community in Moscow, but again, those were richer kids with a totally different background. They wore fancy brand sweatshirts ordered from the States (that was long before the later economic boom in Russia) and were not interested in science—they all studied in the economics department. I was more or less doomed to become a crypto hardcore kid, a loner, and that didn't interest me much.

But in 2004, right before I was going to quit that all together, I was invited to visit a hardcore show in Kirov—a provincial city 1000 kilometers east from Moscow, halfway to the Urals. I'm totally a Moscow kid, never actually been in "the real Russia," so that place and its scene was a shock for me. Kirov was a heavily industrialized Soviet city that went totally bankrupt after the perestroika, leaving most of the professional population unemployed. A bankrupt city in the woods. But strangely, it had its own hardcore scene at a time when only a few other cities throughout the whole country did. There were masses of hardcore kids; it seemed it was the main urban subculture there. And more importantly, they were all like me—poor, shaggy, and studying humanities.

Their bands were cool, too. They took all the anger from early DC and Boston scenes and translated the sentiment into Russian, using all the notorious and funny rural vocabulary of the Russian countryside—the philological mixture was like a bomb! The early hardcore narration, the feelings of the impoverished white kids of the Reagan era coupled so well with the post-Soviet Russian realities. God, how I liked it. The place was a Utopia for me. They had numerous local DIY zines, they performed actions against fur boutiques and were politically involved, not to mention that a big number of them were straight edge and vegan. And they all kept jumping around me: "You are from Moscow? We can't even imagine what a great scene and movement you must be having there, guys!"

So when I returned, I felt re-empowered and had a clear view on the proper approach. Another scene was possible, we just needed to bet on different people: on the poor, on the intelligentsia outcasts, on the kids coming from distant provinces, converted ghetto teens, drug abusers, and so forth. Start from the blank page and never let "hardcore" in, if you understand what I mean.

(Important to note: Moscow is a huge city and there had been acceptable hardcore communities within the older scene. One community to be precise—kids frequenting Jerry Rubin Club, a non-commercial youth center. They were really nice, they had some good bands, but their influence was very limited and numbers very tiny for years).

We registered a webpage called Sxe.ru. Not that we were all straight edge, but it was a good keyword to start with. There we were mostly uploading translations of interviews with the hardcore speakers of the 80's, articles from old American sxe zines, very retro stuff. But mostly that website was used as a platform for communication with the regions, since we started to receive responses from all over the country (almost nothing from Moscow). In every big city there was a kid who had lived the same way we did—he was straight edge, vegan/vegetarian, anarchist/anti-fascist, very active, and alone. They considered our shaggy website as a blessing, a real chance. I was even exchanging emails with some kid who lived on an oil platform in the Arctic Ocean! Slowly, but steadily, there were more and more people from Moscow, too.

In 2004 I first met Fedor. He was a lonely, self educated skinhead from the suburbs who worked all his life as a draft worker. He was older than all of us, and really bitter at the fact that the Russian skinhead scene was provincial nazi shit. We were all ready to wage a war. First of all, because crowds of nazis effectively were a symbol of stagnation for all urban subcultures. They *were* the main urban subculture and would never allow another group to exist. Second, war has a great unifying potential for a small, young community. Third, it was also a definitive filter for the new members. Forth, challenging the nazis was the main urban intrigue of that time—the group that would have successfully done it would become a symbol of a new wave and new tendencies for all the youth of the city. And fifth, fighting against nazis is a noble cause.

So we were the first who started the war. I never really cared about the nazis themselves; the aim was not particularly to wipe them out, but to establish an alternative community through a conflict and send a strong cultural message to the youth: the new wave is coming. We employed the sophisticated tactics of the British hooligans, and that made us extremely effective. We were cleaning one spot after another. The nazi community was totally enraged. They started attacking random punk and hardcore shows, but as we never attended those, only innocent victims fell. "We are not anti-fascists, we are just hardcore kids!" people were screaming, but got an iron bar in the face anyway.

At the same time, as predicted, there were more and more people willing to join the group, and as predicted they were from the proper background. In 2004, we reached 30. A couple of new social initiatives were introduced—like Animal Liberation Front actions and weekly Food not Bombs actions, when we would cook 30 liters of vegan soup and distribute it to the homeless near a big railway station. I started to print a DIY hardcore zine. There were mostly short stories and articles on given themes, almost not a word about any music at all. The zine had mostly the same aim as the website— to gather the contacts, to become an artifact-message to our people in the regions. I started with 100 copies, and after two years ended up printing 1500; people were ordering it from all over the country.

What we were still lacking was a band. I always kept in mind that there should be a scheduled ecstatic ritual in a community. So we asked everyone if they had ever played any instruments, and

A protest demonstration against cruelty to animals in front of a store carrying fur (the poster says, "Stop the suffering of furred animals at the farms"), Novy Arbat street, Moscow, 1999. Shot by Sergey Voloshin

ended up having six people in the band and two vocalists including me. We called the band Proverochnaia Lineika, which is a literal translation of "straight edge" but sounds really strange and illogical in Russian. By choosing this name I wanted to underline that we were not a musical band at all, but a blanket for the community. Like being a musician is a sham and we were only forced to play by a functional necessity. We recorded the first demo in one day, and as all the musicians had practically never had any musical background, it sounded really strange. "Oi-like skate-punk" as my friends later referred, broadly some typical college band mixture. The lyrics were simple chants so everyone could sing along, strictly in Russian (contrary to the previous Russian hardcore scene, where English lyrics were dominant) and postmodernistically in-your-face. A lot of provincial vocabulary. I wanted to sound "direct from the ground," for real.

If I were a father
My kids would say fuck you
I would not give them the right knowledge
About the world that is before us
They would not have the money
For a new mobile phone and fashionable clothes
They would conduct their time
In the nearest pig station instead of school
They would go to the rally
Against the garbage and against the system
They would wear knives in their pockets
And never part with baseball bats
They would listen to hellish music
And never know what TV is
Feed the people on the streets
Disseminate straight edge ideas
One would be a pilot, and the other—an astronaut
The third would participate in a terrorist act
The fourth—a surgeon, always unselfish

A fifth would become fucked like me.[180]

---

180 "Papa" by *Proverochnaia Lineika.*

Kristina Doga: At the time before social media—VK and Facebook— there existed a nazi website called "Format 18." I didn't even have a computer at the time, but my photos were all over this nazi website. There were so many photos of anti-fascist skinheads and just me for punks, because I looked the brightest for St Petersburg. I had extra long spikes, a bright jacket, and makeup, so people always photographed me. So of course some of those photos would show up on the Internet. There were like seven or 10 photos of me that had my name, so nazis already knew what I looked like.

A couple of weeks before, I remember we were walking downtown and I remember some nazi skinheads attacked us (I was around 17, in 2006) and this girl with me was maybe 16 or 15. Some guys attacked, and I still remember the moment they beat me. They beat my head on the metal railing parallel to the water screaming, "Ohh Kristina, we recognize you! Ohh Kristina!"

And then at another time I was drinking in the morning— it was before punk bars were a thing—and we decided to drink at a far away metro station. Our friend thought it was a good idea. This day was already crazy because a dog bit me for the first time in my life, coincidentally. I was looking for a place with coverage, and I thought there was just trash on the ground, but it was homeless people, and their dog bit me—I was wearing leopard print and she took a huge chunk out of the stocking. I still have the marks.

So then there were a few of us, two girls and a few guys, anti-fascist tough guys, and I got shitfaced—black out—so I didn't remember all the details myself, but I remember the moment when I was on the ground surrounded by a few people and they were beating me. And then suddenly, one guy—he wasn't a skinhead, he was a pacifist, and he wasn't very strong—he found me. He saved my life, because they turned to him and came off of me. So basically, if it wasn't for one of my friends, I would be dead right now, probably.

Then at some point I found my friends, and they told me I was bleeding; they stopped me. I woke up in a bed full of blood and I was like, "What's going on?" And they told me that a nazi stabbed me. They told me to check the mirror, and I noticed I had a fucking hole in my back. I was shocked, but I was also young and too drunk to care.

So later, I learned the entire story. It went something like this: we met some nazis, I guess they were with a girl who started to tease us, and we teased back. She called her friends, and we all started to fight. Someone had a knife and people started running away, and this girl and I got lost. I still didn't know where this girl went, because they found her later and broke her arm and gave her a concussion. And I remember in the morning, we found a stamp of Dr. Martin's in her fucking forehead. So in the morning, our friend told us to go to the hospital, and we pretended not to care; he forced us to go. And while I was going, I said to myself "Now I'm not scared of anything." The stab wound was four or five centimeters, almost to my lungs. That's it. They fucking stabbed me. Just me.

My friends came and stole me from the hospital bed because I was going nuts there for two days. After some hours, my mom came and gave me her phone and a new sim card, and I don't remember why, but everyone already knew my number and what happened. In the morning I told one of my friends and he told everyone. So when I put the sim card in everyone started calling, offering me money and help for the medical bills. They made a show for me—Crowd Control played, I think. It was really nice.

Ivan WWF: There were lots of violent moments. Once I came to a ska concert in St. Petersburg, and my friends were attacked by nazis. It was maybe 30 people against three. Security did nothing, and we just hid backstage. I sent a text to my band mates, who were separated in different parts of the city (we came there to play a show the next day). In one hour, they gathered a group of maybe 10 people, came to the concert, and fought maybe 30 nazis. It was really funny stuff; I will never forget it. It was, you know, punk-hardcore friendship. We always supported each other in any situation.

What We Feel, Voskresensk, Moscow area, 2009, Used with permission of Ivan kulikov

The New York Times: The 26-year-old victim, identified by anti-fascist groups and Russian news agencies as Ivan Khutorskoi, was shot in the head in front of his apartment building in eastern Moscow on Monday evening, the investigative wing of Russia's Prosecutor General's Office said in a statement on Tuesday. The statement, which did not identify the victim by name, said he was killed possibly because he was "an active participant in the anti-fascist movement."[181]

Pjtor: We had to be conspiratorial when it came to organizing gigs. Luckily, there are a lot of available places to rent in Moscow, including abandoned Soviet cinema theaters, basements, industrial

181 Michael Schwirtz, "Nationalists Suspected in Russian Activist's Death" *The New York Times*, November 17, 2009. http://www.nytimes.com/2009/11/18/world/europe/18moscow.html

Ivan "Bonecrusher" Khutorskoi (1983-2009), Berlin 2007, Suren Kanisterkopf

areas, even abandoned Cold War bomb shelters. For a little money, you could have done basically anything there. And it was much more fun than playing in some shitty rock bar, that's for sure. All attendees were personally invited; the only way to get to the show was to be brought by your friend. That produced a very unique and thrilling atmosphere—yesterday you would have been fighting together with those people, or bribing some local cops while illegally feeding the homeless, and today they were all on the show and there was not a single one who didn't participate in something productive. Risk of being located by the nazis and burned alive in that basement also benefited the atmosphere. Unfortunately, there were not many girls attending (because of the grave risk or because we were really ugly and hopeless), but the ones that went were ultimately cool and enthusiastic.

The Moscow hardcore scene despised and hated us. Not only because they were suffering because of us. You could feel it was a very classist thing: "Bums," "rednecks," "uncultured," "dumb," "primitive," not to mention the awful music and retarded lyrics. Our aim had been achieved; that scene was destroyed and there were new kids coming to our shows from the suburbs, the majority of whom never attended any "real" hardcore show in their lives. For them we became the norm—and violence, Food not Bombs, politics, straight edge, and veganism were parts of that norm.

From the very beginning, we were regionally oriented and the band was supposed to travel a lot to spread the message into the provinces. Kids in the distant cities felt that the new wave was coming and were thrilled to help it expand into their cities. They would book a gig for us in some abandoned movie theater, invite some friends, and hope we brought enough supporters from Moscow so they could stand an inevitable attack from the local nazis. We would bring at least six armed guys to their godforsaken place, but normally we travelled with a much bigger crowd. All the musicians were interchangeable, of course. Every kid could just grab a guitar and play the three chords. We also frequently didn't take guitars at all. Who needs a guitar if you are attacked right off the train?

Roma Sovest: I started going to shows in 2003, and until 2005 I had just been going to pop punk shows. And well, at the time pop punk was huge, but it had nothing to do with slogans, and there was no attitude. In 2005 my friend told me about a Proverochnaia Lineika show that I got really into. I was like, really… for a person not from that sub scene, it's really hard to find out about gigs from that band because they were so-called "closed" gigs. They were really obscure and somehow I managed to go. It was really interesting, and after that I started getting more and more into the obscure Russian scene. I was really attracted to it because my understanding of music was really different. Before then, if you wanted to go to a pop punk show you just went to a show and bought a ticket. The bands were sort of idols, and the hardcore scene was different because people went and talked to their friends freely with no barriers, no boundaries, and it was so fricken cool. Plus there was this cool feeling of danger, because everyone always thought something would happen before or after the show—that nazis would come and attack us. A lot of people carried knives, pistols with rubber bullets, bottles, and whatnot.

Anti-fascism Moscow, 2012, Used with permission of Pjtor from his personal archive

Ivan WWF: "Hardcore is more than music," we understand and made as our slogan, so that the music we play is an instrument of propaganda. It affects those who listen to music for the sake of music. We would like to introduce these people to movements and initiatives that we believe are important and correct: Anti-fascism, Food Not Bombs, or Animal Liberation. Of course, there is hardcore music. But the things that we advocate—which we support through our lyrics, with announcements at concerts—are, in fact, more than music. We are active, for example, in the Food Not Bombs movement. Our singer is a member of an anti-fascist group. And the other guys are also involved in different areas. We play charity concerts and try to support the anti-fascist scenes in different cities. For us, this is far more than just music; these are our views, this is our movement.

You keep silence, when they shout,
They are heard, and you are not.
Do not be aside,
Do not obey stupidly.

With your inactivity you dig the grave for yourself,
Now you do not care, but it will also concern you,
Fascists will never know rest until you show the strength,
Resist, speak aloud about your views.

Good night white pride!

Has fascism already become a norm?
Did you forget, what millions of people died for?
Do not dissemble the problem of nazism,
Do not believe in all these ravings.

Good night white pride![182]

Pjtor: In Volgograd we only played with drums and a bass. After the gig, the venue was stormed by a crowd armed with hardware and bricks. We barricaded the entrance, and in the fuss forgot our second vocalist outside. He grabbed one of the attackers as a hostage and dragged him under a car, smashing his face with a brick

182 "Good Night White Pride" by *What We Feel*, from the album *Last War* (2007), *Karma Mira* record label.

so he wouldn't scream. In Krasnodar, together with the locals, we outnumbered the nazis and were chasing them through the whole city after they broke the windows and tried to storm the venue. In Riazan we came multiple times, every time smashing the local nazis before the show until, on the third time, they didn't gather all possible people they could've, and it ended with massive bloodshed in the center of the city, one of the most brutal I have seen. We also went to Nizhny Novgorod two times, and the last riot was supposed to be so massive and brutal that the local authorities instated a day curfew and called for the army. We also went touring to the emerging anti-fascist scenes in Minsk and Kiev; the virus was spreading internationally.

St. Petersburg had its own established hardcore scene, much more socially oriented than the old scene in Moscow. They had an agreement with the local nazis, a status quo. We played there only once; that was the only relatively big concert we ever played to that point. After the show our local friends were laughing at us: "Look, it's so distinguishable who is from Moscow. You guys are all grabbing empty bottles, sticks, junk hardware—we are in a normal city, common!" After a couple of months, the nazis murdered a kid from the hardcore scene exactly in St. Petersburg, as revenge for our extremely successful season in Moscow. I definitely feel guilty for the death of Timur, along with a couple of other innocent kids murdered during the succeeding years (I don't mean my friends, Fedor, Ilya, and Ivan, who were totally not innocent). If not for the war we started, they would still be alive. But on the other hand, the nazis were routinely murdering tons of innocent people through the decades, including random punk rockers, and the total number of annual murders hasn't ever really changed—with or without us.

Indymedia.org: "Timur Kacharava, a student at the St. Petersburg State University and frequent participant in anti-fascist meetings, was murdered on Ligovsky Prospekt on Sunday night. A preliminary police investigation revealed that Kacharava and his friend Maxim Zgibay, who is currently in hospital with severe injuries to his head

Timur Kacharava (1985-2005), Berlin 2004, Liubava Sharokhina

and chest, were attacked by a group of youngsters at about 18.30 outside a bookstore, Interfax reported.

"'The prosecutor's office is considering all possible versions, including a nationalist attack as both students were active pacifists and took part in virtually all the anti-fascist events in St. Petersburg,' read the statement of the city prosecutor's office quoted by Interfax.[183]

Pjtor: So the war continued. We had extremely successful seasons in 2005 and 2006. The mob was steadily growing in numbers and we became a major violent force in the city. Consistency was very important: every open nazi event, every festival, every show, every nazi friendly venue, or nazi supporting office was being attacked. After two years, they practically ran out of friendly venues. Massive amounts of people preferred to leave the nazi scene and to concentrate on the football intrigue, which was much safer. "Apolitical football hooliganism" became a safe trend—that was a major victory. The remaining core nazis steadily disappeared into

183 Interesting to note that the St. Petersburg Times has taken their original article offline.

the underground, where we previously belonged. Realising that they had lost the street war, they decided to shift to terrorism, accumulating firearms. That was good, because they lost the grip on the urban streetlife and the monopoly for cultural influence. But at the same time it cost the lives of a number of my close friends, who were shot and massacred at their homes later. But that's another story.

Meanwhile, the hardcore scene was growing, and there were more and more bands sharing our position. We started to organize open gigs—first as the formal invitation for the nazis to attack and be smashed, but then they were just open gigs. First open festivals, crowds of people from all over the country, tons of bands. As soon as we got the machine working, I dismissed the band. There was no reason for a fake project to live when the mission was over. I was very annoyed by the sound, too.

Maksim Dinkevich: After the killing of Timur, the cops and FSB knew something was wrong and started paying attention to anti-fascists. And in maybe 2006, they established the Department for Combating Extremism, or *Tsentr "E,"* and both fascists and anti-fascists were considered extremists.[184]

Kristina Doga: Since I started being in the anti-fascist movement, I had fights, but when you're 16 to 18 it's like a game—like, "I'm using you to get some aggression out." So it was fun until Timur died, then you realize this game is fucking serious. By the way, my nose was broken a few times. For me it was fun—get beaten or beat people—I always thought they would never kill me, but when Timur died, it was like fuck. He was so young.

Mitr: I think neo-nazis started to get manipulated by the government and police. They started to use them. Everyone knows there were big fights in Moscow at the marketplace, once there was a bomb at Cherkizovsky market. I think the secret police tried to

184 For *Tsentr* "E" read footnote 5, Introduction.

use them to infiltrate other radical youth cultures. Without this situation, the band What We Feel would not have existed. The idea for the band came because when Timur was killed, we were all shocked. I caught the idea that people like me were struggling with the dark side of humanity, so I wanted to do something. I'm not a street fighter, but I wanted to do something. So it was like my way of kicking ass—playing anti-fascist music. There were thousands of attacks at our shows.

For example, we played a show in Riazan with What We Feel and some other bands. The venue was crowded. The show started, and then some young nazi called the police from his house and told them there was a bomb in the venue. The police came, kicked us out, and all the people (mostly from Moscow) left the venue. They called like that a lot. It was a cop-out for them, because there were too many of us to fight. They kicked people out, arrested some people, but unfortunately for them everyone missed the last train to Moscow. They had money and just started to drink, shoplift, and destroy everything and cause trouble on the streets. While this was going on, the police spent one to two hours trying to find the bomb. Finally, some policeman decided to check the

What We Feel, Moscow, 2014, Used with Permission of Ivan Kulikov

attic of the venue. He put the [police] dog up there, and the dog fell right through the roof on to the policeman! After that, the police realized there was no bomb and the officer realized the chaos he started in Riazan. He asked the organizer, "What can we do with these people?" and the organizer said he didn't know because the train left for Moscow. So the policeman said, okay, you need to start the show again, then. So they went from arresting people to letting them back in. The policeman went on the stage and apologized to the people. Special forces, police, bombs, all that shit happened all the time. At this time it was a hype.

Kristina Doga: We put out all this literature and stuff, and when I hung out with my boyfriend I always had a baseball bat. We were always super scared. Then a lot of new anti-fascist skinheads in St. Petersburg and some bands came to the scene, and we always stayed together, because back in the day we didn't have so many people. At that point, around 2010, everyone was together. Now it's a grey zone again. There weren't many females, and people still remember me as one of the first girls in the DIY scene. And it's nice; it's cool to see people who still respect me.

So I started to become kind of comfortable and forget about those days. And one day, I was riding home with headphones on and I was waiting when some guy and girl came up to me and started saying some shit, so I was sure it was something about my look. I figured, "Ah, who cares, some normie comments." I didn't pay attention. Unfortunately, I had to. At some point I stopped understanding what was going on, and then I saw pieces of glass around and a lot of blood on my face. I was freaking out. They broke my nose, cut my eyebrow (I still have the scars on my face), and there was a lot of fucking blood. It was a spectacle. At 16 to 18, I was looking for it, but at this point I was older and didn't think I would get attacked. I just want to be able to go about my life and dress how I want and not worry about protecting myself.

Characters in the order they appear:

Sasha "Chacha" Ivanov—Frontman for the bands Naïve and more recently RadioChacha (Moscow).

Max Kochetkov—Bass player for Naïve.

Dmitry Spirin—Frontman for Tarakany! (Moscow) and popular contemporary DJ.

Anna Andreeva—Frontwoman for Senkevich (Moscow).

Vova Rodionov—Guitarist for Tarakany! from 1995–1996.

Slavik Dacent—Frontman for Distemper (Moscow).

Masha Kinder—Drummer for Vosmaia Marta (Moscow) from 1998-2001, writer and composer.

Dmitry Khankin—Early '90s fan of Moscow punk scene.

Pavel—Frontman for Uchitel Truda (Moscow).[185]

Il-78 (Ilya Alekseev)—Frontman and songwriter for Ankylym (St. Petersburg). Academically trained observer of the scene.

Ivan WWF—Frontman for What We Feel (Moscow), antifa activist.

Kirill "George" Mikhailov—Guitarist for the bands Svinokop, 01 band, Cut'n'Run, Dottie Danger, and vocalist for Upor Lezha (St. Petersburg). Founder of Karma Mira and NotLG tapes record labels.

Aleksey "Shkobar" Olesinov—Leading member of early anti-fascist movement in Moscow, anti-fascist skinhead activist.

Ribson—Co-singer in the '90s for Piat Uglov, frontman for Next Round (St. Petersburg).

Pjtor—Frontman for anti-fascist band Proverochnaia Lineika (Moscow), activist, and writer.

Kristina Doga—St. Petersburg punk and fan and model.

Roma Sovest—Longtime fan of Moscow hardcore and guitarist for Worshit (Moscow).

Maksim Dinkevich—Cofounder, editor, and writer at Sadwave.com, frontman for Da, Smert! and Mraz (Moscow).[186]

Mitr—Guitarist for Dottie Danger, Upor Lezha, Distress (St. Petersburg), and What We Feel (Moscow).

---

185 *Handicraft Teacher.*
186 *Da, Smert—Yes, Death! Mraz—Crud.*

PART FOUR:
GROUNDSWELL 2000-2010[187]
4.1 Punk in the Provinces

Sergey Sukhinin: The "hero" city of Tolyatti in the mid-'90s of the last century—the "Russian Detroit," *avtograd*—was notorious in the whole country for its *VAZepovskie* light cars of crappy quality and shameful execution.[188] More or less, it was one large sleeping area for hard workers and lay people. It had an extremely low cultural level, in general. A typical provincial dull hole. Somewhere in the distant megacities and cultural centers—Moscow and St. Petersburg—there were some exciting and significant events in regard to underground rock: club life, concerts, visits of famous Western singers, new labels for new alternative rock music, television and radio programs, literature produced and sold, all different freaks walking the streets in the attire they wanted. And most importantly, they had the largest variety of rock music—audio (on any sound equipment), video on VHS, all sorts of different settings. Numerous large and small parties, even then divided by interests. [Tolyatti] at that time was under gopniki dictatorship.[189] For an earring, a shirt with a print of a favorite rock band, for any haircut that was not proper, for a bandana on your head or for any screaming appearance (in the view of prison influenced gopniki) you could get a serious beating right when they took notice. In any part of the city, on walls and fences you could find the ubiquitous inscription: "*Nefory-Lokhi!*"[190]

187 This chapter is the sparsest in terms of interviews for a few reasons. Originally, this project was conceived of with a focus on St. Petersburg and Moscow. It was only after the insistence of a few people that I ventured to Izhevsk and Nizhny Novgorod to conduct interviews. The other reason is that the scenes in each place are of course smaller, and the variety of opinion was lacking. The interviews here were paradigmatic and included the most detailed information. Over time, I began to notice that the interviewees collectively told a story about bored kids in remote provincial islands, isolated from the luxuries of the capitals and determined to have something of their own. This chapter is presented, then, as a testament to that. For a simple example of this, skip to the final section on punk in Izhevsk.

188 The word *avtograd*—auto-city refers to a city where car manufacturing is the leading industry; *VAZepovskie* refers to VAZ. AvtoVAZ, formerly known as VAZ—Russia's largest automobile manufacturer.

189 For a definition of *gopnik/gopniki*, see footnote 4, Introduction.

190 *Nefory-Lokhi*—Freaks are losers! *Nefory*—a contracted form of *neformaly*—was a common name for representatives of various youth subcultures in the '80s and the '90s in Russia.

There were practically no rock concerts. Rock musicians were very, very unfashionable, unprestigious, humiliating, not good, inferior, and the style was actually dangerous for life and health. And also troublesome, expensive, problematic, costly, and still, all the same—in the remote backwoods: hopeless and futile. Extremely rare, clandestine, amateur "sessions" of enthusiastic rockers were always stalked by the gopniki, and they almost always ended with harsh beatings of musicians, their friends, and visitors of the event. At the height of the summer of 1996, the rock-clubbish group in the city was quite big, but it was the only one out there. Everyone was hanging out together in the same melting pot, regardless of different tastes for musical styles, genres, etc.[191]

Anton: [In the provinces] something is missing in people. People are stuck in the year 1988, when heavy metal was the craze. They listen to death metal en masse, anoint their face with black paint, wear chains, iron. It's a fearful bore, nothing to see. As if it was not 1999 now, but the '80s. Now, during the last half of the year, we managed to overcome it somehow. A couple of bands appeared after us; they play in the same vein.[192]

Fyra: I remember when we were engaged in vinyl, that is to say we were going to Nizhny [Novgorod], exchanging LPs. It was around 1988. That's when we got a Misfits LP, then S.O.D. We would take the insert of the S.O.D. LP and read all the thank you notes to different groups—basically to the whole New York hardcore scene. That's how we figured out what LPs to look for next.[193]

Eduard Kireev: Play Hooky! arose from an interest in music and all the resulting musical activities. I was interested in an independent music scene that was not covered well in contrast to popular music. I was interested in musical counterculture and

191 From the history of the band written by the frontman, Sergey Sukhinin. Found here https://wiki.rock63.ru/Turbo_Lax/Interesting_Punk
192 From Olga Aksiutina, *Pank-virus v Rossii* (*Punk-virus in Russia*) (Moscow: Lean, 1999), 310.
193 Taken from the documentary *Goriachee Vremia* (*Hot Time*) about the punk scene in Kirov. Used with permission by the director, Boris Baragozin. It can be found here https://www.youtube.com/watch?v=5ty6rVpcMPg&t=257s

Play Hooky! #2, December, 1995, Eduard Kireev

the lack of information spurred me to publish my own zine, share the information that we had, and receive information that we were interested in. We gathered material for the zine by communicating with music collectives that were possible to contact. Addresses were taken from Western, and less frequently Russian, presses. The layout was created on the principle of "cut-paste." And the main binding was possible, because by then xerox technology was freely available in the city.

We tried to expand our horizon with primitive means. Well, we just needed to communicate with punk and hardcore music enthusiasts (and not only), and those with whom we were lucky enough to get acquainted. These were people from all over the world, including from the former Soviet Union and Russia itself. Deeply engaged people were mostly from the major cities: St. Petersburg, Moscow, Novosibirsk, countries located near the border with Western Europe: Belarus, Lithuania, Latvia, Estonia. In Kirov itself, there lived advanced and educated people who tried to create something, like us and the early Unsubs crew. There was a hardcore scene, so they also crowded up the record-stop, played rare concerts, and even had a hardcore punk radio.

Fyra: And a small crew appeared, they sought to make contact with us, they came to our concerts… We realized that we had already achieved something. And it already gave us joy.[194]

Vlad "Pelsh": I was listening to these sounds open-mouthed, so to speak. Anxious, energetic, driving sounds. I was really excited.

Aleksey "Spik": I liked this ingenuousness in music. This internal protest that was ripping in me and my friends was expressed in an uncompromising way. We did not aspire to be seen as geniuses or to represent some spiritual culture. It was like speaking my mind. Screaming actually in a maximum, quick-and-dirty way.

Fyra: At that time, I used to chat with a girl from the US. I think she was from Texas. She had her own fanzine. This one time she sent me a copy of *Maximum Rocknroll*. That's where I found addresses of the labels or distributors of different groups. We made up a letter saying that we were a radio station that wanted to promote groups—hat's why we asked them to send us promo albums, shirts, and other shit.

---

194 Aksiutina, *Pank-virus v Rossii,* 310.

Eduard Kireev: They wrote something like, "We are a bla-bla radio from a small town and we are poor, we don't have money, send us this and that."

Fyra: So we sent those letters to like 150 different addresses, and within half a year we got a shitload of discs, vinyl LPs, shirts, stickers, and other shit.[195]

Artem "Tommy Gun": There was no punk in Arkhangelsk before the '90s. It is a small seaport with a small population of 380,000 people. It's been a very gopnik-city ever since the '80s. You know who they are right? At that time, they made up about 99% of the youth in the city. There are many prisons in the Arkhangelsk region, so once they were released from prison they went to the closest city. Consequently, the crime rate was enormously high in the '80s.

In the late '80s, a lot of new music appeared in the city. It was brought by seamen, as Arkhangelsk is a seaport. TSo they would go abroad and bring back records and cassettes. So these kids would listen to this stuff, including heavy metal and Russian shit-rock, and try to make something on their own based on it. The important thing is that we never had a scene here. The distinguishing part of our scene is that it's self-contained and reserved. People were mixing with other people from their own city, from their own region, not really sticking their necks out. When some of the groups from Moscow or St. Petersburg came, they very happily took the money and never came back.

Roman Farik: The punk scene in Nizhny Novgorod has existed for a long time, but over the years it has changed a lot. The years 2008–2012 were more ideologically charged—the groups that formed were interested in playing angry and ideologically loaded punk rock. Part of the reason is that there were frequent skirmishes with nazis. There were hardcore bands, anarcho-punk, you name it. Voennoe Polozhenie was the sickest band at that time.[196] They

195 Boris Baragozin, *Goriachee Vremia.* https://www.youtube.com/
watch?v=5ty6rVpcMPg&t=257s
196 *Voennoe Polozhenie*—Martial Law.

created a feeling of real unity in the scene. So much so that people got comfortable. Then at that moment, repressions started and they began to close gigs. Many people dropped out of the scene, continued with ordinary life, lost interest, or began to worry about their safety because of the nasty things that law enforcement started to do. The activities of nazis on the streets also started to fall over time, probably also from pressure by the cops.

Bulat Ibiatov: In Kazan, the punk rock scene started very late, in 2002. There were punk bands in the '80s, and in the '90s, but there was a punk rock scene with labels, fan-zines, and DIY ethics only in 2002.

I went to my first punk rock show that year. It was Naïve and Smekh in Nizhnekamsk, a small town near Kazan. It was a rock festival.[197] I was 14 years old. Later on, I met the singer of Parasites from Nizhny Novgorod, and I booked a show for him. He would bring me discs with punk rock, hardcore, and emo. He talked to me about straight edge, vegetarianism, etc.

Then the first serious DIY punk band in Kazan was a pop punk band named Spory?[198] It was founded in 2002 and I started to be the vocalist for it in 2004. From 2003–2005 the most important punk shows in Kazan were with Spory? There was also 12 Marshrut, but they played, like, The Exploited-type punk.[199]

Diliusa Gimadeeva: The first group that impressed me was Spory? When I decided to start a girl band, which was new to Kazan, the lyrics and music were playful and had a feminist character. But above all, during our concerts they encouraged people toward kindness.

---

197 *Smekh*—Laughter.
198 *Spory?*—Quarrels/Spores? In Russian these two words are homonyms in plural. According to the band, they didn't decide which of these words the name refers.
199 *12 Marshrut*—Roote №12.

Spory?, Aviator Club, 2011, Bulat Ibiatov

Your government and parents
And everyone around you
Has constructed your personality
Independent of you.
Your thoughts are projected
And your brain can't think by itself
And you are so self-assured.
In a position to see only sexual objects![200]

Timur Sloboda: Frankly, we were impressed with music in Ufa city. We were shocked by the fact that there were many fashionable folks, who listen to a lot of music, and adequately dance and perform in concerts.

Nikita "Nikitoaster" Mekhanoshin: I got into punk rock through skateboarding. My first experience was watching skate videos and hearing some tracks from the Misfits, 7 Seconds, Dead Kennedys, and Agnostic Front.

Most bands in Izhevsk, in my opinion, were very banal and boring—musically and lyrically. We wanted to play something more technical, stylish, and serious. There were too many people who absolutely didn't care about music and ideas, they were only interested in fun, drinking, and violence (everything is okay, but

200 "Sexual Object" by *Off-Key.*

without music and ideas it all means nothing). Most of them quit the scene very quickly a long time ago.

Dania Baykov: I was fourteen when I heard punk rock, and it was because my classmate showed me bands like Naïve, Turbo Lax, Klowns, Unsubs, Changes… And then I found for myself other foreign music, particularly Ska music. The first show I saw was Ricochet and My Crazy Days, which later became my band, Reasons. That show was in Izhevsk, and it was something crazy that I didn't understand at first. People were going crazy, fighting without any violence. And this atmosphere, this spirit… you can release your anger or something else… To feel that in your life… it's hard to describe. But I felt something. And then I started to meet people at shows, and it was a long way from there when I finally started to listen to hardcore punk. Now I can say I really believe in hardcore. It's not only the music; it's how people are doing things and how they look at the world and what they see in it. The place where you can do anything—you can write a book, paint a beautiful picture, you can start a band and do a show by yourself and invite friends and friends can invite you. You can go to any city, any town, and find people who will help you, and then you will help them without any difficulty.

Sasha Shmakov: I started to listen to punk rock when I was 13 or 14. I listened to Korol i Shut. My first show was in 2004 and it was *Naïve*, in Izhevsk at the house of culture, the old Soviet style place with seating. Punks broke the first five rows, and everyone was standing because of that. I was really impressed by their show, because the Izhevsk scene at that moment consisted of boring Russian rock bands that played blues or something in a Russian way. Naïve was about teenage life, about how parents don't understand you and about unsuccessful love. And some songs were really aggressive.

I can say that in the provinces people are more relaxed; they don't care about how they look when they are dancing, how they support bands. For example, I played with Minefield in Dimitrovgrad, and their scene was young at the moment and everyone was so supportive. All the people were dancing and hanging out. And then you go to big cities with old scenes like Moscow or Kiev, and people just watch you. They're not as supportive because they've already seen it all.

Scrap Monsters' Sasha, October 9, 2016, photo by Azat

Aleksey Kotikov: I got involved in the punk rock scene pretty late, though I had friends who were part of it, and one time our band was invited to a hardcore concert (at that time we were playing post-rock and the band was called Chayka Sterkh).[201] The guys invited a band from Kaliningrad called Dice. It was my first hardcore concert, and I was fucking amazed how fast the cafe turned into a gym when other bands were playing. Hardcore and punk seemed very primitive back then—four chords and unchanging lyrics about friends. At that moment I liked two bands—Ray and Feeding The Fire. I thought that melodic youth music was the only music acceptable for listening to at home. It all changed after I heard Ricochet. Like many others, my first thought was "How can you listen to this high pitch singing and strange music?" But that's exactly what got me hooked. The music and the lyrics were very outstanding for punk

201 *Chayka Sterkh*—Gull White Crane.

rock. I still see them as the best punk rock band in Russia's scene. Then one thing led to another, and I got involved in the scene. I had friends in the hardcore band Party Breaker. Unlike other styles of music, people seemed more united in this one. At least more than the other concerts I'd been to and arranged. The atmosphere was completely different. Earlier, like every schoolboy I came across Grazhdanskaia Oborona and Purgen. But all that was subconscious and far away. For me, punk rock is the guys next to you, you see them in the streets and concerts, and not in the pictures or on stage.

Artem "Tommy Gun": We didn't know much about punks from other places. We knew that Moscow was something like a skinhead city for us. We also knew that there were many cool punks in St. Petersburg. So every time someone came back from a holiday in St. Petersburg, we would ask them about their punks: "Did you get to see them? What are they like?" One of the most famous legends about St. Petersburg punks, that fully reflected our views on them at the time, was that they played two games for fun: *piatnashka* and basketball. Piatnashka is a game where a bunch of people gather around a piece of shit and smash a brick against it to see who ends up having more shit on him, ultimately winning the game. Another legend about St. Petersburg punks stated that they would take yellow bottled lemonade, pour it in a three-liter jar, and take it to the hospital for a urine analysis. When they were asked, "Why did you bring so much?" they would respond by drinking down the content. So in our view, St. Petersburg was a wild and free, emancipated city with TaMtAm club and Korol i Shut. Moscow was more about histrionics and cruelty to us.

Dania Baykov: We didn't play St. Petersburg, and we didn't like Moscow, really, because it was poorly organized, really bad. The first mistake we made was to travel with our stuff. We were tired and it was the last time we went to the club, and the man who organized left in a car with girls. He just left. And when we went to the club, he said the venue changed and we had to go somewhere else.

Ribson: Next Round played in Moscow and St. Petersburg, and many provincial cities in Russia. For me, there was no difference—only the clothes were richer in Moscow, they have more. The crowd was incredible everywhere, in Izhevsk even. Better than Moscow. There weren't a lot of people, but they were nuts. They were hungry, poorer, they were like me when I grew up in Leningrad. We were hungry for information, we wanted to see everything, to participate. Moscow is more comfortable with its scene; they're more familiar with it all. In the provinces they come from everywhere—from villages, it's incredible. The kids say, "We listen to you in the countryside, thank you so much." For me it was like, bahhh! Wow.

Party Breaker, Moscow, December 2012, used with permission from the band

Alex Distress: In the big cities, we have more opportunities in terms of clothing and money. Last year we did a tour across Russia and it was an interesting experience for us. We went to Kazan. The scene there is different, but it was fun. I like going to new places, meeting new people, opening something new for myself. Sitting around in one place is boring, there are no emotions, and you get tired of it. I like going to concerts and touring; I like changes. We don't have opportunities to go on tours very often, but when we do, we are always up for it. You meet new people, you talk. Give something to people and they give something back, you know. This communication means a lot.

Sasha Shmakov: Minefield's first Moscow concert was really not successful. We planned our tour one and a half months before it started, and Damir, our singer, said that "It's okay… everything is good for our Moscow show." He had a friend who was supposed to make it for us, and he said it was the only show that we didn't have to worry about. And we were headed back from Ukraine and it was about two weeks until the show, and I asked Damir, "What about the Moscow show? Why don't we have a flyer for it, an event on *Vkontakte* [Russian social media] or something like that, no advertisement, is everything okay?" He said, "Yeah it's okay, I'll just write to my friend."

One week before the show, the promoter said he didn't know a place to do it, and we told him, "Man you can do it anywhere, we don't care, in a garage, rehearsal spot, not necessarily a club." And he said, "No, I don't know such a place." And we thought, "Oh fuck, what's gonna happen?" And with a week left, I wrote to Bagi and he made us a show.[202] I wrote him in the morning and in the evening he responded, "Yeah, your show will be in Moscow, don't worry, I'll try to do everything," and he booked a show in a club, but there was no time to advertise or spread the word about it. And there were about 60 people at the show.

Daut Yuzovka: Ufa has always been relatively quiet in terms of fascism when compared to other cities in Russia. There have been a few cases of people getting jumped before or after a show, but nothing serious. As for *Tsenter E*—we've never dealt with them, although I assume they probably keep tabs on the scene. I was in an oi band called It's a Can though, and we were supposed to have a concert with some anti-fascist bands from other cities on Hitler's birthday, but somehow the authorities got wind and the bands were warned not to go to Ufa. It went ahead with local groups and there

202 DJ Bagi (Bagi Boev) is co-owner of the punk-label East Beat Records.

was heavy police presence, and they pulled anyone who stage-dove into the paddy wagon. Ironically, while all the cops in the city were at our concert, neo-Nazis jumped some kids downtown after an emo concert. We've been attacked in other cities, though. In Tolyatti we played a show right after I got jumped by about ten football hooligans in the parking lot of the club, and somebody in Barnaul started chasing people around the club with a knife while we were playing.

Sasha Shmakov: Around 2008, the crowd was bigger... maybe all people were younger than now, and they started pits, got crazy. We got good feedback. About a hundred people were there. And the most successful show in Izhevsk was with *Turbo Lax*, an old hardcore band from Tolyatti. When they played, there were about two and a half hundred people who showed up. And some nazis called the police and said there was a bomb in the building.

We knew it was nazis, because nobody else could do it. Because at this time, there was a lot of tension between anti-fascists and nazis. And this was a completely anti-fascist gig and nobody else could do it. Police came and spent two hours looking for the bomb, said they didn't find it, but they closed the concert. And after that, people moved to a theater that we used to practice at, and it became a very underground, very DIY show with 100 people or more hanging in a place like a squat, but it was not a squat. It was completely illegal, I think there was no protection or guards. And I think this show was like... eh, like the best Izhevsk show. We didn't play, but it was really great.

Dania Baykov: I actually think the whole process of distribution and whatnot being based on friends is not good. Because some bands became more popular, and I can't understand why—they're not bad at all, but we are trying to do the same things and it could never happen. We need to know people, yeah, to spread it out loud. But to establish connections, just because you need to spread word about your band, is not so good I think.

Roman Farik: Now, the situation in Nizhny Novgorod is like this: a small group of punks—the people left over from the time when there was real punk rock that was at the vanguard of the scene I mentioned earlier. There is a hardcore scene, usually apolitical, but many of them also maintain anti-fascist views to this day. They have their own concerts and their own tours. Their scene intersects with pop punk, skaters, and several groups of musicians with a similar style. And there are already a lot of subcultures—hipsters, post-rockers, some kind of children in my opinion. It's clear they have nothing to do with any of the ideals of punk. I actually think that this is all temporary. The fashion will go away, some other mods will appear, and real punk rock as it was in our city—as some 20 to 30 people represent it—will remain. It would be desirable, certainly, if the scene grew and developed on a larger scale, but with some enthusiasm and genuine feeling. In any case, while we are here we won't let it die.

Andrey Bakhmetyev with Putin at a Kazn' show, Kazan, 2012, photo by Anna Bushmits

Characters in the order they appear:

Sergey Sukhinin—Frontman for Turbo Lax (Tolyatti).

Anton—Drummer for Unsubs (Kirov).

Fyra—Frontman for Unsubs.

Eduard Kireev—Writer and creator of *Play Hooky!* fanzine (Kirov).

Vlad "Pelsh"—Drummer for Topograf! Zemlemer (Kirov).[203]

Aleksey "Spik"—Frontman for Tochka Kipenia (Kirov).[204]

Artem "Tommy Gun"—Music fan from Arkhangelsk.

Roman Farik—Frontman for Criminal State (Nizhny Novgorod).

Bulat Ibiatov—Frontman for Spory? (Kazan), founder of record label Siyanie.[205]

Diliusa Gimadeeva—Frontwoman for band Off-Key (Kazan).

Timur Sloboda—Frontman for Indikator (Izhevsk).[206]

Nikita "Nikitoaster" Mekhanoshin—Frontman for Unbroken Bones, and founder of record label Drunk with Power Records (Izhevsk).

Dania Baykov—Guitarist for Reasons, frontman for Misery and Milligan (Izhevsk).

Sasha Shmakov—Frontman for Scrap Monsters, guitarist for Minefield (Izhevsk). Founder of fanzine Teenage Waste.

Aleksey Kotikov—Frontman for Zagon dlia Sobak (Nizhny Novgorod).[207]

Ribson—Co-singer in the '90s for Piat Uglov, frontman for Next Round (St. Petersburg).

Alex Distress—Bass player for The Pauki, frontman for Distress (St. Petersburg).

Daut Yuzovka—Frontman for *Aybat Halliar* (Ufa).

---

203 *Topograf! Zemlemer*—Topographer! Surveyor.
204 *Tochka Kipenia*—Boiling Point.
205 *Siyanie*—Shining.
206 *Indikator*—Indicator.
207 *Zagon dlia sobak*—Pen for Dogs.

4.2: *A Brief History of Punk in Izhevsk, Russia*[208]

If you've ever heard of Izhevsk, it probably had something to do with the Kalashnikov rifles (also known as AK-47s) that its factories introduced to the world. What is less known is that Izhevsk—the capital of the Udmurtian Republic—is home to one of the youngest and most invigorating punk scenes in the Russian Federation.

Easily a sixteen-hour train ride from Moscow, and a 24-hour drive from sumptuous St. Petersburg, Izhevsk is a small, isolated city on the outskirts of European Russia. The majority of Udmurtians living in Izhevsk are loyal communists, who unhappily witnessed the Soviet regime topple. A brazen statue of Lenin outside the local library serves as both a rallying point for the conservative left wing, and a popular late-night destination for bored, drunk, and disorderly punks looking for an easy scuffle. The city, like something out of a Lloyd Kaufman movie, is built around a man-made pond that has accumulated generations of industrial waste from its aforementioned rifle factories. Everything about the city is artificial. But the punks stalking the shores of Izhevsk Pond are the definition of real. Together, they embody something more profound than small-town political dissidence and obligatory "fuck you" antics. They recognize and hold something tangible in punk rock—something that is often lost in the consumerism of big cities, and that is not entirely communicable to the average Udmurtian, let alone the average Russian. To them, punk rock is a community powerful enough to provide a real alternative to local conservative culture. That community has produced a very refined cohort of bands, labels, and fanzines, which have orchestrated a *coup d'etat* in punk scenes from Udmurtia to San Francisco Bay.

---

208 This article originally appeared in *Razorcake* on Thursday, July 02, 2015. It can be found here: http://archive.razorcake.org/columns/a-brief-history-of-punk-in-izhevsk-russia. Since 2015, Izhevsk's punk scene has quieted down again, and Nizhny Novgorod has taken its place. In that case, the article is meant to be an example of a typical provincial city's rise and fall.

It's hard to gauge how punk rock made its way to Izhevsk. Like many cities in the Soviet Union, punk was initially enmeshed within the local culture of rock bands belching out their best rendition of Western classics in local nightclubs (the Sex Pistols, the Clash, and all the early greats heard on BBC radio became standard covers for Soviet and then-Russian rock bands). By the late '80s, the city became known for its electronic music scene, which may explain how cassette copies of Yegor Letov's innovative punk act from Omsk, Grazhdanskaia Oborona, found their way into the hands of some local rock aficionados. However, that rumor can't be substantiated by anyone who may have experienced it. What is certain is that as punk scenes in Russia's major cities consolidated in the late '90s and early 2000s, their influence spread to more remote, provincial cities, such as Izhevsk.

If the city's administration in any way encouraged the germination of punk rock in Izhevsk, it came in the form of a metal skate park in 2001. The park was replaced in 2007 with a dilapidated wooden skatepark, wrought with loose nails, decaying wooden ramps, rats, and the occasional rusty syringe. The park was not intended to foment counterculture, but to keep troublesome kids from loitering in "family friendly" parks around the city.

Despite the decrepitude, the skate park did become an inconspicuous place to hang out and exchange music and ideas. In their effort to master new tricks, people like Nikita "Nikitoaster" Mekhanoshin, front man of Unbroken Bones religiously watched skateboarding videos dubbed over with punk tunes. "I didn't even know that it was called punk rock or hardcore, just cool music," he recalls. Unsurprisingly, the music was conducive to a successful skate session, and it wasn't long before Naïve, Korol i Shut, the Dead Kennedys, 7 Seconds, and Agnostic Front became required listening for Nikita's rapidly growing entourage. One had to be really determined to get the music you wanted back in the days of Izhevsk's dial-up internet. Nikita each day meticulously downloaded each song. The process consumed most of the day, if it even worked at all. Another way of getting at the new music, albeit a surprisingly longer and more unreliable path, was through mail-order catalogs from Moscow and St. Petersburg. Distros such as Old Skool Kids, Karma Mira, and Neuroempire served as important engines through which Russia's "provincial" youth could hear new sounds.

Nikita wasn't alone in his penchant for "cool music." Something about punk's raw energy conveyed the bottled-up boisterousness found in the outwardly laconic miscreants. "In your own small town if you don't have anything else, you have something in punk rock" says Dania Baykov, one of those twenty-something-year-old punks stalking Lenin's statue at night in search of a conservative communist to scrap with. Dania is known throughout the city as the greatest guitar player, and the list of bands he plays for attests to that: Misery, Sea Devil, Reasons, and most recently, Milligan.

Another important figure, some might even say the golden boy of Izhevsk's punk scene, Sasha Shmakov discovered the music from a stranger while in the hospital. The story is told by him like a plot twist straight from a Gogol short story, "When I had a rotten finger, I got put in the hospital. A guy who was ill near me was listening to Korol i Shut. I copied the cassette tape and fell in love with this music. So thanks to my rotten finger." But Sasha's real punk christening occurred at a show headlined by the Moscow-based group Naïve at the city's Dom Kultury, where the crowd was expected to sit and stare aimlessly at the stage.[209] Soon after the band started, "punks broke the first five rows, and everyone was standing because of the broken rows." Sasha was consumed by the power of Naïve's show compared to local rock shows. To them, Naïve, was about the problems of youth, and unsuccessful first loves. Sasha understood the relevance, and while the lyrics of Naïve might seem rudimentary to him now, the music's ability to distill teenage angst into a sonic, ear-splitting punch resonated.

209 For a definition of *Dom Kultury*, see footnote 31, Part 1.1.

By the early 2000s, punk was a pervasive genre in the city, but few local bands maintained an actual scene. Indikator, which is widely viewed as the first punk band in Izhevsk, only played a few concerts because, as the band's frontman Timur Sloboda said, "There was no scene really, only a group of friends who played Sex Pistols covers." Whatever semblance of a scene that did exist, it was stitched together by a plethora of joke bands like the Speedy Toasters and Dianetica (a reference to Scientology).

The first local band to successfully metabolize punk's energy into something profound was a Red and Anarchist Skinhead (RASH) oi band, Red Card. Performing songs like "Proletarskaia Mest" and "Idealny Rab," the band invited their fans to think for themselves and stand up to the omnipresent conservative culture rampant in their city.[210] The band actively promoted vegetarianism and straightedge through a rough-and-tumble punk ethos that transformed their fans into a conscious community, mutually responsible for each other in the fight against pervasive and often dangerous nationalism. Up to that point, most Izhevsk punks had only heard bands from Moscow, St. Petersburg, and the West. The opportunity to experience a local show, with local musicians, singing relevant songs, became a reality for fans seemingly overnight.

Bands like Indikator, Red Card, and My Crazy Days paved the way for what would become Izhevsk's golden generation of punk rockers. Punk festivals and concerts were a regular occurrence around the pond by 2007. They also drew a number of people from surrounding cities. "All of our community in Kazan, around forty to fifty people, were going to Izhevsk for shows like Indikator, Sudny Den, and Unsubs (Kirov).[211] In Izhevsk, we had seen for the first time so many skinheads and punks in one place," said Bulat Ibiatov, originally of Kazan but now of the Moscow record label Siyanie. More importantly, it gave locals like Dania the opportunity to experience their first real show. It left him with a feeling of absolute

210 *Proletarskaia Mest*—Proletarian Revenge; *Idealny Rab*—Ultimate Slave.
211 *Sudny Den*—The Day of Reckoning.

stupor, to see people fighting without anger. It was the moment he realized that hardcore was something worth believing in.

Izhevsk entered Russia's punk periphery from out of nowhere. Nikita put together Unbroken Bones in early 2008 with the aim of claiming a spot for Izhevsk on the punk rock world map, and it was also the year eighteen-year-old Sasha formed Scrap Monsters to make punk more germane to everyday life in Izhevsk. Daut Yuzovka, front man for Aybat Halliar (Ufa) remembers playing a show with Red Card in Izhevsk in May 2007, in which more than one hundred and eighty people attended. "[Izhevsk] was always one of our favorite places to play," he said. Scrap Monsters played their first show in 2008 with Mister X (Belarus) and Red Card. More than one hundred people packed themselves into the local Dom Kultury. That's impressive for a city with around 320 square kilometers of land and a population of less than 650,000. An underground punk gig at the time in Moscow, with a population close to twelve million, typically brought around two hundred people.

The scene swelled so much that it generated animosity amongst local neo-Nazi groups, who habitually attempted to sabotage shows. At a Turbo Lax (Tolyatti) show, with over two hundred and fifty people—arguably Izhevsk's "most successful show," according to Sasha—neo-Nazis called the police and

Danya (Center, thumbs up) and friends, August 8, 2015, Anatolyi Polozov

reported a bomb in the venue. "Police came and spent two hours looking for the bomb. Then they said they didn't find it but closed the concert anyway," he remembered. Sasha, ever the resourceful and determined one, reconvened the band and its fans at *Scrap Monster*'s former practice space, a squat-like abandoned theater outside the city's center.

Fascist activity wasn't the only obstacle to the budding scene in 2008. Agents for Russia's Department for Combating Extremism also sought to stifle all "fascist and anti-fascist youth movements," which is as vague as it sounds. "They would go to a show and say, 'The show is over' or they could find some, for example, mistakes in the 'fire safety code' to kick us out," Nikita recalled. There was another time in 2008 when the cops "came and beat the public," forcing everyone to disperse. In a small, ideologically conservative city, any gig that deviated from the standard colorless rock ensemble replete with a comatose audience constituted a potentially subversive gathering.

Despite the persistence of some, the scene's relegation to the (illegal) underground meant less fans at concerts, and the local scene started to decline around 2010. The next best thing for bands like Scrap Monsters, Unbroken Bones, and Reasons was to forge close connections with scenes in places like Ufa, Kazan, and Yekaterinburg, where locals had cultivated a comparatively irrepressible subculture. In that way, the resulting outward movement of bands only made Izhevsk's scene more exportable, and it incentivized bands to record their first releases: Unbroken Bones—*Demo* (2009), Scrap Monsters—*Total Control* (May 2009), and Reasons—*Road to Home* (May 2009).

"We would travel and sleep in the van or in the flat of people who organized the show," said Dania about touring with Reasons. Not all bands could afford to tour unpaid, so Dania said "When our friends went on tour we gave them cassettes to distribute." If a local group went abroad, they took practically the city's entire discography with them.

While playing shows in Izhevsk became increasingly difficult, recording got easier and cheaper starting in 2010. That year, after recording his own band's album, Nikita decided to open his own record label, Drunk With Power Records. "I contacted some bands about trade and distribution and started to find some money for that by selling some old things from my own collection," he says. According to Nikita, the label's purpose is not only to promote his own band, but also to release foreign bands in Russia.

Sasha also seized the opportunity to expand by starting Teenage Waste Records in late 2010 and published the city's first fanzine under the same name in 2011 (his first attempt was in 2008 under the name *Cheers and Beers*, which he refers to as a "teenage mistake"). The new zine adopted a mantra from an Abrasive Wheels song by claiming to be "Just another punk fanzine, just another Teenage Waste," although it couldn't be further from that. After the first issue in 2011, *Teenage Waste* had climbed *Maximum Rocknroll*'s list of top ten fanzines in December of 2011. Rightfully so, as it typified the DIY spirit it endorsed. All prints come from Sasha's personal printer and all editions continue to be loaded with interviews, album reviews, and commentary about DIY bands from the post-Soviet world and abroad. Sasha also reached out to American zines and distros to exchange music. "I started to write them. 'Hey we are a band from Russia and want to trade CDs,'" he recalls, adding that "some would reply, 'Oh, CDs aren't popular anymore. Write me back when you have vinyl.'"

It is impossible to make vinyl in Russia—the country simply lacks the facilities. The only option for Drunk With Power and Teenage Waste was to reach out to European and American labels to get vinyl pressed. "I can't really take distribution in Russia seriously like I do in other places around the world," said Nikita after listing his label's resulting international connections. The challenge, in the end, turned out to be a good thing for Izhevsk's burgeoning labels, because, as Sasha said, "When you trade with some people from another country, you understand that punk rock is international... it's like a net spread all over the world. All of the touring and entrepreneurship made the scene into something cohesive, and it received a reputation throughout the country as a particularly unusual case of small-city ambition. The excess of outward growth partially stemmed from the abundance of creativity confined to such a small area, but it was also a consequence of the city's aversion to punk rock itself. Clubs simply refused to allow punk bands to perform, and there is nothing more appealing for artistic kids than defying the status quo.

Then something changed in 2011 when Dania formed Misery, and Sasha, along with friends Damir, Misha, and Serezha formed Minefield. Even Nikita admits, "It was my favorite time in Izhevsk's scene." Minefield in particular resolved the conflict between youth disenfranchisement and the city's disdain for punk rock by telling all authority to "fuck off." They proceeded to book shows anyway. (The band's first 7" was characteristically called *Otyebis!* which translates to "fuck off" in Russian. It pictured a punk smashing a bottle into his own eye with another writing, "God listens to Minefield" on a building in the background). The first demo came out in 2011 and it was a powerful discharge of exuberance in the form of lively traditional hardcore complemented by youthful vigor. The jolt of energy came just in time.

With that in mind, part of the reason Sasha and Dania claim they formed Minefield and Misery was to bring the city's own fanbase back to life. As Sasha says, the only way to improve the situation seemed to be "to wait for something to open or open it yourself."

Sasha and Dania's outgoing tenacity exemplifies the subculture's propensity to embolden those who feel trapped in a system they don't endorse. In Izhevsk, this means devoting every day to furthering a scene that has provided its loyal followers with so much. "For people involved in this, it has become a part of their personal history. Punk and hardcore taught us to be ourselves, to have another opinion," Sasha said. For others, the experience with punk is more transcendental, "Don't know how to describe it really, but it's something new, like I opened another, freer side of my mind and my thoughts," says Dania, never failing to assume the role of drunken philosopher. Even one of the city's veteran punk rockers, Ruslan Khrust of Red Card, regards punk rock not simply as music or a style, but "primarily a people, their actions, their principles of life, and their ability to defend their beliefs and fight for their ideals."

Minefield and Misery's responsibility for rekindling Izhevsk's punk scene in 2011 cannot be overstated. Sasha began booking shows at clubs that detested punk rock. The club owners shut down shows and forced the crowd to move out in a giant exodus once they realized what kind of music poured through their speakers. But the kids couldn't be stopped. Sasha and the crew always finished the show in the woods or a practice space, adding a new dynamic to the already enticing subculture of rebellion. The re-emergence of activity also gave preexisting titans such as Unbroken Bones and Reasons the chance to play more shows at home, reinvigorating the interest of many who left the scene a few years before. Instead of recreating what was lost, Minefield and Misery inadvertently erected a larger, more powerful movement. Izhevsk, with their help, went from an anomaly in Russia's greater punk scene to something comparable to Russia's most active.

Minefield, Dimitrovgrad, 2012, used with permission from the band

As Izhevsk rose in awareness in the eyes of Moscow and St. Petersburg, bands seized the opportunity to organize their first long-distance tours using their own money. Their DIY antics and small-town spirit made an impression on big city bands and their energy was contagious. "We played with Minefield in Moscow and they destroyed the whole place. The vocalist jumped like crazy, the drummer beat the shit out of his drum set, and the guitarist just couldn't stay at the same place for more than two seconds," recalled Maksim Dinkevich of *Da, Smert!*, and online music publication Sadwave.com

Moscow's large scene and proclivity for diversity reciprocated the liveliness Unbroken Bones and Reasons transmitted for Nikita and Dania. However, it also brought in highly unorganized and often sleazy promoters. Minefield's first experience in Moscow almost ended abruptly when an amateurish promoter backed out of the situation altogether. Sasha was forced to contact one of Moscow's most well known punk rock promoters, Bagi Boev of East Beat Records, to set up a last minute, un-promoted concert. As enticing as the story of small town punk in the big city is, the differences between them run deeper than flakey promoters and tolerable venues. Truthfully, Moscow crowds never quite sated the bands' hunger for crowd participation and enthusiasm, unless they opened for bands like Power Trip (US), which Unbroken Bones managed to do. There is a spirit in cities like Izhevsk, Kazan, Ufa, Perm, and others that, for whatever reason, seems more palpable than other places.

Izhevsk is a peculiar case because of the attention it has received beyond Russia. For example, Minefield and Scrap Monsters have gained the attention of *Maximum Rocknroll* more recently (an interview with Minefield is featured in *Maximum Rocknroll* #385, June 2015), and Nikita's label has issued releases in Canada, Japan, and Germany. Unbroken Bones, as previously mentioned, has played shows with Power Trip and Onslaught (U.K.). Dania's new project—Milligan—is yet to break out of Russia, but he maintains hope in knowing that a man from Brazil and another from Australia purchased Reasons shirts online.

The scene today is still limited locally, but it has continued to experience outward growth, which is important, considering there are still no clubs willing to host punk rock bands. (The city's only club, BVI, is a decidedly unfriendly spot for punk rock, as it caters more toward a wealthy clientele).[212] In summer 2014, Unbroken Bones, Scrap Monsters, and Milligan played their first local show in some time in a bedroom-sized practice space. Underground efforts like this are rare, but they seem to be the only way of keeping locals interested in punk rock.

This story of an emerging punk movement is most likely just like anyone else's small-city tale. Punk culture is reinforced by decades of history in almost every Western city. In New York, your dad's dad could have been a punk rocker. But small city scenes experience a cyclical boom and bust that often occur in rapid succession, giving rise to a particularly energetic and rambunctious group of kids, who are then remembered and emulated by succeeding generations. Izhevsk's scene is not interesting because

Unbroken Bones, Izhevsk, Podval club, 2015, Sofi Gusarova
212 Abbreviation for *Bar Veselykh Istory* (Bar of Festive Stories).

Milligan show, Pole Chudes, Izhevsk, August 5, 2017, Anatolyi Polozov

of its originality, but because it is a contemporary example of that aforementioned generation-to-be-emulated. In Izhevsk, we are experiencing the birth of something that will be remembered, if even just by future kids in a remote city.

Amongst the rumors that "punk is dead" and the increasing marketability of dissidence, Izhevsk reminds us that punk rock is still inherently organic and self-perpetuating. It gives isolated, disenfranchised youth the opportunity to push back against Russia's increased censorship and radical conservatism, in a way that is both constructive and communicable across the world. In Izhevsk, the future will test whether a movement fomenting such passion and inventiveness can endure in an increasingly disparaging environment, and whether or not creative cultural dissidence can ever really be quelled. Even Sasha "Chacha" Ivanov of Naïve, one of Moscow's first punk acts, can't help but admit that Izhevsk's punk scene embodies "something strange" when compared to the rest of Russia. For Nikita and others, the city's story offers a particularly compelling "micro-Russian" paradigm for understanding Russia's broader history with the subculture. No matter the extent of political or ideological restriction, punk rock has a certain staying power that resonates with creative individuals who feel they are on the outside looking in.

PART FIVE:
RUSSIAN PUNK TODAY 2010-2015

5.1 Raw Energy

Ankylym, Free-bo 2 Fest, 2013, Oksana Mironova

At once—as if there haven't been new places, no new names.
As soon as you turn back,
You seem to be sitting in the same car again,
To hear the same monotonous voices,
Long tired of an endless dispute about anything

And time will pick up the advance again,
Once given to you as a memory,
And old-timers will embrace you
With cold hands.[213]

Timur Yenaliev: Since the end of the '90s I have faced the problem of fascist low lifes, and did everything in my power to counteract them. Not because I was ideological or anything like that, I just saw it even then as the essence of shit—gopnik times during which I did not want to live, as I could make the world around me better.[214] I must admit that it turned out well, despite the horrors and death.

---

213 From the song "Dniam," *Derzko Ukradennym u Smerti* (To the Days Saucily Stolen from Death) by the Moscow based band *Ricochet*, written by Alexander Lyubomudrov.
214 *Gopnik/gopniki*, see footnote 4, Introduction.

So how did I get into punk? I was born in hell. Almost everything from family to school teachers, friends, and foes contributed to my distrust and rejection of the false reality that was being offered. To some extent, I was lucky to register all sorts of violence and obscuration. All the systems of personal and social, and later subcultural values, contributed to my burdensome awakening; I could offer nothing to this universe other than my pure energy. It was sometimes lonely and regrettable. But mine and others' paths were filled with sincere love.

Alexander Lyubomudrov: Since the very beginning, Ricochet was an anti-fascist band in the broadest meaning of that term. We were standing against all kinds of oppression, intolerance, and violence— including homophobia, sexism, ageism, racism, nationalism, and authoritarianism. So we ended up being in opposition to many people within our own hardcore community. The cases of homophobia, sexism, and traditional authoritarianism, unfortunately, were not very rare and were accepted by many militant members within the movement. We tried to stay away from bands and labels that we were not sure we are on the same page with. However, we were always ready to explain our position.

Singing along with Ricochet—Lubomudrov and fans, February 2012, Rashkovsky

Maksim Dinkevich: I started listening to punk when I was in school, like everybody else. I just bought fanzines, music magazines, and read about some bands. I bought some tapes in some special rock shops, and one day I bought the book *Punk Encyclopedia* written by the Russian journalist Oleg Bocharov. There was a description of classic punk and hardcore bands from the USA. Then I bought my first pirate tape of NOFX. I never heard such a fast record before. That's how I started to get into DIY and this kind of punk. In terms of Soviet punk, I'd listened to it many years before because Russian punk was similar to Russian rock, since they came from the same tradition where the message is more important than the music. My father listened to Russian rock a lot, so I knew these bands when I was really young. Then I moved to faster, more radical, more energetic music and I discovered some old kind of Siberian punk like Grazhdanskaia Oborona, and Moscow underground bands like Banda Chetyrekh, and St. Petersburg bands like Avtomaticheskie Udovletvoriteli and others.

Max "Scum": Well, I think first of all we were influenced by the environment we grew up in. We were children in a fucked situation in the '90s, and I suppose growing up in a single-parent family while a lot of other children were rich. I didn't waste my time playing video games at home, instead I was stealing copper with my friends from plants and locomotive depots. And I think that if not for punk rock, I would be still doing the same thing—many didn't have any other option and we had no image of the future. I got the idea of a way out through punk rock. I didn't use the money I got from stealing for port wine or anything like that, but on cassettes of Grazhdanskaia Oborona and guitar strings. It was the first band that I heard and loved.

Alex Distress: Distress started because we wanted to play music that was different from what was being played in St. Petersburg at the time. It wasn't that the music was bad, it was just that after The Pauki, I wanted to start something louder and more aggressive. It

Distress's Alex, Arkhangelsk, 2010, used with permission from Alex

was classic '77 punk, street punk, '87 punk. I wanted something more.

Sergey Rebrov: I got into punk around 2002. My college friend gave me Naïve and Tarakany! tapes and I liked them. Then I bought Tarakany!'s *Strakh i Nenavist*, and I found inside a list of bands that inspired the guys.[215] It was a starting point. A few months later I discovered the Ramones—the band that changed my perception and whole life.

Vic: I was a teenager or younger I think, and the first bands I heard were like Sektor Gaza, Naïve, Korol i Shut, Grazhdanskaia Oborona, and Purgen.[216] I lived in a small town eighty kilometers from Moscow and I had no access to Western bands. The only place I could buy a record was a tiny store where it was easy to find any Soviet or Russian bands, and it was quite hard to find anything else but The Exploited. I lived far from Moscow, and the only image of punk that I had was so-called *govnopunk*.[217] I really tried to copy the style. All my friends who called themselves punk were govnopunks. We fought with those who listened to rap music, and most of my

215 *Strakh i Nenavist* –Fear and Loathing.
216 *Sektor Gaza*—Gaza Strip.
217 *Govnopunk*—Shitpunk, the equivilant to saying poser punk in the West.

friends were—well, I wouldn't say they were right wing, but for example they didn't like black people. Probably they never saw a black person, but they said they didn't like rappers. But then I moved to a town closer to Moscow and I got access to Moscow's distribution market, so I had an opportunity to go to *Gorbushka* and buy records of any foreign band.

Roma Sovest: Gorbushka used to be a huge bootleg market where you could get tons of punk rock and hardcore. It's not so big anymore, in that not a lot of people go there for music because of the Internet, but it used to be a huge place where people from different backgrounds and subcultures went to hang out.

Vladimir Panov: There was no Internet back then, and in the neighboring district (about a 40-minute walk from my house) there was a music store with some heavy music, mostly metal. They also had punk music, so we became friends with the shop assistants, who later allowed us to copy cassettes. We didn't really have a device to listen to CDs on, so we would take cassettes without a deposit or take them home to make copies. The first concert I went to was Tarakany! at Tochka club in 2004.[218] I was very inspired by the concert. I was young, I drank a lot, and I went on my own without any friends. I met some people, danced, enjoyed myself, and later it turned out that all the people in my group were at that concert, but we didn't know each other.

Bagi Boev: I grew up in the Murmansk region in a town called Apatity. It's a northern region where winter lasts for nine months with polar nights, where it's always dar, and in the summer it's the polar day. When you are a schoolboy you spend a lot of time outside because it doesn't get dark, and so from early childhood I started listening to rock music—like the Beatles and Boney M— and hung out on the street a lot, and I eventually came across the term punk rock. Living in a vacuum without anything, I started to search out this term. I came across people I can call pseudo-

218 *Tochka*—Point.

punks: getting wasted, sniffing glue, and they were listening to Purgen and Grazhdanskaia Oborona. My girlfriend's brother had a huge collection of their tapes, which I took and listened to. One day I came across a punk compilation and heard Tarakany! and Elysium—a more melodic style of punk rock. Soon I got an Internet connection and I could search for information there. So I spent the long nights downloading music, and I eventually moved to Moscow where I discovered the Ramones.

Alex Mitin: When I was a kid I started going to punk shows. The first was Korol i Shut. I also started spending time around the shop Zig-Zag near Arbat street. It was a spot for subculture guys, and there was no Internet, nothing. In this shop there were many posters with gigs and stuff. Many guys were hanging around drinking—punks, metal guys, etc. There was only a small, traditional-skinhead scene in the early 2000s; most skinheads were actually pretty right wing. Then at the age of 17 or 18, I heard Tarakany!

Maksim Dinkevich: A guy I studied with invited me to an underground DIY show, at the oldest and the only DIY club in Moscow, called Jerry Rubin. It was maybe 2004, and it was a *Proverochnaia Lineika* show—their first gig. Their singer, Pjtor, was one of the most charismatic leaders of hardcore punk then. He gained political momentum for the scene. They had a passion. They always said, "We don't play music, we are here to fight for our scene and say something." In the early 2000s, nazis started going to shows to beat the shit out of everyone; they didn't care about anything else. So Pjtor was the first who said we could fight back. He started forming anti-fascist brigades at every gig. So I remember I went to the gig, and it was impossible to get information about it unless you knew someone—invites were only sent through SMS. No flyers, no posters, no anything. It wasn't like that in the late '90s or early 2000s, only in the mid 2000s.

Before going to shows, people always met near the metro station to avoid getting beaten up, because there were nazi scouts everywhere. Some years later, nazis killed three guys because they were alone. I remember a guy who just handed weapons to people in the crowd. After each show, singers would warn people about rumors and urge people to travel to the metro station together. I didn't really understand what hardcore was in 2004, but I opened a door for myself and I was, like, amazed. It was my first time in Jerry Rubin Club and, as it turned out, the first show of Proverochnaia Lineika. There was a half naked guy jumping, screaming, yelling "Beat me up! Beat me up!" and I was like a hippie with long hair like, "What the fuck is this?" It was kind of embarrassing.

Bagi Boev: The atmosphere at concerts has been changing with the course of time. When we started Cretin Boys we were all teenagers, we made concerts for our people, for our crowd; that's why only friendly people came, and there were never big problems. When Give'Em the Gun appeared, more people came and it was hard to control the situation at punk concerts. But still most of the concerts had a friendly atmosphere because we had many songs about unity and we've always tried to stick to peaceful resolutions to conflicts. Of course, there was violence at the concerts, among the public I mean, but the violence was usually brought from the outside—when some nazis or gopniki attacked. With Give'Em the Gun we took a position of anti-fascism. We were socially active, and yeah, there appeared people ready to resist us. But the situation has changed so much that now when people hear there is someone with violent intentions at a show, instead of being afraid and avoiding it, all the punks actively seek out this person and punish them. But generally over the years, the problem has decreased.

Vic: Ten years ago a show could set a fire in my chest. Now I think that I'm just older. And I still go to shows, but much less. What has changed is the number of bands and the quality. It's easier to start a band, and it's easier to discover hardcore punk music. Ten or even more years ago there was a filter—it was harder to find the music,

Dancing at a Dottie Danger show, April, 2010, Rashkovsky

to download—and now anyone can join the punk community with just two clicks.

Stresshold in *Maximum Rocknroll*

Katia: We realized that in Russia the term "feminism" is not approved of and people are afraid to use it, but for me this was the main guideline. The patriarchal system is very convenient for capitalism (and I hate capitalism!) as well as cops. I wanted the band to be as close to my inner world as possible, and I wanted nobody to weigh upon me.

Some people do not understand what our message is and just slam dance to the music, but their ideas may not fit ours. I still hear mean jokes, even from close friends. When I react sharply to them, I often hear another joke about me having PMS. Now I realize that we need to beat the shit out of such people, even if they are close to you. I have always been against violence, but eventually I realized that being a hippie is not for me.[219]

219 *Maximum Rocknroll* #415, 2017. Interview conducted by Nikolay Kemaykin.

Aleksandr Sankov: In Russia, almost all music can be downloaded for free on the Internet. Selling releases is not a very profitable business. CDs are sold mostly at concerts, but they are bought as a memory, or for a collection, and you can even copy the disc, put it on a shelf, and continue to listen to everything on the Internet.

Sergey Voloshin: The profits for Old Skool Kids went into releasing new records.[220] I never lived from this money—it's very DIY. I've spent more money on the label than I earned from creating the records. I had a lot or records that were hard to sell, and I'm stuck with them. I used to send my releases to *Maximum Rocknroll* and other places for foreign reviews. I got a lot of letters—for example, people in American prisons who read *MRR* sent me their contacts. Most contacts throughout Russia were made through the Internet.

Actually, now I release one physical record a year because it's become impossible to sell them. I don't do CDs anymore because nobody buys them. I think it's a bad thing for the label, but a good thing that people can find any music they want on the Internet and download it. It was hard for us in the '90s to find music; now it's easy. So this is a good thing. For a label not so good, because I cannot continue it—I used to release 20 records a year, but now only one. That type of paying-for-downloads doesn't work here in Russia. You can always find it for free. Maybe it works in the USA, but not here.

Bagi Boev: Now we no longer have big problems with the police. Sometimes it happens, but not like in the '90s or early 2000s when there was so much chaos and the police could come to the concert, beat the punks up, and close the show. Now it's like, if the police want to come to the concert they can come and try to shut it down using administrative means, by means of pressure on the club's administration, but all in all the police's attention to punk rock is not the same. Punk concerts are freely arranged in Moscow, including big punk shows. The police pay more attention to events like political

---

220 Old Skool Kids—Moscow-based record label, founded by Sergey.

or anti-fascist activities, those that bear some social protest. Police may come, but it's not hard to make arrangements with them. We have a special police department fighting extremism. They follow up issues of extremist activity, and somehow youth social activity is considered extreme or nearly terroristic to them, though it's very stupid. Some events come into the oversight of this department and they visit them, but more as observers.[221] I don't know what the purpose of their visits is, maybe to control the subculture, but all in all there is no big problem with them in Moscow.

I know that in smaller cities, this police department has nothing to do but to focus on youth events. They can come to a concert, beat people, take them to the police department, and keep them for a night on some grounds. For example, I know that in Nizhny Novgorod this department is very fierce; there are many frame-ups. So yeah, there is such a problem in the regions. Everything depends on the situation—if you are lucky and everything is calm, then it's good. If the police come, then so be it. People have grown up and don't get frightened by the police anymore; they try to solve the

Alex Mitin and Bagi Boev, East Beat Records, 2014, Alexander Herbert

221 Bagi is referring here to Tsentr "E", referred to in footnote 5, Introduction.

matter and to let the show happen. Open fights with the police are very rare. But still, everything is circumstantial.

I remember one time there was a concert in Riazan. It was during the spasmodic development of the punk rock scene when a lot of people from different cities came, plus several buses, and there was supposed to be a big show. During the concert some nazi idiots called the police and said that there was a bomb in the club. So the police came, kicked everyone out, and searched the club. Of course they didn't find any bomb, but they said, "Dudes there won't be any concert." They got the reply, "Okay, you've brought OMON here, you are the bosses now. But look, there are 300 to 500 crazy punks who came to the concert. Do you want us to break windows instead of attending the show?[222] Or maybe it's in your interest to let the show happen? We can gain a permit and everything will be peaceful and without any trouble." And of course the police decided that it would be safer to have the show. This is one of the examples I remember when the police understood that they were not the only ones to decide what happens, that people have their own self-organization and that they are ready to do something. In Russia, the police have a lot of authoritarian grip; they can arrest you, beat you up. The examples of this are plentiful—my friends have been held in prison on some invented charges—this all is typical in Russia. Though there are examples of resistance to the police, not in an open fight, but if people have numerical advantage they can solve an issue without violence.

Max "Scum": To be straight, our guitarist was cut by a gang and our drummer was fucked up going to practice by a mob of hooligans. But they are alive and well now. Since this is a problem in principle now, we have to learn to fight back. In the early 2000s it was much different—we had no big scene like now. But we must understand that the problem still exists, because we all live in the same city and walk the same streets, and we can never know when another conflict will arise.

222 For a definition of *OMON*, see footnote 112, Part 2.1.

Alex Mitin: In Russia now we've got all these subcultural styles, they support the anti-fascist scene, and now fascism and nationalism can be considered a criminal thing. In Russian law it's called extremism. But if you are anti-fascist you are also considered extremist. If you start to beat someone on the street or get in a knife fight with a nazi you are an extremist—even if you are defending yourself, your friends at the gig, whatever. I actually try not to discuss these things, because if you start saying you are anti-fascist and there is a cop around you will get in trouble. Because they have a special department about these things called Tsentr "E." They deal with politics and religion; it's their business—a dirty business.

Aleksei Firsov: In the '90s fascist went to punk shows, as there was little politics or protest in the scene. Now everything has changed. Now fascists are sought out and eliminated.

Tima: [Whether or not punk is as dangerous as it was] depends on the conditions. At the time of Pjtor and Proverechnaia Lineika, the most popular subculture in Moscow was the boneheads, and the most important task was to oppose them—and now everything is about nothing.

Vova: We also have a super task, and I think we are one of the few worthy groups. To do something serious, some kind of organization, we need an organization of the working class.[223]

Everything modern will turn to dust
All young people will perish in internal protest
At such times many songs are not in public view,

But they will be sung by all in a century or two.[224]

Max "Scum": We never had a problem booking shows; if you wanted it bad enough, you could get it. Even a small tour in Russia is not always easy, but it's possible. We have huge fucking distances between our cities compared to Europe, but we don't even imagine

223 Interview with *Pank-fraktsia Krasnykh Brigad* (*Punk Fraction of Red Brigade*) conducted by Maksim Podpolshchik, published here http://sadwave.com/2015/07/pfkb-rockets/.
224 "Gde Vziat Kachestvo" (Where to Get Quality) by *Pank-fraktsia Krasnykh Brigad* (2012).

Dmitri 'Sid" Spirin (Tarakany!) guest singing for Give Em The Gun, April 2010, Rashkovsky

touring in central Russia or in Ukraine. You just need to understand that nobody will do it for you—you have to do it yourself.

Bagi Boev: Well, now it's a new age. The total insufficiency of everything before was replaced by an era where you can buy any equipment, good or rare. People appeared who assemble equipment, but you still need money of course. It's not a problem of buying equipment anymore, but of renting a rehearsal space. In Moscow, specifically, there are great problems with renting. It's hard to find and arrange a rehearsal place because you need specific resources and money, and rent is expensive. Sometimes several bands collect money together and open rehearsal spaces. In some other cities maybe they still have problems with equipment, but it's 2014, not the '90s.

Roma Sovest: In ex-Soviet countries, the equipment situation works different than anywhere else. In Europe or the States, even a shitty band has their own equipment. You can get amps and everyone has cars. Here, getting your own equipment is growing, I have my own for example, but it's an exception. Most people expect clubs to have their own equipment.

This is Moscow – Worshit's Roma Sovest (guitar) and Sergey Rebrov (vocals), February, 2012, Rashkovsky

Bagi Boev: Every time we arrange a tour, we contact the promoters and tell them that we need equipment, and they take care of it. And since it's not typical to travel in a van around with your own equipment like in Europe, people try to help and provide stuff locally.

Vladimir Kotliarov: The source of income is concerts. The revenue from them is divided equally between each musician and manager. This money, to put it simply, goes to rent and food. If there are tours, we have money. If there are no tours, we get into debt. Everyone lives on this money for three to four months. If you count by months, you will get about 15 to 30 thousand rubles. Our income is very unstable. Not every one of my friends is ready to lead such a lifestyle. We are in business only because of a great love for music.[225]

Stresshold in *Maximum Rocknroll*

Katia: At first [touring] was so damn stressful, because we set off so abruptly, but everything was a blast! To be honest, I did not expect anything special from the tour, as the tour happened by chance

---

225 This is taken from an interview conducted by Maksim Dinkevich for Russian media outlet *Afisha*. It can be found here: https://daily.afisha.ru/music/4105-skolko-zarabatyvayut-rok-muzykanty/

and many things were not up to us. There was one show that we missed because of one of the supporting acts. We refused to play because we did not like the band's sexist cover. There were also some weird gigs where they could have potentially involved nazis. Political indifference is very common in the scene. We received some messages that said that we had canceled the concert there in vain, but none of their arguments could convince us to change our minds.

Sonya: On the road, we were stopped by cops who told us that we had violated the driving regulations (which we did, in fact, violate). We had no money and it was early in the morning, so the cops were satisfied with the money for just two cups of cappuccino and let us go.

Katia: The funny thing is that they wanted to get a bribe or take our bass player's driving license. They asked for thirty bucks, but we had no money. From the whole car we managed to find only about ten bucks, so we told them we had no money.[226]

Anton Obrazina: We never had a distinct business model. We instead used our salaries from our daily jobs for the band. Sometimes it feels just shameful to demand a payment or royalties. For instance, when it's about bringing a Western band we know and like, and it is clear that the concert would pay off. It's the same story regarding charity concerts and DIY-festivals. It doesn't have to do with money! Recently, of course, [we] oftener asked at least for minimal sums; we're not seventeen anymore, indeed. Thus, one gets enough for the cost of the rehearsal facilities—we have our own place, which we share with our fellow-bands. I mean, a sum less than ten thousand rubles. Concerts that we arrange on our own for ourselves make it to that point. Making presentations of our releases helps to cover the expenses of the recording and mastering. Although we don't spend too much on that. Almost all Jars albums were recorded in two days maximum. Honestly, I cannot see any point in spending

226 *Maximum Rocknroll* #415, 2017. Interview conducted by Nikolay Kemaykin.

Ricochet, Club Zoccolo, 2008, Egor Rogalev

weeks in a studio and pouring huge amounts of money in creating the sound that will be branded "like in the West." Take a look at the bands of the "new Russian wave"—nowadays one can fill concert-halls just using tape recordings. I like this much more than the polished albums of the bands that gather no more than 50 people. We always went to other cities in return for the travel, food, and accommodation expenses. The charge fees are out of the question here. An opportunity to see other cities and play for a new crowd is precious itself. If we talk about a tour, for that end we calculate the cost for gas and the driver's service, and then divide this sum by the number of the cities. The tour concerts come rather cheap, therefore it becomes possible to see nontrivial places. On the road we spend money that we get from selling merchandise. Most of the tours we've made on the "Gazelle of Death" with Denis Alekseev.[227] For me long trips mean primarily adventures, and only secondly a commercial undertaking. Though, in the last tour in Europe we went into debt a lot. I've been paying up since then—had to sell the guitar. But one can buy a new guitar, and the experiences during the trip I would not change for anything.[228]

---

227 *Gazelle* vehicle—Russian light commercial vehicle, minibus.
228 From the interview conducted by Maksim Dinkevich for *Afisha*: https://daily.afisha.ru/music/4105-skolko-zarabatyvayut-rok-muzykanty/

Denis "Siggi" Alekseev: I bought my first van, a really shitty old Russian car, but at that time very few people in the Russian punk community had vans or were able to drive them with random bands. So people quickly learned that I was driving bands around and asked if I'd help them. It was really easy. After some time I just wrote to bands I really liked, "Hey, do you want to tour in Russia? Seven to 14 shows, I'll pick you up at your house and drop you in front of the venues. All you need is to sit and play music every night."

I never asked for money, because seven to 14 shows is enough to collect for gasoline, visas etc. Well, it also depends on the band. But basically it didn't cost them anything. Traveling by car is much cheaper in Russia than the train. Gasoline here cost three times less than in Europe. And honestly, it's very hard to make a good tour on train here because our train network is rather strange. Russia is a centralized country... Sometimes if you want to go from city A to city B, and the distance between them is only 250 km, you need to connect in Moscow, which can take you 800 km out of the way.

Alexander Lyubomudrov: Obviously, there is a strong relationship between the St. Petersburg and Moscow scenes, and these are the big cities with over 12 million people, so there were more kids at the shows. It was always more exciting to play away than in Moscow— see old friends, make new ones. St. Petersburg was, and still is, a renowned city for its cozy venues, bars, and clubs that were super friendly to have our motley crew going wild on the dance floor (as opposed to "plastic" Moscow, with its greedy venue owners and picky promoters that would not let any punk bands in). However, we were bringing crowds of youngsters, and they figured out pretty quickly that there was money to be made. Moscow kids were more spoiled and got bored pretty fast, since we played way too often. Being the only band with good backline and a van, we were getting lots of requests to play.

Shows in the provinces differed from place to place, so it's hard to compare Kirov or Vladimir punk with other places. Kids in the provinces were usually less spoiled and more excited to see DIY touring bands. There were less of them and they had varied music preferences, from nu metal to college rock, but they would still come and check you out. Wwe loved to play in front of these stereotype-free kids.

Kirill "George" Mikhailov: Touring is a little different now. Because in Russia there is now a punk scene in more or less every big city, some people bought a van and made touring possible. In any case, it's still a problem because the country is so huge. The first Dottie Danger tour in 2006 was only five shows, and covered 5,500 kilometers by train.

Dima: In Moscow and St. Petersburg, I think people are not as into it as they used to be. ou have a show like everyday, and you can choose which one you want to go to. In other cities, you can't choose. You have one concert per month (or three months), and the people have a stronger community—punks, anarchists, metal heads, skinheads. They are together, not separated.

Alex Distress: I don't know. It's not the same anymore. The first time we went to Europe was very interesting. It was a memorable experience, because it was 2005; it was a different scene. Even the appearance was different. I am not talking about mohawks, more about leather biker jackets and things like that. It was all a little bit different. The first time we went to play at Puntala in Finland. The way they looked wasn't really a revelation for me because I grew up listening to the English punk, so I had an idea what punks looked like. But when you travel from one world or scene to another… you can instantly tell the difference. Now there is no big difference.

Lena Panama: I chose punk and will end this way. When I die, if I live to be 50 or 70 years old, even then I will be flipping off those who embody everything evil about society. All concerts and all the guys that organize them and all who come—I love these people; they are for me, my brothers and sisters no matter where they live. Many wars are happening in our world, and it's cruel and wrong when civilians are killed, when leaders cannot share their power and cause innocent people to suffer. But I think if we can use the punk scene as an example, then we'd be better off. Always help each other, don't give up on each other.

Dottie Danger, Mrachek (vocals), April 2010, Rashkovsky

Diliusa Gimadeeva: The perception of women in bands will undoubtedly be different. If the group has at least one woman it will increase interest, because it is not typical. But it's not all taken seriously, and if someone liked the performance or recording, they're sure to say something like: "Cool female voice," or "A good beat, and even from girls!" But if you do something you love, you shouldn't care what others think. There were a few times we heard screams from the crowd, but in general I think women's bands are good.

Anastasia Kobesh: It's like when we were in Europe, sometimes people screamed "Show me your tits!" In Russia nobody really cares—you're a girl, you just sing, and that means you just copy Paramore, because nobody knows any female vocalist bands. People come to me saying, "You're so cool... you sound like, I don't remember the name of the band, but the girl with red hair." And I finish their sentence with "Paramore," and yeah.

Katia: I do not think I can speak for the scene as a single organism. I know for sure that there are many activists who raise the problem of discrimination, but groups that are openly talking about this are very few. There are a number of women's advocacy groups, but they do not exist within the framework of the scene we are talking about. Therefore, I can't say that there is any kind of centralized or cohesive formulation of ideas that develop the scene as an alternative to society—primarily, to the consumer society. I believe that some people, even those I personally know, may very well progress as individuals. But the scene does not move in this direction, because the "scene" does not have such a goal. I still don't understand the goals of this "scene." I clearly know the purpose of all my own projects, but my last project also belongs a bit to another crowd, and Stresshold generally never associated with any crew or belonged to one. It was important for us not to associate with anyone, but then people started associating with us. In general, I want to say that you cannot be a person, or a group of people, and progress in one thing. Progress must be complex, and only after some time can you see some kind of overall trend. I'm not trying to say that all the efforts amount to nothing; there just aren't people who unite groups or provide inspiration for creating educational content and sources that many kids and girls would read and understand. Earlier all those who came to the movement were sitting for hours on some blogs, translating texts, and making zines. Now I can count zines on my fingers. Electronic zines are also very small. The common mistake is that we do not give each other anything new, but linger in the same place. I took all the cool ideas from the texts of certain groups and from the zines of friends and strangers all over Russia; they paid much attention to ecology, politics, and discrimination. I formulated the consciousness in a different way.

> *"There are only four of us who are desperately trying to realize ourselves in this vast universe, covered with suffering, fear, and pain. We are against state borders and attributes. Fuck sexism, racism, homophobia. No one has the right to limit you. Security is just an illusion."*[229]

Scarlet Pills, Club Zoccolo 2014, Vitaly Kolotsey

---

229 This is an announcement that Katia makes before each *Stresshold* performance.

Maksim Dinkevich: I started to get interested in fanzines in high school. I always read from newspapers, and I started to write and read about music. And when this wave of fanzines came, and I got involved in DIY, there was a huge wave of zines. In 2010 almost all zines were dead because of the Internet—you couldn't beat the speed of the Internet—it was too fast. It was the time when *Vkontakte* came to life, and all the zine makers just put their stuff there and it was really apathetic. But somehow I still had this passion, and I wanted to translate and write, and I still wanted to interview. But I didn't know where to put it. So I started to write my blog and Livejournal. One day my friend recommended doing a website— not my personal blog, but an actual media outlet. And there was nothing like that until we made it. There was no regularly updated punk online media. People who did online zines usually stopped after a few months or so, or their writing became too simplified. It was not interesting and nobody got feedback. When the initial wave of zines died, people stopped writing emails and stopped commenting because it got so boring. So we wanted to make quality

Stresshold's Katia (drums), Sonya (vocals), and Denis (bass guitar) in Žilina, Slovakia, 2017, photo by Slimáčik Jonátanovy

media about punk rock. We were only three guys, but we tried to be like *Maximum Rocknroll* for Russia, to cover the news as fast as it arrived—so it's updated every day. It's our project; we work every day because there is still no other option. At the end of last year (2014) big media started to give us attention. They discovered that we exist and they started to give us different offers: "Hey would you mind writing to us about punk?" So yeah, now we write to them about punk and make some stuff for them. Sadwave.com was the first to be discovered by big media.

Alexander Lyubomudrov: On the global scale, everything got pretty much shaped by the retro trend in the hardcore punk scene. Technically, bands started to play better; they do not need to spend as much time breaking through with record pressing and distribution, if you know what I mean. There is less space left for musical and lyrical experiment in modern punk. Everyone is back to good old clichés in the music and the message. The political message is a bit outdated. I haven't heard a single song directly or indirectly related to the conflicts in Eastern Ukraine, Crimea, or Syria. I do really miss the spirit of late '90s European hardcore.

Characters in the order they appear:

Timur Yenaliev—Bass guitarist for Ricochet (Moscow).
Alexander Lyubomudrov—Frontman for Ricochet.
Maksim Dinkevich—Co-founder, editor, and writer at Sadwave.com, frontman for Da, Smert! and Mraz (Moscow).
Max "Scum"—Frontman for 4Scums (St. Petersburg).
Alex Distress—Bass player for The Pauki, frontman for Distress (St. Petersburg).
Sergey Rebrov—Frontman for Worshit (Moscow).
Vic—Bass player, songwriter for Worshit.
Roma Sovest—Longtime fan of Moscow hardcore and guitarist for *Worshit*.
Vladimir Panov—Frontman for The Poseurs (Moscow).
Bagi Boev—Guitar player for Cretin Boys and Give'Em the Gun (Moscow), and East Beat Records co-founder.
Alex Mitin—Co-founder East Beat Records, frontman Hopes & Disasters (Moscow).
Aleksandr Sankov—Frontman for The Agitators (Moscow).

Sergey Voloshin—Founder of hardcore band B'67, *Old Skool Kids* zine, and Old Skool Kids Records (Moscow).

Aleksei Firsov—Frontman for Komatoz (Moscow).

Tima—Drummer for Pank-fraktsia Krasnykh Brigad (Moscow).

Vova—Frontman for Pank-fraktsia Krasnykh Brigad.

Vladimir Kotliarov—Frontman for Pornofilmy, frontman and guitarist for Jars (Moscow).[230]

Katia—Founder and drummer for Stresshold (Moscow).

Sonya—Frontwoman for Stresshold.

Anton Obrazina—Frontman and guitarist for Jars.

Denis "Siggi" Alekseev—Tour driver of "Gazelle of Death."

Kirill "George" Mikhailov—Guitarist in bands Svinokop, 01 band, Cut'n'Run, Dottie Danger, and vocalist for Upor Lezha (St. Petersburg). Founder of Karma Mira and NotLG tapes record labels.

Dima—Compiler of zine *Holiday of Dissidence*.

Lena Panama—Moscow based punk fan.

Diliusa Gimadeeva—Frontwoman for Off-Key (Kazan).

Anastasia Kobesh—Frontwoman for Scarlet Pills (St. Petersburg).

---

230 *Pornofilmy—Porn Films.*

5.2 THE PARADOX OF PUSSY RIOT

Pussy Riot, photo by Igor Mukhin

On February 12, 2012 five members of the feminist art collective Pussy Riot entered the Cathedral of Christ the Savior in Moscow to perform their song "Bogoroditsa, Putina Progoni."[231] The song posed a direct challenge to the Russian Orthodox Church's (ROC's) call for Russians to support the re-election of Vladimir Putin. Barely getting more than forty seconds of attention, the women were seized and arrested for felony hooliganism, under the pretext that they "caused profound insult and humiliation to the faithful."[232] Their performance and subsequent arrest also caused a hailstorm of media attention as feminist groups around the world turned their attention toward the artists who were imprisoned and shut out from their family and friends. As Western media emphasized Pussy Riot's self-identification as punk rockers, punk rock activists and musicians in the United States and around the globe responded with public demonstrations of support. Pussy Riot had brought

---

231 *Bogoroditsa, Putina Progoni* –Mother of God, Drive Putin Away.
232 *Pussy Riot! A Punk Prayer for Freedom: Letters from Prison, Songs, Poems, and Courtroom Statements, Plus Tributes to the Punk band that Shook the World* (New York: The Feminist Press, 2013), 53.

Russian punk rock to center stage. But how much did these women represent the Russian punk scene?

The paradox of Pussy Riot is precisely their place in the history of Russia's punk rock scene. On the one hand, the band displays the anti-conformist and disestablishmentarian ethos typically concomitant with other members of the punk pantheon, and their guitars certainly emit a muffled, incoherent sound that parodies the ad-hoc performances of early punks so ardently admired by Leningrad's early provocateurs. On the other hand, Pussy Riot is an enigma of Moscow, born more from political activism than the punk rock subculture they claim to be of. Indeed, while most all interviewees regarded Pussy Riot's commandeering of the label "punk" as an insult to the "real" grass roots music-oriented subculture, other groups, particularly those seeking to profit from punk rock, embraced Pussy Riot's brand of the genre and hailed them as true revolutionaries. How should we place Pussy Riot into the history of Russian punk rock? Are they merely, to paraphrase the words of former President Dmitry Medvedev, seekers of attention and notoriety, or are they a genuine example of the punk ethos? Does Pussy Riot represent something more than the Russian punk scene described thus far?

This article makes no attempt to provide a definitive answer to any of these questions. Instead, the goal is to present two images of Pussy Riot based on interviews that seem, but are not, mutually exclusive. As mentioned in the introduction, the definition of "punk" is inherently subjective, and it varies depending on who is employing the term and and how someone is using it. Of course, there are certain requirements for what "punks" are willing to define as "punk rock." Everything from social and political dissidence, a particular style of music, or even a style of dress, constitute at least what the West typically considers to be punk rock, and none of these elements can be easily disaggregated from the other. And yet we can say the exact same thing for "art"; it is subjective, stylistic, and, at least the successful forms of it, non-conformist—transgressive.

Hence, I present here what I see to be the paradox of Pussy Riot—that is, their conscious embodiment of the Russian punk ethos, and that community's uneasy acceptance of their membership.

> *The Church's prayer to rotten dictators*
> *The cross-bearer procession of black limousines*
> *A teacher-preacher will meet you at school*
> *Go to class—bring him money!*
>
> *Patriarch Gundiaev believes in Putin*
> *Bitch, better believe in God instead!*
> *The best of the Virgin can't replace mass meetings*
> *Mary, Mother of God, is with us in protest!*

In an interview with T*he New Yorker's* David Remnick, Nadia Tolokonnikova and Masha Alekhina present their protest as an artistic expression of defiance against the ROC's endorsement of President Vladimir Putin. They trace the roots of their act to Boris Groys' idea of "Moscow Romantic Conceptualism," which stresses the mystical side of collective action that provides a lucid alternative to scientific experimentation through the "unity of the collected spirit."[233] For Pussy Riot, their brand of activism could only be conveyed and experienced collectively; a number of women screaming lyrics at a gathering crowd. But, as Nadia describes in the interview, Pussy Riot added a level of vigor and protest unheard of to Soviet and contemporary conceptualist art. They had imbued their art with a politically conscious character that capitalized on a level of antidisestablishmentarianism that echos Naïve's "Boris Yeltsin is an Assohole" outside the White House. In effect, as the members describe, they had smashed together the artistic pillars of conceptualism, direct action, and punk rock shock aesthetic, producing a unique brand of in-your-face avant-garde activism.

Hence, in unraveling the paradox, it's important to consider how Pussy Riot conceives of itself before the media. First

233 Boris Groys, "Moscow Romantic Conceptualism," *A-YA* 1 (1979): 4.

and foremost, Masha, Nadia and Katia speak of their collective as part of a nascent protest culture. When giving a closing courtroom statement, Katia remarked, "In our performance we dared, without seeking the patriarch's blessing, to unite the visual imagery of Orthodox culture with that that of protest culture, thus suggesting that Orthodox culture belongs not only to the Russian Orthodox Church, the patriarch, and Putin, but that it could also ally itself with civic rebellion and the spirit of protest in Russia."[234] The task of Pussy Riot, then, appeared Herculean, if not entirely self-sacrificial. In fact, a major theme throughout the court case became the personal faith of the members on trial, who viewed themselves as martyrs for a just Russia ruled by law, and not the "vertical power" of Putin.[235] This explains why, in one of her letters from prison, Nadia quotes Matthew 10:17—"But beware of men: for they will deliver you over to the courts." She then goes on to compare the sacrifice of Pussy Riot to that of Christ Himself, admitting only that their goal was "much more modest."[236] That modest goal was quite simply to lay bare the contradictions of the current Orthodox hierarchy, and at the same time take a stab at Putin's regime and media, not entirely unlike Christ's challenge to the Roman state.

> Masha: "Religious symbols and Christian symbols and Christian Orthodox symbols are not something which the government should have a monopoly over. The government should not have a monopoly to speak on behalf of the Church and Orthodox Christianity. Christianity is in many ways a protest religion and there's a lot of values that are shared, for instance the values that everybody was protesting for at the end of 2011, which is freedom of speech and fair elections.
>
> "And this was truly painful for us to watch and to observe, and it wasn't a one time occurrence that the Patriarch Kirill suddenly decided to do this, this was a well thought out line of policy that he was carrying out and

234 *Pussy Riot! A Punk Prayer for Freedom*, 89.
235 *Pussy Riot! A Punk Prayer for Freedom*, 105.
236 *Pussy Riot! A Punk Prayer for Freedom*, 22.

expanding, which was to support Putin on behalf of the entire Orthodox Church."[237]

Whether the band members were sincere in their plea for the Church to remain apolitical, or their deployment of religious imagery simply served to make a broader political point, their actions addressed deep rooted socio-political issues—and that's all that really mattered. Punk rock embodied a transnational ethos and identity that provided the most familiar and palpable outlet to encapsulate and transmit that message.

In so far as punk rock provides a platform for public expressions of dissidence, Pussy Riot probably accomplished more than any recent punk band, definitely in Russia, and maybe even in the West. In fact, some punk musicians and activists at the center of Moscow's punk scene applaud the courageous deeds of Pussy Riot. When asked who the five most influential Russian punk bands in history are, Dmitry Spirin of Tarakany!'s first answer was Pussy Riot:

> *[Band mate] Tolik: Is it a joke?*
> *Dmitry Spirin: Why? We are talking about the most important Russian punk rock bands. I specifically asked for whom our choices are important. For me Pussy Riot is an important punk rock band. Despite the fact that they are only a notional punk rock band, they've never released any album, and their songs are just some declamations, still they performed a civil feat. And it makes me respect them greatly. Who's gonna go to jail for our songs. Lesh? [turns toward a band mate] Will you go?[238]*

While Moscow punk rockers are anything but representative of Russia's scene as a whole, Spirin's point was spot-on. Pussy Riot didn't play punk, they never released any albums, never

---

237 *The New Yorker*, "David Remnick Interviews Pussy Riot - Conversations - The New Yorker," Youtube, uploaded July 22, 2014. Found here: www.youtube.com/watch?v=fy4FHCE0z-A 27:50
238 Tolik's question is indicative of the polarization within the scene over *Pussy Riot*. He sincerely thought Dmitry was just being difficult for an American interviewer.

demonstrated any level of involvement with the scene, and they appeared out of nowhere, but they still attributed their "civil feat" to their own feminist punk ethos. To Spirin, a veteran of the scene, that was enough to induct them into the Russian punk hall of fame.

But for others, Pussy Riot's use of the label "punk" is a slight to the grassroots DIY bands trying to create a real underground feminist subculture. One particularly glaring issue between Pussy Riot and the underground scene is the band's apparent disregard for feminist punk that has been striving for recognition since before Pussy Riot made it big. The whole thing would not pose an issue if it were not for the band's claim to be Russian feminist punk progenitors:

> "We decided to pick the topic of political punk feminism; we were sure that something like that must exist in Russia and so we already scheduled our talk and the time and the place. So as usual we do everything at the last moment, and about 12 hours before the talk we start researching and we discover that there's no such thing in Russia. And so in those 12 hours we suddenly found ourselves with this task of historical and epic importance, which was to create Russian feminist punk, so we recorded a song…"[239]

In fact, women played punk in the Soviet Union long before Pussy Riot donned their masks and hit the streets. In 1987 Irina Lokteva helped form the all-women punk collective Zhenskaia Bolezn, hoping to bring something new to the Soviet underground and shock the cultural police, otherwise known as the *Komsomol*.[240] Their act was also one of social protest, in so far that it tested the boundaries of how women were expected to behave in both the mainstream and underground music scenes. It was not easy to get a scene dominated by male egos to take them seriously. During their first concert they received a little help from members of the biker gang Night Wolves, who came on stage and sat around the girls as

239 *The New Yorker*, "David Remnick," Nadia, 15:20. My own emphasis added.
240 A live performance of *Zhenskaia Bolezn* in 1992 can be seen here www.youtube.com/watch?v=DVlmwVq56Zc.

if at a campfire, in order to grab the attention of everyone in the club. As people soon found out, their music was powerful enough to make an impression, and succeeding generations of female musicians continue to remember them as innovators of all-female punk bands in Russia.

"From where did these girls in Pussy Riot come? This is not even close to music and they fall short of being punk," Lokteva quipped when asked about Pussy Riot. To be sure, her criticism was not over the political act of Pussy Riot, but more toward their music credentials. Actually, Lokteva inadvertently filtered her opinion of Pussy Riot's brand of "punk" through her own definition of the genre. "Punk rock," she says, is "energy, courage, good music played which you can play however you like—fast, slow, using different musical styles and approaches, but the message is one of power, fun, fire, and availability of good taste." This shows the inherent nature of the paradox; such a vague definition of punk does not, in fact, exclude Pussy Riot. They certainly have "energy and courage," and their music is categorically unorthodox, maybe without the fire.

Another political feminist punk is a little lighter on Pussy Riot. Tamara Nechepaeva of Diet Pill and Pincher provides the same musical criticism of Pussy Riot, but concedes on roughly the same point made by Dmitry Spirin. Here, Nechepaeva is worth quoting in full:

> *Pussy Riot—without a doubt a very interesting phenomena on the Russian stage. These are incredibly brave and strong women who are not afraid to express their views and protest while many others have failed to do so. That made me really admire them. However, I would consider their project in the realm of contemporary art events and political struggle, rather than music. As I understand them, the girls are trying to use art to draw public attention to the problems of our country; they don't need to concern themselves with developing as musicians, writing in the best studios or creating legendary hits.*

But a female punk rock music scene goes back to the '80s in Russia, when Jean Sagadeev (EST) contributed to the creation of the Zhenskaia Bolezn collective. Generally, women's groups in Russia have experienced a few climbs and waves, and they still successfully persist in a variety of ways.

For me, the legendary female punk rock groups of the '90s include Vosmaia Marta, Dzhan Ku, and Thaivox.

I would consider the early 2000s to be the general flowering of female punk culture—there was a whole movement of female riot groups in grunge style. Those who first come to mind include Pretty Pills, PMS, Diet Pill, and more specifically "punk" might include Dochki-Materi and also Pincher.[241]

Perhaps where Pussy Riot is a first for me is at their level of protest. I do not know of any other all-female groups in our scene that would have struggled with the system so violently.[242]

Woman's home is in the kitchen
Being there makes her feel alright
There's no need for her to be pretty
Cause no one gives a flying fuck

Woman's home is in the kitchen
Being there makes her feel alright
There's no need for her to be happy
Cause no one gives a flying fuck

Woman's home is in the kitchen
No friends or pals of any kind
Woman's home is in the kitchen
No career and no foes[243]

Evidently, Spirin and Nechepaeva have no issue admitting that the acts of Pussy Riot are significant and courageous in general,

---

241 *Dochki-Materi*—Daughters-Mothers.
242 Nechepaeva certainly could have claimed her band Pincher, formed in 2009, to be the first political feminist punk band, but her failing to do so is indicative of the admiration garnered by Pussy Riot in the political realm.
243 "Mesto Zhenshchiny na Kukhne" (Place for Women is in the Kitchen) by Pincher

Zhenskaia Bolezn, Left to right- Natalya Terekhova, Vasilina Malyshevskaia, Olga Suvorkina, Irina Lokteva (center), Used with permission from www. guitaristka.ru

and Spirin certainly appreciates the international attention garnered by their public protest. The only overwhelming criticism is unequivocally musical—no interviewees willingly ascribed the "punk rock" label to Pussy Riot, even though definitions of "punk," such as Lokteva's, are vague enough to apply to Pussy Riot. Perhaps the members of Pussy Riot were aware of the definitional ambiguity and found it to be an endearing element of punk rock. After all, it's not entirely dissimilar to abstract art's inherent interpretive nature and openness. Maybe claiming their music to be anything but punk rock would have made their political protest less palatable

Pincher, (left to right- Jannet, Tamara, Masha), Tver punk open-air, 2013 Used with permission from the band

to a national or international audience. Or more simply, maybe the interviewees refused to ascribe the label in the interest of not seeming too disagreeable within the (predominantly male) underground community. Either way, while many take issue with Nadia's claim to be Russia's first political feminist punk act, the addition of the adjectival *political* makes the claim largely true, if one believes that feminism is concomitant with *political* activism. Russian feminist punk certainly existed before Pussy Riot, but how overtly political was it?

With that final note, we have elaborated fully on the paradox of Pussy Riot. Their actions and attitudes denote an unabashedly "punk" attitude, and yet the community doesn't accept them because their music doesn't represent "punk rock." What's more, membership in punk's society draws a lot on communal effort and mutual trust, but Pussy Riot has never belonged to that community or shown an interest in communicating with it. As Nechepaeva's band mate and vocalist for Pincher, Jannet Maylo said that claims like Nadia's "depreciate the musical breakthroughs of the female sex. I don't know who was first, but I can say that when we started in the early 2000s, there were even then quite a large number of female musicians."

In the end, deciding whether or not to include Pussy Riot in this book posed a serious dilemma for exactly that reason. As I contemplated whether public dissidence and self-ascribed labels outweighed the lack of communal and musical belonging, I found myself unwilling to side either way. The paradox of Pussy Riot is therefore left open for the reader to take a side.

For my part, I believe that Pussy Riot has brought the *idea* of Russian punk (not the sound) into a new level. In Soviet times, the State served as an abstraction that one could never clearly and definitively articulate an opinion in opposition to. As we have seen thus far, the neo-nazis became the mortal enemy of post-Soviet Russian punks in the 1990s and early 2000s. Pussy Riot has mobilized some Russians to inject their music with a dose of political consciousness that turns the abstract neo-Nazi and bureaucratic state into concrete realities, not distant boogimen.

Dasha Kholobaeva, the translator of this book, suggested that perhaps Pussy Riot "is bigger than punk." The idea that their non-participation in the scene and absence of musicality is made up for in their daring protests simply challenges Russian punks to be more engaged with their government's politics and culture.

CONCLUSION

There were a few moments that I thought would be ideal for writing a conclusion to this book. After all, going to Russia for long durations at a time to collect interviews brought me to some strange places, made me rethink how I understand punk rock, and gave me access to a side of Russia that most people will never see. It also introduced me to some interesting people—some who only wanted to talk to me because of the research, and some who couldn't care less about the research. To many I was merely a walking excuse to get their band some recognition in the States, to others I was simply an ear willing to hear their story, mosh at their shows, and contribute to their scene. I garnered somewhat of a reputation as "that American writing a book on Russian punk rock," the one that cared about the humble scene of a non-Western country. So there were many times I thought writing a short and sweet conclusion would be possible—to end the project, to renounce my reputation, to hang up my boots, if you will.

The first moment I thought of writing a conclusion was on my plane ride from St. Petersburg to Frankfurt on August 3 of 2017. Weeks in advance I thought about what a proper ending to such a work should entail, if there should be a conclusion, and the ideal time to write it. It was only on that plane ride that I definitely realized the researching portion of the book was finished, as if the seatbelt click was the light going off in my head. Sure, I used it as an excuse to drink the free booze on board. I was worn out. That summer was so packed with new names, new sounds, and new experiences that I instinctively reflected on all the places my interest in punk had taken me.

My first experience with Russian punk occurred in an abandoned warehouse in Nizhny Novgorod in 2012. I knew absolutely nobody; I had nothing but my stupid accent, a pack of cigarettes, some cheap beers in my backpack, and a love for punk rock. Even the friend who brought me slid out of view, because he personally didn't like punk, but only knew that the concert was happening. At that point the idea of compiling a book on the history of Russian punk was the furthest thing from my mind. It was long before Pussy Riot made international headlines, when the Western media didn't care much about punk in Russia—when they didn't pretend to know—and when I still had no idea I was capable of even compiling such a book. I do regret not taking photos at that concert, but I was so enthralled by the experience, so taken by the raw energy of the crowd and bands, that I didn't even think about photography. This was actually the beginning of a recurring pattern.

On my second trip to Russia, I had the luxury of living in Moscow. I initially thought Moscow was too big, too intimidating, and that its scene was way out of my orbit. How would I, an American intern at the Russian History Museum, enter into Moscow's punk scene? The answer was, as most things in punk rock, a jean jacket. When I went to buy a jean jacket I was approached by a tattoo-clad employee, who popped the question: "Do you listen to punk rock?"

The summer of 2014 changed everything. I found out that Russia didn't have a "punk scene;" it had many: hardcore, crust punk, ska, '77 punk, psychobilly, thrash metal, you name it. I met more people than I could remember, and even had to open a Vkantakte page in order to keep up with them all. I'm not bragging here, because my inability to treat everyone equally continues to be a point of anxiety. But it nevertheless indicated that compiling a book on Russian punk rock was possible. I had the resources, I knew the people, and I just needed the initiative. The kind of push that only those who know you better than you know yourself can give you.

One's ambitions on a long flight are always greater than their abilities. Writing a conclusion on that flight didn't happen. I drank too much, lacked sleep, and had too many thoughts on my mind. I believe I started two lines, and they were probably the best lines I wrote for this entire book—but I deleted them, so they are forever lost.

The second time I thought about writing a conclusion was a month after I'd returned from St. Petersburg and was settled once again in Chicago. In the news, alt-right activists gathered in Charlottesville, Virginia, and were confronted by anti-fascist activists. A lot of people were hurt, one person fighting alongside anti-fascists died, and *The New York Times* photographed one of my childhood best friends proudly standing next to the person that drove their car into another human being. Only a month earlier I had concluded interviewing for the "Anti-Fascist Movement" chapter, and I remember being utterly stunned by the real violence these Russian punks and skins had to confront on a daily basis. To tell the truth, I actually thought Pjtor was embellishing his stories, and that the violence couldn't have been as bad as people described it—street wars? Brigades? It seemed like the language of kids a little too obsessed with military culture.

When all my interviewees' stories started to overlap, I began to capitulate. When I saw photos of the brawls and street marches, I believed. Although Russia's anti-fascist movement is a shadow of its former self, it still exists in the memories of its champions, and there are far more than those I included in this book. People today are proud about the endurance of their scene, and happy to have sacrificed themselves to keep it. In all the shows I attended, all the people I met, I never once ran into a neo-nazi, and it is likely thanks to them.

There was one memorable show where I confronted the caprice of Russian police. In St. Petersburg, I went to a show around the corner from my apartment where the Nizhny Novgorod band Criminal State was supposed to play. The bands played on the third floor of a building that had two exits—one leading to a courtyard, and another leading out to another side. When I was out socializing, I saw a car trying to leave the courtyard being blocked by some young punks, and I suspected that they were simply stirring trouble.

I went back inside to watch the next band, and as I climbed the stairs people were running down, holding their shirt collars over their face and nose. I began to feel a relentless itch in my throat. I immediately stopped and asked someone what was going on, and found out that the police entered through the back and raided the place, gasing the entire venue with no warning. I felt trapped. If I went inside, there was a possibility the police would stop me, find out I was foreign, and bring me in. So I looked out the window into the courtyard and saw that two cop cars had the exit blocked, and punks were throwing bricks, rocks and other objects at the officers and the cars. I waited it out—absolutely frozen—until Kristina Doga, of anti-fascist fame, came and grabbed me. Her and I, with a few others, managed to escape and cross the street, where we bunkered down in an abandoned factory until 4 am, after the cops stopped circling the vicinity.

I thought that I was lucky as an American to not have to deal with street clashes between neo-nazis and leftists, to not have to experience the murder of a friend or the threat of a Tsentr "E." As a kid I attended punk shows without a problem. I played a few shows in my youth and attended many more, but only on exceptional nights did a show get closed down (and even then, never raided, gassed, or surrounded by the police or neo-nazis). I began to think that I grew up in a coddled scene, protected from the struggles that others had to go through.

Then I came home and witnessed what happened in Charlottesville—what my former friend was involved in. At that point, I understood the personal investment that these Russian activists put into their struggle. I realized how the death of their friends impacted their everyday lives, how it continues to haunt them, and how it also pushes them to persevere. At that point my life and my research intersected, and I, being the opportunist I am, thought it was a good moment to write a conclusion.

I was too emotional, too angry about my former friend, too shocked by my own naivety to write a conclusion. I was incapable of reflecting on the totality of my experience and the narrative of the book, and too focused on the parallels between what Russian punks had experienced, and what American punks were preparing to confront.

I don't know why I feel capable now. Perhaps it is because I can finally say something without reducing the book to a political statement about Putinism, and I don't feel compelled to describe my personal experiences in excess (although it's probably too late now). Perhaps that merits another project altogether. This book was never about politics or me. I merely wanted to demonstrate that Russia has a deep history of punk rock that goes almost as far back as any other. It is just as variegated and present, just as energetic and alive. I wanted to show how, despite what we think about the late Soviet Union and early Russian Federation, a bunch of kids persisted in creating something of their own. I wanted to show that there is more to Russia than politics and Petrine mimicry—that the scenes, images, sounds, spaces, and personas that Russian punks relish and create mean something very real to those who've participated, past and present. I wanted to demonstrate how punk rock, as a subculture, music style, fashion, ideology, and more, empowered kids who forever remain lost, kids who live in the middle of nowhere, kids who literally witnessed their country collapse, enter into economic anarchy, and resort to desperate expressions of identity. I wanted to show that the reality of punk rock is more important than the psychology of punks.

Many people have asked me what the grand narrative of the book is. I know that any answer to that question is loaded with political, cultural, and social implications. Is the history of Russian punk a drama? Did the early struggles with official Soviet rock, the aggression of Generation TaMtAm, and the fascist yoke remind you of a dramatic play? Was it a tragedy? Did the scene's development as a political and ethical objection to Soviet monotony decline into a meaningless replica of its Western counterpart? Perhaps it can be read as a comedy—all of these people investing their lives and skills into a trivial movement that seems devoid of long-term meaning and value.

In the end, I think that every participant and onlooker of punk rock around the world will base their understanding of this narrative on their own subjective experience. I'm only glad I could contribute to the conversation.

As for tomorrow, I am just as unsure as any punk. There is no future, only today. Russian punk has lost much of the unity it exuded during the anti-fascist years, but it still confronts a highly conservative society. In the past ten years women have gained more of an independent voice in the scene by fronting bands, creating zines, and maintaining a feminist library in St. Petersburg. Homosexuals, unfortunately, remain conspicuously absent still. The "elders" are beginning to fade in the background, and what is emerging is a punk scene that is more willing and able to learn from its own history. Bands are being discouraged from singing in English, not because of some pseudo-nationalistic sense, but because they see the importance of maintaining a specifically Russian brand of punk. Capitalism in the age of the Internet presents the same problems to Russian bands as it does Western bands, requiring new forms of marketing and new sources of income, but it is not stopping them from making music and touring. The future of Russian punk is indeed unwritten, but at least now we are better poised to hope for the best.

APPENDIX 1:
Fuck the Legacy: Life as a Soviet-Punk Dissident

by Tommy Dean.[244]

Feddy Lavrov is the son of Aleksandra Lavrova, a single mother who supported her two children through her artwork. The family lived near Teatralnaia Square, home to the renowned Mariinsky Ballet and Theater of Leningrad. During his childhood, Feddy was introduced to classical music, but it was the jazz records that a family friend sent from the United States that piqued his interest. Jazz was common in Russia in the Soviet Union, but contemporary American artists like Horace Silver, John Handy, and Miles Davis were redefining the genre and had a progressive appeal. "[Russian] jazz was too old and simple with standard improvisations," says Feddy. "Fusion was an escape from reality, parallel harmonies and hell-knows-what notes."

Feddy entered adolescence in the late '70s, when mainstream records were rare and difficult to acquire—not only were they expensive, but every artist had to be approved by the State and released on the single Soviet-run label Melodia Records. The only other exposure to Western music came from Western radio programs picked up by shortwave units, despite the Soviet government's attempts to jam foreign transmissions with artificial sounds.

While listening to a BBC music show, Feddy heard the Ramones's rendition of "Do You Wanna Dance," from *Rocket to Russia*. To Feddy, the fast, no-frills music had the energy of jazz fusion melded with the primitive drive of mid-century American rock and roll. Then, through scant coverage by the Soviet media, Feddy learned about the burgeoning punk scene in London. The music's untamed energy and image appealed to the adolescent's

---

244 This article uses interviews conducted by Tommy Dean and Alexander Herbert, primarily in the summer of 2014.

smoldering sensibilities, which had already grown weary of the repressive culture. "It was exactly what I needed," Feddy recalls. "There were so many rules and regulations. We all needed something." At fourteen years old, Feddy Lavrov proclaimed himself a punk rocker and fastened a single safety pin to his school jacket.

Along with a newfound affinity for punk, Feddy was endowed with a subversive political consciousness. His grandmother Dolly frequently talked politics, read copies of banned books, and clandestinely tuned into BBC news programs on the shortwave radio. Listening alongside her at a young age, Feddy heard reports of persecuted Jewish citizens fleeing Russia and the rampant escalation of Soviet weaponry. He learned about Soviet dissidents like nuclear physicist and Nobel laureate Andrey Sakharov and Aleksandr Solzhenitsyn, the decorated army officer turned exiled author whose depictions of Siberian gulags earned him a Nobel Prize in Literature.

The homegrown education instilled a sense of political purpose in Feddy. "When you live in the Soviet Union and hear about these bad things happening in the country, you decide politics is a part of your life," he says. "It's not just something to think about. It's something real."

But there was a difference between harboring dissident sentiments and explicitly expressing them. Since Stalin's reign, the Soviet government had garnered a reputation for intensified censorship. From poet Osip Mandelshtam to writer Boris Pasternak to theatre director Vsevolod Meyerhold, numerous artists in the USSR faced execution, exile, or imprisonment not only for their views, but for the works they manifested.

Furthermore, the KGB maintained an omnipotent specter with its ever-growing army of citizen provocateurs—civilians who reported their neighbors' anti-Soviet activity to the agency in exchange for penal leniency or career advancement. This forced many people to practice "inner emigration," a political radicalism that was more mindset than actual activism. "Any friend could betray you back then if they were caught or charged with a crime," says Feddy. "So all of the good people were living in disguise. Protest wasn't an action—it was a way of thinking." Even Dolly, the aging political firebrand, was wary of her words. At her work, when she entertained company and was among trustworthy people, they hung a dry rose on a chandelier to let them know they could talk freely, but when the flower was absent, the confidants understood that a potential informant was present and politics were stricken from conversation.

Feddy's first punk band, Rezinovy Rikoshet, was a collaboration with schoolmate Aleks Akensov, who shared his friend's fondness for Italian films and avant-garde plays. The two boys enlisted a guitarist named Oleg and recorded a demo, despite their inability to formulate a cohesive song. "We just got together and decided, 'We have two verses, three choruses, and one solo.'" Feddy recalls.

As the '70s gave way to the '80s, a small group of local youths formed Leningrad's original punk scene. Like Feddy and Akensov, most of them were part of the city's neo-intelligentsia, the sons and daughters of educated and relatively well-off professionals, many of whom were artists, professors, and military officers. Unlike their parents, the dawning generation saw little appeal in the complicity inscribed into the collective Soviet consciousness they still recall as oppressive. "We were the most free people in the least free country in the world," says Feddy. Instead of engaging in the daily regimen of school and work, they spent their days causing mischief on the streets, imbibing alcohol, beating each other up, and riling the public with their untamed energy and at night they congregated at apartments for illegal "drinking parties." The smutty image they co-opted from mainstream acts like the Sex Pistols, and abrasive nature of the music was the ideal soundtrack to their resistance

At the helm of this nascent subculture was Andrey "Svin" Panov, a lanky, handsome guy a few years Feddy's senior. The son of world-renowned ballet dancers, Panov had a high-culture background, but eschewed an air of aristocracy in favor of notoriety as a drunken miscreant. He was epitomized in his eponymous moniker, Svin (meaning swine or pig), which he attempted to earn through a string of shock-value stunts, which ranged from displays of public nudity to making tea out of toilet water to allegedly shitting on the doorstep of a fellow musician—in addition to an unhealthy penchant for smoke and drink. "He was the first among the older generation to accept the rules of self destruction and follow them literally," recalls Feddy in an interview with *Maximum Rocknroll.*

Svin was also the frontman for the city's first punk band Avtomaticheskie Udovletvoriteli—an approximation of "Sex Pistols"—and would later be dubbed the "Grandfather of Russian Punk" by his peers and future fans.

One night, Akensov showed up drunk at Feddy's apartment accompanied by Svin. Before passing out in Dolly's bed, Svin read a futurist manifesto that Feddy had written about an utopian world of art and culture to be built from the ashes of the USSR's cultural wasteland. In Feddy, Svin recognized a fellow foot soldier in the unofficial war against the Soviet state's malignant hold on expression and proclaimed, "He is one of us," officially initiating young Lavrov into the scene.

Feddy's participation in the salad days of the Leningrad punk movement was crucial. During the early '80s, the only sanctioned rehearsal spaces were the government-run Houses of Culture, and the sole official venue was the recently opened Leningrad Rock Club. To gain access to these spaces, a band had to be approved by the government. While commercial rock was gaining the partiality of the State, the authorities and the general public rebuffed punk as a brutish bastardization of the country's rich artistic heritage. To survive their scene, the early Leningrad kids played shows in their cramped apartments with whatever instruments they could get their hands on—a minimalist version of the do-it-yourself ethos practiced by their American and English counterparts.

In his tiny apartment near the docks of the Baltic Sea, Feddy assembled a recording studio with a single-track recorder and plastic *Oktava* microphones, along with a drum set his mother bought him. Svin and other punks added to the studio's collection: "Somebody would bring something stolen or borrowed," recalls Feddy. "Everyone knew that I had no money to buy anything, so they would bring another tape recorder to combine with mine."

"We had no remotes, no good musicians, no pedals, no preamps—nothing," says Yevgeny Titov, the bassist for Avtomaticheskie Udovletvoriteli and Narodnoe Opolchenie. "These guys often made their own guitars and pick-ups by manually twisting the copper wire. It took a lot of patience."

Feddy dubbed the makeshift one-track system Begemotion Records. He produced demos and compilations of the city's few punk bands, some of the only sonic documentation of the original Leningrad scene.

In 1982, Feddy was introduced to a short Jewish kid with piercing brown eyes, colorful clothes, and a contagious sense of humor named Aleks "Ogoltely" Strogachev, who was nicknamed "Donkey" by his peers. When they first met, Donkey's head was shaved bald and he had just ended a two-week stint in jail for public intoxication. Both boys were songwriters and decided to start a band, but upon hearing each other's material, they decided to start two bands—Otdel Samoiskorenenia, and Narodnoe Opolchenie—to accommodate their diverse writing styles. Narodnoe Opolchenie bared a resemblance to punk-infused second-wave ska, while Otdel Samoiskorenenia was the voice box for Feddy's radical politics.

Despite his heavy involvement in the Leningrad scene, Feddy was a pole apart from most of his contemporaries. Svin and his entourage were heavy drinkers, whose rebellion was their daily existence of unemployment and playing punk rock. Conversely, Feddy was sober (having started drinking at an early age, he decided at 13 years old that he would abstain) and used punk as a channel for his aggressive political views. In Otdel Samoiskorenenia songs like "Voyny dlia Voinov" and "Voennaia Monarkhia," Feddy criticized the leaders on both fronts of the Cold War and lambasted the Soviet state for its amassment of nuclear weapons, as well as its involvement in Afghanistan.[245]

So when Feddy set out to record the first and second Otdel Samoiskorenenia albums at Begemotion, his bandmates worried for their personal safety. Ogoltely feared KGB agents would recognize his voice if they got the tapes, so he refused to share vocal duties, and Svin called the songs "over the top," though he played bass as an unofficial member on some of the tracks.

The cassette-recorded albums lacked fidelity, but they showed an honest effort of young punks honing their skills, emulating the Sex Pistols and the New York Dolls with a sneering swagger, an occasionally offbeat drum, and shaved-down straight rock 'n' roll backbone. When the albums were eventually finished, they were copied and then distributed to friends and fellow scenesters. Years later, Feddy discovered that the Otdel Samoiskorenenia tapes reached Siberia, where a separate scene had also blossomed, led by the indomitable anti-Soviet political poet Yegor Letov, whose shows were routinely under the surveillance of the KGB.

In 1984, Feddy's musical ambitions were curtailed when he got a fateful call from the military to report for government-mandated two-year service. He hoped his wife's pregnancy would exempt him, but after arriving at the government headquarters, he was detained. Feddy's mother and wife watched, crying, as he was shipped to boot camp. Meanwhile, Feddy's mother-in-law, a Russian Orthodox devotee who disdained her son-in-law, smiled and waved.

At the rank-and-file military training base, Feddy was an outlier, mingling with soldiers from different Soviet countries and vocalizing his radical political beliefs. Some of the soldiers respected his antithetical stance and labeled him a "refugee," but his superiors were unimpressed. Once, a sergeant dragged him into a bathroom and threatened him with a chain wrapped around his fist: "He asked me if I was going to serve or not," recalls Feddy. "I asked him if I was doing anything wrong, while training, while studying,

245 *Voyny dlia Voinov*—Wars Are for Warriors;

while cleaning." He hadn't technically violated any protocol and the sergeant "admitted that he found no reason to 'give me a lesson.'"

As the Russian occupation of Afghanistan escalated, Feddy began looking for an exit strategy, lest he relent the pacifist politics he preached in his songs and take the army's oath of allegiance (the last step to making him an official member of the military). He got his chance when he was sent to the medical ward for blisters he developed on his feet. A young doctor tended to Feddy and asked him about his political beliefs and ideals. Feddy knew the physician's genial demeanor was an attempt to seek out troublemakers, but he knew it as an opportunity for discharge. He talked openly about his opposition to war and the military while the doctor scribbled in his notebook. Soon after, a high-ranking officer visited Feddy and asked him the fateful question: "Are you going to take the oath?"

"I finally felt that my future was in my hands," recalls Feddy. "It took me seconds to make a decision. With cold and wet hands I responded, 'No!'"

The repercussion for refusing to join the army was punitive psychiatric treatment. Days after he refused to sign the oath, Feddy was transported to a holding unit. "Hell was there," he says, describing the dirty cell to which he was confined. "I saw so much pain, anger, and violence. Some people died." While there, he attended to the other inmates, some of whom were strapped to beds, helping them urinate so they wouldn't soil themselves, as the apathetic guards stood by talking and smoking.

After a few days, Feddy was transferred to a unit in a mental hospital that consisted of a small corridor lined with rooms that held approximately ten patients each. He was heavily medicated—"They gave me so many pills I couldn't control my arms and hands"—and for the first two weeks he was not allowed outside. Eventually, he developed a daily regimen of exercise and writing to ward off boredom and combat the sedative effects of the medication. He also made the acquaintance of many interesting people, including a *stiliaga*, or Russian hipster whose generation developed its own unique brand of fashion and music in the '60s. "They also tried to create some special world," says Feddy, recalling the camaraderie he felt for his forbear of Soviet subculture.

Less than two months after being admitted, Feddy was discharged and escorted to his hometown by the same military doctor who brought him to the hospital. But Feddy knew the most severe repercussion for his recalcitrance lied outside the hospital walls on a piece of paper. His schizophrenia diagnosis would be noted on his permanent file, which Feddy compared to being a "dead man." People with the mark had little chance of getting a good job or even a driver's license, a particularly daunting prospect considering unemployment was illegal in the Soviet Union at the time.

Yet, when Feddy arrived at the local medical center in Leningrad to collect his paperwork, the distinguishing mark was absent. The doctor noted that the records were mysteriously lost, and as far as Feddy's paperwork was concerned, he was sane and employable. Later, he learned that his clean record may not have been a mistake of Soviet bureaucracy, but that his mother slept with a Soviet doctor to clear her son's name. "I know my mother," says Feddy. "She would do anything for me."

After Feddy was released from the military in the summer of 1984, his life quickly changed. He divorced his wife and his son Ilya was born. Before the month expired, Feddy was once again in the crosshairs of the Soviet system.

"We all got telephone calls from the KGB officers at the same time, the same day," says Feddy. He and his band mates were summoned to the local KGB office, commonly referred to as the Big House, for questioning. "Everybody was scared. One after another we went to the interrogations, which could last for two hours or more." In the interrogation room, two officers played the KGB rendition of good cop, bad cop. "One is shouting at you, walking behind your back cracking his fists while another is sitting and smiling, asking his colleague to let him talk alone with you." The most disturbing part of the interview was what the officers had in their possession—Otdel Samoiskorenenia tapes, photographs, and lyric sheets, which slandered both American and Soviet politicians with lines like, "Reagan and Andropov fucked the whole of Europe from behind." No one claimed to know how the agency obtained the memorabilia, but Feddy surmises it was either a friend who betrayed their confidences, or someone who happened upon the evidence at a party and turned it into the KGB for personal gain.

Despite the USSR's reputation for harsh reprisal, Feddy was not exiled or imprisoned, and neither were his friends. Instead, he was forced to a sign a contract that stipulated he would disband Otdel Samoiskorenenia and never make radical political music again. To this day, he is not certain why he was granted leniency.

During the late '80s, under the rule of Mikhail Gorbachev, the Soviet government issued the liberal policy reforms perestroika and glasnost, which allowed for unprecedented cultural expression as well as an increase of commerce with Western countries. The country's punk bands, which had lurked in underground practice spaces and cramped apartments for nearly a decade, were granted access to public venues. Many of Feddy's old scene cohorts became regulars of the Russian rock circuit, touring and playing the Leningrad Rock Club and music festivals. Political radicalism became a popular theme in Soviet punk repertoire. Svin and his group Avtomaticheskie Udovletvoriteli, who had continued playing throughout the '80s unhindered by the KGB, even had songs that smacked of political and cultural critique, such as "Reagan Provocateur" and "Bourgeoise."

Otdel Samoiskorenenia had been broken up for nearly two years by the time Gorbachev's reforms were instituted. Feddy spent the next two decades being a spectator of the scene from the periphery as he weaved a jagged thread of employment, adventure, fortune, and mishap through the '80s, '90s, and early 2000s. He built subways in St. Petersburg and severed the middle finger from his right hand. He toured Europe with the Mariinsky ballet as a stage carpenter and illegally immigrated to Paris. He built furniture, released an Electronica record as well as couple solo albums, and coordinated exhibits at Moscow's contemporary art gallery, Triumph. He released five albums in an indie-punk-prog-rock act called Begemot, wrote soundtracks for films made for Mexican Catholics, and played keyboards in Pink Floyd and Depeche Mode tribute bands. He founded the synthetic art production company Shtuka, and created a film about Soviet punk with Triumph Gallery founder and Cold War Moscow scene veteran, Dmitry Khankin.[246]

He married again, had another child—a daughter—then divorced again, and then married two weeks later, this time to a young art school student who was more than twenty years his junior.

In 2012, nearly thirty years after the KGB ordered *Otdel Samoiskorenenia* to disband, Feddy revisited his group's material. In the interim three decades, through the do-it-yourself means of mail orders, record distros, and zines, and later, the internet, Russia's once-insulated scenes had become a nationwide network. After unearthing the cassettes, Feddy remastered the tracks and released them to the public through torrents, YouTube, and *Vkontakte* (the Russian equivalent of Facebook). The result was a novel appreciation from the present generation of punks, who had a renewed interest in their Soviet roots.

"This is the beginning of punk rock in our country," says Valentin Popov, co-founder of the Russian-based label VDV Records (named after the *Otdel Samoiskorenenia* song *Voyny dlia Voinov*).

In 2014, VDV released three re-mastered Otdel Samoiskorenenia songs on a 7", and later that year another young Russian label, *Izdatelstvo Siyanie*, released the band's complete '80s discography on a double-CD set, "Anti-All/Full Dossier 1982–1984". Then in August, Otdel Samoiskorenenia played its first ever public performance at a club called Kamchatka in St. Petersburg, which was once a makeshift practice studio for early participants of the

---

246 *Shtuka*—The Thing.

Soviet punk scene. The band then played shows in Moscow, Nizhny Novgorod, and a few more performances in St. Petersburg.

Feddy and his band are undoubtedly artifacts of Russia's punk past, but their access to public audience and recently-released records endow them with a yet-to-be determined legacy of what they are, and for some, what they could have been. Titov, the bass player for Avtomaticheskie Udovletvoriteli and a close associate of Feddy since the early Leningrad days, believes that his friend had great potential, but was inevitably hindered by circumstance. "Even back then, I thought Feddy and his songs were born at the wrong time and in the wrong country," he says. "I'm sure that if he played his music somewhere normal when he was twenty years old, with his talent, he would have become very popular."

Some believe that Feddy's importance to Russian punk origins rivals that of Siberia's Yegor Letov, who has been the subject of numerous academic texts, history books, and documentaries. "Right now every young music lover in Russia loves and respects Yegor Letov," says Bulat Ibiatov, founder of Izdatelstvo Siyanie. "Unfortunately, because of the problems with the KGB in the '80s, and the many years Fedor spent in France in the '90s... his influence to modern Russian punk is not very powerful. But I am sure that the wind of history will put everything in its place."

But for Feddy, recognition, in the past or present, is of no importance: "I don't want pop charts and radio rotation," he says. "My bands were not a way for me to get popular, fuck more girls, and get more free drinks. I only wanted to create something new." Nor does he believe that his ethical outlook makes him extraordinary. "If you stand for something, spread the word. You have to follow your ideals till the end, whatever happens. This is nothing special."

Rather, Feddy perceives his involvement in the dawning days of Leningrad punk as the inevitable byproduct of being a carefree youth with a rebellious zeal. "I was just having fun, trying to do my best not to care about anything," he says. "I was too brave, or let's say too naïve to give a damn about tomorrow."

Yet what endears the first wave of Russian punks, and the music they made, to the new crop of kids is how their willingness to create persisted despite the harsh political and economic climate of the time. "What the young generation of punks like about it is the *freedom* of creation," he says. "They say that it's amazing how we managed to create such things when nothing was allowed and nothing was available."

It is that symbolism of liberation implied by the music that Feddy wants people to take away from what he and his friends created more than thirty years ago. Recently, during one of our correspondences on Facebook, I asked Feddy if the idea of freedom (a word he persistently uses when talking about his music career and Russian politics) is just as important now as it was when he was a youth. He responded with a resounding yes, because although the Iron Curtain may have fallen long ago, he understands that the country of his birth is still full of people fighting for *their* freedoms, whether it's the members of LGBTQ community, dissenters of State, musicians hampered by "religious fanatics," or just the common man looking for a job that pays the bills and fulfills him.

And for Feddy, freedom starts and ends from within— "The inner censor is in every Russian Citizen," he says—a lesson he may have learned while covertly listening to the shortwave radio, practicing "inner emigration" alongside his grandmother Dolly all those years ago. This may be why for Feddy, music continues to be his main passion—no matter who listens, how it survives, or what it's recorded on, there is *that* freedom one has while playing it, a feeling no government official or religious fanatic can take away.

"Playing music is the most wonderful thing ever," says Feddy. "You can't get a better feeling skiing in the Alps or riding a motorcycle. It's all about being free. Fuck the legacy."

APPENDIX 2:
We're Not Made of Paper: A Reflection on Punk in the Cultural Capital
by Kirill "George" Mikhailov

Translated and Edited by Alexander Herbert

The common cliché "lost generation" is often associated with the punk movement. In a certain sense, the Russian (or more precisely, post-Soviet) punk movement can be called lost twice.

When the Soviet Union collapsed and the pressure of the system ceased, the rock underground turned out to be in a two-pronged situation. On the one hand, recent bans were lifted, and Soviet rock musicians received an unlimited space for self-expression. On the other hand, the musicians were like fish out of water; they suffocated in the new and unusual conditions of freedom and the nascent capitalist society. In one instance, the entire Soviet reality in which they were born and raised ceased to exist. It became necessary to look for new outlets for creativity, new opportunities, and to establish an identity in their new life.

Before getting into the turn of the millennium, it should be emphasized that Soviet punk rock was very specific. Most Soviet rock music originally carried a social or political protest message. Soviet punk, therefore, with few exceptions, was more of a purely stylistic offshoot of rock than the actual ideological subculture it connotes today. And for lack of "genuine" punk, punk rock was often championed by artists who had a rather indirect relationship to it. Take, for example, Mike Naumenko from the Leningrad group Zoopark, who played traditional rock and roll rhythm and blues in the style of the American 1960-1970s, but looked fresh and vigorous in comparison with conservative Soviet rock bands.

The first Russian punk group, Avtomaticheskie Udovletvoriteli, naturally and organically connected a new style of music and life to a quintessentially Russian buffoonery. They managed to mix features of Russia's national character and folklore with the cynicism and nihilism of punk, creating a unique fusion in which the music itself, the worldview, and the way of life became closely intertwined. The main figure in the group was, of course, Andrey "Svin" Panov. In addition to him, almost a hundred musicians played in the band.

Oleg Kovriga (head of the label Otdelenie Vykhod, a publication of the Soviet and Russian rock underground) wrote in his memoirs that at the funeral of Svin in 1998, he called him "the main Petrushka of the Soviet Union," which sounded like a standard reaction to the meaningless farewell ceremony for the Soviet punk pioneer.[247] This comparison was all the more accurate and successful, not only for Svin, but the whole early Leningrad punk canon, among which there were such names as Aleks "Ogoltely" Strogachev (Narodnoe Opolchenie), Fedor "Begemot" Lavrov (Otdel Samoiskorenenia), Aleksandr "Rikoshet" Aksenov (Obyekt Nasmeshek), and Nikolay Mikhaylov (Brigadny Podriad). Also, one should not forget the fact that the early Leningrad punk clique was closely connected with the group of young directors and conceptual artists (the most famous of them was Yevgeny "Yufa" Yufit), who later became known as "necrorealists."

In a sense, this generation of the first Leningrad punks can be regarded as proto-punk, like the American garage groups of the '60s or the New York rock scene of the early '70s, famous for its being the forerunner to punk.

By the beginning of the '90s, new opportunities and unlimited creative freedom, coupled with the depth of despair and a drop in the standard of living, firmly entrenched the "dashing '90s," eliciting nostalgia in some, and horror in others.

247 *Otdelenie Vykhod*—Department Exit; Petrushka is one of the main characters of traditional Russian folk theater, a jester.

The decade was an extremely eclectic and controversial time. From the TV screens, to the radio and the pages of the print media, a flood of new music, new information, and all the products of the Western showbiz machine confronted Russian citizens. And of course, it was impossible to intelligently digest this avalanche of information in such a short time. Russia in the '90s had to catch up to America and Europe in a single decade in many realms of social existence and culture, including music. Of course, punk rock was no exception.

"Genuine" punk started, as a matter of fact, only in the '90s, when conditions permitting such a genre appeared and people were able to unite in a common worldview of non-conformity and aesthetics. Soviet rock music of the '80s in a moment became an anachronism—something shameful—like a backward village relative that looks ridiculous in an urban environment. But the problem turned out to be that by that time punk, as a form, was already somewhat late.

For the new generation, fresh heroes were important, and it did not take long for them to appear. The decade began with the explosion of grunge music, which in the West had deep roots in punk rock, but for the unsophisticated Russian public, this music and movement began life as if from a tabula rasa. Russia essentially inverted the timeline; grunge gave way to punk.

New music, new styles, and new subcultures replaced each other every year—grunge, industrial, rapcore, nu-metal (received in Russia in the mocking name *mazafaka*, because of the frequent use of the word in the lyrics of fashionable American groups), alternative, and Californian pop punk. Music videos from MTV were collected on tape and sold, circulating hands and teaching the youth how to dress and act the part.

In these conditions, traditional punk and hardcore, as non-commercial and non-conformist subcultures, were inevitably forced to the sidelines. They became a heaven for outsiders and the antisocial, or a few ideological enthusiasts who attempted to harness them into a powerful and serious movement.

The development of punk throughout the world has been parallel and unequal. In almost all countries, national characteristics have influenced music and subculture, giving rise to a huge variety of sub-genres. (Thus we get British punk '77 and '82, Deutsche punk, Californian punk, Finnish hardcore, Japanese "burning spirit" hardcore, Swedish crust, New York hardcore, etc). Russia arrived late to this holiday, with the exception, of course, of Siberian punk, successfully called by the Moscow rock journalist Sergey Guryev "existential punk," as well as St. Petersburg's "TaMtAm generation" of the '90s.

St. Petersburg (1703–1914)—Petrograd (1914–1924)—Leningrad (1924–1991)—St. Petersburg (1991–) was originally conceived and built as an outpost of the Russian Empire in the West, a "window to Europe." Independent, self-sufficient style was inherent in the city from the very beginning, which further emphasized its distinctiveness and set it apart from the traditional Russian way of life. In the Soviet era, the status of the former Imperial capital was lost, but in time it became redubbed the cultural capital of the Soviet Union, and then the Russian Federation.

Being a major seaport, Leningrad has always been inundated with a lot of tourists and sailors who brought records. It was important that the city was close to the borders of Finland and the Baltic States. For example, Lekha Nikonov from the Vyborg punk band Poslednie Tanki v Parizhe said that in the '80s and '90s he learned about new music through foreign imports, particularly Finnish radio intercepted along the border.[248]

Finland is also connected with a phenomenon known as the "vodka-tourist," when Finns, suffering from the high cost of alcohol and the almost absent nightlife in the '70s and '80s, came to Leningrad to drink and have fun. They also brought in rare records.

---

248 *Poslednie Tanki v Parizhe*—Last Tanks in Paris.

By the early '90s there were a lot of "punks" in St. Petersburg, but there was no general movement as such. With the breakdown of the state came street punks (literally punks living in the streets), who were absolutely antisocial and had no unifying factor, except resistance to their surrounding world.

As Seva Gakkel rightly wrote in his memoirs about people going to club TaMtAm, "Nobody could believe that someone would do something specifically for them. Therefore, they had the strongest desire for destruction and they did not have any place to contain themselves. For them, every concert in a new place should have been the last." The mistrust of punks toward the state, to any social structures, was massive, and the internal level of nihilism was too high for life and creativity. Therefore, it is not surprising that many of them eventually went down the path of crime, ended up in jail, and died of a drug overdose. Everyone who was around this in the '90s—more than a dozen friends and acquaintances—stayed stuck in this decade forever.

But in spite of the whole color of street punk and the noise produced by it, music of the '90s became defined by more intelligent groups that went down in history under the conditional name "TaMtAm generation." Although it was less straightforward punk, many more interesting and unpredictable bands played a wide range of guitar music, from post-punk to hardcore with punk roots. This was partly due to the fact that some of the musicians started playing in early childhood, and really only developed the scene in the '90s.

First and foremost, it is necessary to name the group Khimera, which is often associated more directly with the "TaMtAm generation," especially as the group was a resident of the club and played regular concerts there. The group played psychedelic noisy hardcore. For its five years of existence, Khimera recorded several albums, including a split 7" with the Swiss anarchopunk group Steine für den Frieden, and they went on several European tours.

The group existed until 1997, when its leader Eduard "Redt" Starkov committed suicide, attaining posthumous cult status.

It is interesting to note that many St. Petersburg bands from this generation created an elusive sense of community from the gloomy sound and atmosphere, regardless of the style they played, as noted, for example, by Moscow witnesses. This also revealed the specific connection of the musicians with their native city, which at that time was undergoing a major transition with massive restructuring and reconstruction projects. As a typical example, in the '90s there were still streets in the city where films about World War II were filmed without any set props.

By the mid-late '90s, the popularity of rave and other new dance styles reached the Russian public. Many musicians were carried away by electronic music and DJing, which contributed to a certain crisis in guitar music. In addition, by the end of the decade it became clear that for most punk and indie bands there was still no hope in achieving anything big. Thus, many groups from the '90s broke up early, or were worn out by punk— musicians who have played since the '80s have grown old, started families, and have careers; they are no longer willing to give all their strength and time to music.

But this was more or less a global process. The underground remained in the underground, but the emphasis shifted. For example, Konstantin Nesterov, who was in the mid-'90s hardcore band director Marradery, switched to electronic music, assuming the name DJ Gvozd—the best-known drum & bass DJ in Russia.[249]

We must admit that in the '90s the national underground network of punk activity—connected and cooperating with each other through regular fanzines, labels, clubs, etc.—failed to form on a scale in proportion to the country. But apparently it was impossible in the mad Russian whirlpool of the '90s, in the face of unpredictable political policies and constant economic crises,

---

249 *Gvozd*—Nail.

occurring within the whirlwind of a new culture, new styles, new fashion, one by one, to an unprepared public.

We can say that Moscow and St. Petersburg were the exceptions, as the largest cities with their own atmosphere, where conditions permitted the existence and development of an independent music scene. The rest of Russia's regions were more concerned with everyday survival. Regional scenes were left to their own devices.

The transition between the '90s and 2000s was distinct, trenchant, and symbolic in many ways. The end of the "dashing '90s" was marked by president Yeltsin's stepping down and empowering—like out of nowhere—the then unknown Vladimir Putin. It also saw the commencement of the Second Chechen War, the cause of many explosions in cities across Russia. Perhaps it was the first terror threats that the new Russian Federation faced. The avalanche economical crisis of 1998, when the exchange-rate of the ruble plummeted several times, still lingered in everyone's memory.

In the beginning of 2000s the Russian punk-hardcore scene was in a decline. Almost no significant bands played anymore. Most of the active bands from the '90s fell apart, or were decaying.

In general, a wave of pop-punk made its way through Moscow most actively, (with dozens of pop-punk and ska-punk bands) supported by several labels and youth media sources that published subject collections (Tipa Panki i Vse Takoe and others), albums, and sponsored regular concerts and festivals.[250] Pop punk bands dreamt about commercializing their music like their icons from Epitaph Records and Fat Wreck Chords, and their point, their message, was clear—to have fun. They often disrespected the punk and hardcore underground and the ideology of DIY that it supported. Correspondingly, the punk underground treated them negatively in return, and labeled them "sellouts."

---

250 *Tipa Panki i Vse Takoe—Sort of Punks and All That…*

Once more, St. Petersburg needed new people and new ideas to develop its hardcore and punk movement. And they appeared.

The generation of young St. Petersburg punk rockers, who drew inspiration from the DIY ethics of European and American punk and hardcore movements, started to express themselves in the middle-end of '90s, when their crew got acquainted with the first punk fanzines in the Russian-language: *Bezumets* (Riga, Latvia), *Play Hooky* (Kirov), *Kontr Kult URa* (Moscow), and English-language: *Angelheart* (Finland), *Aversion* and *Ripping Thrash* (UK), *International Straight Edge Bulletin* (France).[251] There was *Maximum Rocknroll* too, of course, but it was rather a sacred cow, more known by ear than seen and read.

This print media had a big impact on young minds, and local fanzines quickly started to appear—among the first *Nozhi i Vilki* (1998–2006), *Elefantboy* (1997–1999, later renamed to *V Moem Supe Pechenye v Forme Zveriushek, Sean Penn, Paddington*), *In a Free Land* (1999–2000), *Vozduh* (1998), *Ten-Chan* (1999), *Zorry for the Delay* (1999–2000), *Voice* (2000–2002), *Get Up!* (2004–2005), and *Novy Svet* (the oldest newspaper of Petersburg anarchists, published 67 issued from 1989–2006).[252] And surely this influence was related intimately to the music, to the emergence of new bands.

One of the first bands of the new hardcore wave was Til I Die, gathered in 2001 by myself, Kirill "George" Mikhailov, (earlier from SvinoÐop) and Pavel "Mrachek" Sasin (*In a Free Land* zine). They were also joined by Maks Ionov from Moscow (since 1994 he played in the first Moscow-based hardcore bands—Step Back, Skygrain, later XXX, Yarche 1000 Solnts, nowadays—in the concert line-up of Pussy Riot), who lived in Saint Petersburg that time.[253] Til I Die existed until the end of 2003.

In the beginning of 2000s the hardcore/punk crew was small, but unanimous—what can be considered "united." There

251 *Bezumets*—Madman.
252 *Nozhi i Vilki*—Knifes and Forks; *V Moem Supe Pechenye v Forme Zveriushek*—There are Animal Crackers in My Soup; *Vozduh*—Air; *Novy Svet*—New World.
253 *Yarche 1000 Solnts*—Brighter than 1000 Suns.

were few bands and concerts, and hence all the shows were attended by everyone—by punks, hardcore kids, skinheads, crust punks, anyone—there was nothing to quarrel about back then, and this music was really unifying. Surf, oi!, crust, folk-punk, hardcore bands could play during one show, and the audience would listen to all of them; nobody complained about bands that didn't fit the bill. This was also how the uniqueness of the time and the unity of the scene showed itself, and nowadays, when the scene has already been divided according to the styles, crews, and interests, one can barely imagine such diverse line-ups at an average concert.

Some of the clubs were quite friendly to hardcore/punk bands, as they had been opened by musicians from the bands of the '90s, but there were also clubs that were reluctant to host hardcore concerts because of the aggressiveness and unpredictability of the audience, and they said no to bands and promoters.

Sometimes concerts were organized in casual premises, such as a series of shows held at School №32 on Vasilyevsky Island and in a regional library just steps from Ladozhskaia metro station. Such opportunities appeared when the parents of somebody from the crew worked there, and they allowed their child to use the premises. Those events always had a glorious atmosphere, attended only by inside people from the crew. But there were certain organizational difficulties, as only a few musicians had their own equipment, except for guitars.

It was a unique time, full of idealism and enthusiasm, when almost all the members of the scene were young, naïve and thoroughgoing, and gave their all for its development.

After the breakup of Til I Die, three bands were started by their members—Engage at Will, Next Round (who successfully developed the style and the brand of hardcore), and—a while later—Dottie Danger, also founded by Mrachek and myself, who diverged from traditional hardcore to explore other horizons of punk. At the same time Aleksandr Yakovlev (bass player from The Pauki's original lineup and bass-player for Vibrator during the transition from the '90s to 2000s) gathered the first members of the future legendary Russian d-beat/crust band Distress.

Basically by 2005 a new hardcore/punk scene had formed in St. Petersburg: there existed several dozens of bands who were playing all kinds of styles—from traditional punk to dub metal and surf punk. (For instance, Ankylym, Igray Garmon, Komatoz, More&Relsy, Poslednie Tanki v Parizhe, Svinyi v Kosmose, Coffin Wheels, Distress, Dottie Danger, Engage at Will, The King Kongs, Mass Murder, Next Round, Sandinista!, and Skafandr).[254] Concerts were held on a regular basis, and people started to organize tours for local and foreign bands (generally in northwest Russia—Petrozavodsk, Petersburg, Pskov, Novgorod). A total of ten to 20 fanzines, circulating anywhere from 50 to 1000 copies, had also been started.

In the beginning of 2000s the first local labels and distributions appeared. Direct action groups also came into being—Food Not Bombs, animal rights activists, anti-fascists, etc.

The scene was developing quite rapidly, and the process went on not only in Petersburg, but throughout Russia—almost every city seemed to explode. But at the same time the punk scene advocated for leftist politics and anti-fascism, a profascist and neonazi scene, atune to antifa movement (in the way it understood it) developed. The two sides grew more tense, until the murder of anti-fascist activist Timur Kacharava (guitarist for *Sandinista!* and *Distress*) on November 13, 2015, in the middle of Saint Petersburg, after Food Not Bombs action, created a point of no return.

The radicalization of these two sides led to a street war by the second half of the 2000s, during which several people died and dozens more were seriously hurt. That created a sense of danger in the scene, and paradoxically attracted more people; furthermore, by the end of 2008 the so called *Tsentr "E"* was created—Russia's special police force for combating extremism, entrusted with the task of "preventing extremist activities." In practice their tactics

254 *Igray Garmon*—Play Accordion; *More&Relsy*—Sea&Rails; *Svinyi v Kosmose*—Pigs in Cosmos; *Skafandr*—Armor.

consisted of raids in clubs, cancelling concerts, arrests of musicians and visitors. As a result, the practice of "closed" concerts sprang up, when neither place nor time were mentioned in advertisements, and often the information was spread just among friends. Social media by that time, in particularly *Vkontakte*—the most known and popular in Russia—was a major help to that.

Yet another spiral of police brutality initiated after an incident at the festival "Music Of The Streets," which gathered Russian, Belarusian, Finnish and Swedish punk bands in the club *Roks* in October 2007. Neo-Nazis brought a homemade bomb inside, but failed to detonate it.

A northwest Russian tour of the veteran Finnish hardcore band Terveet Kädet in 2010 is an example of how concerts may have happened at that time. Their St. Petersburg concert was supposed to take place in the club *Zhelezny Lev*, but the day before the show the club was attacked by neo-Nazis, there was a mass brawl with shooting, and the club was closed by police. The concert had to be moved urgently to another place, and there was an agreement brokered with the club *RusKomplekt*.[255] That same evening the club was hosting a noise festival before the punk show, but the punks showed up early and created a scene. The police came again, and the band didn't get to play. In the end the concert happened at an anarcopunk squat that was located in the former rave club *Mama*.

In 2005 a tradition of summer open air festivals *KronFest* in Kronstadt (a town on Kotlin island in the Gulf of Finland near St. Petersburg, which is also the base of the Baltic Fleet) started. The festivals were held illegally on the territory of abandoned forts in the Gulf of Finland, which were built in the middle of 19th Century to defend St. Petersburg from the sea. The festivals were absolutely illegal, held without any agreement with local authorities or the police. And they didn't have any publicly available advertisements, no ticket sale in advance; information about the time, place and lineup was spread through friends on social media. If the police

255 *Zhelezny Lev*—Iron Lion.

came to a festival spot (and it was always a remote, hard to access place), they encountered hundreds of punks, which they physically couldn't arrest or chase. Thus, they had to agree to turn a blind eye on condition that there would be no criminal activity.

The amount of the audience varied from 100–200 people on the first fest in 2005, and up to 1000+ on the last one in 2009. There were many reasons for closing the fest: from the mass brawl with Navy men in 2009 (the day of the fest synchronized with the Navy Day in Russia), to the rising popularity of the festival and the increasing amount of people. A higher level of organization, which already demanded the festival's legalization, was needed. And the legalization was, in turn, impossible due to absolute noncommercial ideology of the fest the inability to obtain approval from the authorities.

The essence of domestic politics, particularly for the past 20 years, is to control everything, to be aware of any citizen activism, and to direct and to control it. In practice this requires an enormous bureaucratic apparatus, suppression of each and any grassroots movement, and overall sluggishness in making decisions.

The experience of the preceding years and other festivals showed that all the initiatives of open air punk/hardcore fests legalization would end in nothing. A fest may have been approved by local authorities, but it would be cancelled by *Tsentr "E"* as soon as it would get information about it. That's why it has always been easier to organize an illegal fest, or, in a pinch, to make an agreement with local police.

As a result, all the last festivals—United Help Fest, *Yebi Sistemu Fest* and others—were held in forests of Leningrad region, far away from the city, to maximise the difficulty of finding their location.[256] Transit to a fest usually looked something like this: two-three hours on a commuter rail, and an hour on foot through the forest.

---

256 *Yebi Sistemu Fest*—Fuck the System Fest.

After the fascist problem quieted down and things began to be organized, the Russian punk scene seemed to finally be united—it was no longer limited to a few venues or restricted by any censors. The late 2000s was a long way from the days of Avtomaticheskie Udovletvoriteli, but we valued it more than the past. For that brief moment we weren't a lost generation, but very much where we wanted to be.

APPENDIX 3:
I Shouldn't be Here: Moscow's Punk Scene in the Early 2000s

by Maksim Dinkevich

Translated and Edited by Alexander Herbert

This text was not supposed to be written by me. The story of Moscow's punk scene written for the English-speaking world for the first time? What? Are you laughing? I can name more than a dozen people who have done more, seen more, risked more, and could highlight themes much better than me. However, without the persistence and perseverance of the compiler of this book, the history of the capital's punk scene in the beginning of the millennium would probably not be written in the foreseeable future. Such a text is currently unavailable, even in Russian.

I must say, my story does not pretend to be objective. The last thing I wanted to do was to engage in meaningless name-dropping in the spirit of "Wikipedia," so some of the people and bands described below are not referred to by name. If you want to listen to real Moscow punk bands, email me at mpodpolye@yandex.ru, I'll make a playlist for you.

The energy that was bubbling and stirring in Moscow's DIY scene that I observed was tied to the music only in part. Perhaps not even so. The most *interesting* things that occurred in my eyes from 2000–2015, as a rule, did not take place during a concert, but rather before, after, or in place of them. Many certainly will not agree with me, and, well, I'll listen to their stories with pleasure.

The task put before me in writing this was, first of all, to bring up some themes that underlined the *fragmented* Moscow DIY scene that I became a part of (well, and to tell some funny stories so you don't get bored). Moscow is a huge city, and many punk groups in the second half of the 2000s spawned, like mushrooms after the rain. I'm sure many of them did not know about the existence of each other, and I am no exception.

What was Moscow, and for that matter "punk," in the beginning of 2000s for me—a seventh grader? A nightmare and horror. If you were an ordinary schoolboy who drew information about music from two or three glossy music magazines published in the country, the broadcasts of two rock radio stations, and cassettes sold in stalls near subway stations, you were completely disoriented and frankly embarrassing—like a nerd pushed by his evil classmates into the women's locker room after gym class.

Punk in the 2000s was called a lot of different things indiscriminately. These cultural and musical forms had little or nothing to do with the Western understanding of the genre and the culture of DIY. The choice was between either native music, or flat and one-dimensional copies of foreign punk. The former includes, for example, bands like Sektor Gaza (obscene sketches from the life of a provincial youth with a synthesizer and often stolen music), Krasnaia Plesen (bawdy sketches, with practically no songs at all), Grazhdanskaia Oborona (existential depths, darkness, and horror under low-fi recordings).[257] I could not get into the last one for a very long time. And I still don't understand the other two. Bands of the second category, as a rule, were guided by the most prominent representatives of Californian punk (Pliazh, Supermarket, Tri 15 and many many others), or mohawked punks in the spirit of The Exploited and the Casualties (like Purgen and Az).[258] There were practically no exceptions to these rules, except maybe Orgazm Nostradamusa, a truly unique diamond, which in appearance, unfortunately, did not differ from the garbage heap that surrounded it.[259] Rarely did any of these groups have any idea of the "punk attitude" in its Western (classical?) understanding.

---

257 *Krasnaia Plesen*—Red Mustiness.
258 *Pliazh*—Beach; *Tri 15*—Three 15.
259 *Orgazm Nostradamusa*—Orgasm of Nostradamus.

Musicians from the overwhelming number of pop punk bands believed that Californian punks sang exclusively about love, girls, and skateboards (of course, because in California, unlike Russia, it's always warm! It's incredible! And it's a big beach, at least according to films). Most of these artists wanted to become famous, dreaming of becoming a domestic Green Day or The Offspring (which was in fact impossible for almost anyone). Their more embittered grimy "colleagues" could not offer anything more interesting than to get drunk with cheap beer, piss under the door, and fall asleep in their own vomit. For them, *that* was considered punk.

Also around the same time, our country was overtaken by ska and ska-punk, which had existed in the rest of the world for over ten years. This mischievous music with wind instruments attracted not only punks and skaters, but also football fans—most of them right wing. So in the first half of the 2000s, we Muscovite punks proudly stood on par with Indonesia, being one of the few amazing countries in the world where xenophobic ska-punk existed (and to some extent still exists).

The top of this pyramid was crowned by stadium punk bands like Naïve, Tarakany! and Korol i Shut, who were on the radio and even television. However, I do not consider these bands, who called themselves "punk," particularly influential for me because I didn't understand the cultural context that the musicians referred to. It was simply boring rock for me. Still, I am friends with some of the members of Tarakany!, Naïve, and Korol i Shut, whom I met many years after first hearing them.

Finding records of domestic punk bands in the beginning of the 2000s was easy—most of them were labeled "punk"—but they were a bit misleading; music stores were overwhelmed with domestic collections with names like Pank-Revoliutsia, Tipa Panki i Vse Takoe, Russky Pank-Obstrel, Pank-Bratstvo, like direct translations from English.[260] Each of them had groups from one of

---

260 *Pank-Revoliutsia*—Punk Revolution; *Russky Pank-Obstrel*—Russian Punk Firing; *Pank-*

the two categories mentioned above—particularly imitators trying their best *to be punk*. Almost all of their songs had stereotypical "punk" features, the works of such bands could be arranged on the shelves as "deliberately stupid songs," "songs with *mat*," "deliberately stupid songs with *mat*," "songs about skateboarding," "songs about summer," "songs about unhappy love."[261] All of these were released predominantly through sub-labels of Russia's "major" record labels that were oriented toward the youth. Quite humorously, the compilers of many of these compilations with the word "punk" in the title did not even ask the musicians for permission to release their songs. Participants of these groups, however, were not particularly frustrated—getting into such a hodgepodge was considered (and for some, it was) the start of a career.

It was thanks to these compilations that most of my peers were introduced to punk in their time. I think that if in those years one representative of each group of "punks" were put at a table, they would not have recognized each other as brothers in subculture and music. All of these "punk" gangs did nothing but turn me off of the scene.

With my hand over my heart I swear that Moscow, in contrast to St. Petersburg and Siberia, never received notoriety for its punk bands. We can be proud only of "Formation" (described below), which was close to the National Bolshevik Party (NBP)—a total underground, which could not be found by chance, and individual representatives of the Moscow Rock Laboratory in the '80s and the beginning of the '90s (such as the early Nogu Svelo!, little known Pogo or NII Kosmetiki).[262] Almost nobody recalled their albums though, at least not in my cohort. It was almost impossible to explain to teenagers of the 2000s—to those self-described punks—that some generally recognized classics of Russian rock of the '80s like Zvuki Mu, Nol,

---

Bratstvo—Punk Brotherhood.

261 *Mat* is a particular group of Russian swear words and phrases, not as encompassing as the English phrase "swear words," and perhaps more severe than English words.

262 *NII Kosmetiki—Research Institute of Cosmetics.*

and Sergey Kurekhin were much bigger punks than their idols, both in terms of creativity and in life.[263] Few people understand this today. The lack of continuity of generations is a serious problem in Russian punk, and not only in punk. Unfortunately, it is still an issue.

Due to a complete rejection of the public version of the "punk" in the 2000s, all the legendary stories and places that many of my peers today remember with nostalgia and a gleam in their eyes, walked right past me. For example, I had never been in the notorious Moscow club, Estakada, a huge barn on the outskirts of the city, which is famous not only for the fact that all the meaningful punk concerts happened there in those years, but also the fact that punks went there as if for a war.[264]

The place was located far from the metro station, in the industrial area of town, so getting there was not an easy task— the local gopniki and nazi skinheads (there were practically no other skinheads at the time) waited for defenseless subculture kids between the metro station and the club.[265] Getting away from Estakada, avoiding an attack, was even more difficult given that it wasn't until a few years later that an active militant antifa movement was capable of organizing the fragmented and vulnerable masses. Instead, at this time, thugs armed with chains chased crowds of several dozen people in plaid pants and pirate NOFX T-shirts.

I also never went to the no less odious R-Club (as I said, I shouldn't be writing), where in the first half of the 2000s DIY hardcore groups, whose records could only be obtained at specific points on the huge music market Gorbushka, and a pair of punk-distros frequently played.[266] But someone from outside the circle had almost no opportunity to learn about them.

However, I do not much regret that these stories passed me. I had the ability to make up for all the urban guerrilla fighting

263 *Nol—Zero.*
264 Overhead road.
265 For a definition of *gopnik/gopniki*, see footnote 4, Introduction.
266 The music market was located near the Gorbunov Palace of Culture.

and fleeing from armed opponents that I missed a few years later, in 2005–2008.

In 2004, in R-club, Boston's Out Cold, strengthened the then metropolitan DIY underground (Unconform, Loa Loa, Uchitel Truda, No Copies). I found out about this only six months after it occurred through reading a detailed report about the show on Rockmusic.ru. It was a unique anomaly in the history of the Russian media—a glossy and accessible volume—which by an amazing coincidence covered punk and was made by enthusiasts of independent music. If it were not for this magazine and its authors, whom I was lucky to meet years later, I do not know for how long my search for "the" underground world would have lasted.

To get into the existing (rather, striving to exist, according to Western rules) DIY underground, required insider connections, which I did not possess. It sucks being the only music nerd around.

What concerts did I go to in 2001–2004? It's a shame to say that the most accurate responses to my search for something gloomy, powerful, and desperate were the Russian rock-bards. (These might be compared to the American riot-folk artists, only with a completely different background; as a rule, they were either former NBPs or imitators and successors to the Siberian and Russian Leningrad school of rock). At that time they were the most unkempt, frostbitten, and violent Russian artists I knew. In those same years, from the then-released rock encyclopedias and the books about rock and musical *samizdat* released in the '90s, I learned about the existence of Moscow punk bands that continued the tradition of Siberian groups like Grazhdanskaia Oborona, Instruktsia po Vyzhivaniu, and Chernozem.[267] These were the "Formation" groups like Rezervatsia Zdes (later renamed the Banda Chetyrekh) and Solomennye Yenoty. Despite the fact that the peak of activity and popularity of these groups came in the '90s, their history and music was what I was seeking for so long, and later found in the DIY underground.

---

267 *Chernozem*—Black Soil.

Perhaps it was Rezervatsia Zdes that became a bridge for me from the verbose and abstruse acoustic underground to a much more winding and audacious music, which for all its simplicity was sufficiently intellectual and desperate. The album *Gorod Znoy* still remains for me one of the best punk records in Russian; most of the songs on it were written in the first person, the number of chords were strictly limited, but most importantly—no one tried to present their music as revelation, and no one read out notations and morals; musicians just exuded blood and sent everything to hell, not trying to seem smarter and more virtuosic than they are (which, unfortunately, can't be said about the later albums of *Banda Chetyrekh* that grew up on the ruins of the Rezervatsia Zdes).[268]

In addition to the bared decadent romance, which was broadcast by the Rezervatsia, Banda and partly Yenoty, these groups were once at the epicenter of exciting and dangerous adventures. Reading the stories about them in samizdat and on the Internet was breathtaking. Most concerts of both groups were held in an atmosphere of unrestrained drunkenness and were accompanied by fights, wild antics, crazy trips, and every foreseeable way of crossing boundaries. These people had not only powerful songs, but also a grandiose and vivid context in which they existed.

It's funny that, a few years later, when I met anti-fascist leaders who were also looking for a way out of their isolation, they too were fans of Banda Chetyrekh. Teenage infatuation with skinheads and football hooliganism (which came to anti-fascism later), was for them only a cover under which laid *the fun*. "Nobody gave a Hitler salute at the festival Sibirskoe Vtorzhenie like you and me," one authoritative anti-fascist jokingly said to another with warmth.[269] A significant part of the audience of Banda in the beginning of the 2000s were red-brown members of the NBP and football fans. It was in this environment that some of the most aggressive and active anti-fascists grew up.

268 *Gorod Znoy*—City Heat.
269 *Sibirskoie Vtorzhenie*—Siberian Invasion.

A third factor that shaped the face of Moscow's Siberian punk followers was total underground-ness and secrecy, frequently bordering sectarianism. The leader of the Solomennye Yenoty, Boris Usov, strictly forbade the distribution of the group's recordings outside the circle of fans, where only the closest people entered.

Healthy anger, intelligence, energy, danger, and secrecy from extraneous eyes—these are the things I had been looking for and discovered in the hardcore punk community, finding my way in it around 2004–2005.

"Beat me, beat me!" shouted a shaved Asiatic-looking vocalist running around the room in his underwear while his musicians made such a deafening noise that I had never heard before on an improvised stage.

Of all the people at that moment in the hall, I was almost the only one who, after hearing the boy's calls to injure him, cowered frantically to the wall. The others readily accepted these screams as a signal to action. They started jumping on the vocalist, yelling at him into the microphone, knocking him to the floor. In March 2005 I went to the debut concert of the odious straight edge hardcore band Proverochnaia Lineika (the name is a free translation of the phrase "straight edge") in the oldest surviving Moscow DIY club named Jerry Rubin.

Jerry Rubin Club, the basement on Leninsky Prospekt, led by the tireless Svetlana Yelchaninova under different names and in different places, existed since the early '90s. At one time, the musicians of Tarakany!, Chudo-Yudo, and other not-so-known not-so-punk bands participated in its construction, arrangement, as well as preservation from the city authorities, who are still trying to close Jerry.

Jerry Rubin Club was a major epicenter of Moscow DIY punk in the early to mid 2000s. The holiday ended in the second half of the decade, when a violent audience once again broke through the low ceiling of the small hall while crowd surfing, and the drunk skinheads who came to the concert smashed the cars parked in the yard near the club. After that, the owner imposed a strict veto on punk concerts in her club, and the long-term nomadic punk bands began moving around different urban areas that were not accustomed to punk shows, but generally reserved for rock concerts. At the moment, Jerry Rubin is a children's art club. If there is music here, it is modest bearded men on acoustic guitars with their wives.

I remember what then became the three main points: the club Vse Svoi, a typical place with karaoke for managers, directly in front of the zoo and police departments (with a lovely smell and appearance); club Zhivoy Ugolok, a functioning kindergarten with a small hall; and finally a bomb-shelter.[270] The punks themselves broke the lock on the shelter, pumped out the water and dirt, let it dry, and rigged the wiring. One New Year's Day the party was over: illegal immigrants, who had been living next door to the guys and were afraid of noise and strangely dressed people in the neighborhood, denounced them to the police. Ironically, punks were among the few in those days who tried to defend the rights of migrants.

After finishing the performance, the singer of Proverochnaia Lineika reported that it would be suicide to leave the venue alone, so he recommended the audience to stick together. Nobody wanted to die.

Having waited until the last group finished performing, all present orderly lined up. We collectively got out of the basement and headed for the subway. On the road were completely empty bins; punks took glass bottles, stones, sticks, and other implements for self-defense in their hands. I clearly remember that one of the participants of the march brought reinforcement bars in a plastic bag and gave them to those who already knew the drill with joint street clashes with neo-Nazi skinheads. In the same year,

270 *Vse Svoi*—Everybody Common; *Zhivoy Ugolok*—Pets' Corner.

Proverochnaia Lineika wrote in one hour their debut album *Dzhey Pilit Armaturu*.[271]

Such conspiracies at punk concerts were well and good, but did not make life much easier. Already delving into the subject and having read about all kinds of joys and attributes of DIY punk in magazines and books (thanks, not least, to a Russian translation of Craig O'Hara's *Philosophy of Punk* in the beginning of 2000s), I could not go to a single concert for about a year because they were not announced. As an example, this one guy, who had access to the inner sanctum and knew all the right and important people in Moscow sat at the same desk as me, and I had no idea!

We talked about everything, including music, but at some point he inevitably said that he had to do something and then disappeared. And the next day I read in (of course) closed posts on Livejournal that there was a hardcore concert in Jerry Rubin, and I surmised that my colleague was there, but that he hid it from me. My resentment and bewilderment was over the limit. As a result, I finally gathered the courage to ask him to introduce me to the guys from the hardcore scene. He retorted a definitive "No."

This was another less pleasant face of DIY punk in the early 2000s—the notorious secrecy, which for most was a recognized necessity, a matter of survival, but for some was used for the sake of scoring cool points during the get-togethers, making the punk community a snobbish and private club for the elite; all that punk rock rejected, in essence.

There was even a half-joking term "hardcore elite," referring to musicians, activists, and their entourage. It was believed that it was very difficult to get into this circle, but it was also very honorable if you did manage to get in. It took time to realize that those who used such terms did so to bolster their own social status. There was actually very little substance to it.

Another consequence of this closed life, where information about gatherings was spread by word of mouth, SMS, and instant

271 *Dzhey Pilit Armaturu*—Jay Saws Reinforcement Bars.

messenger from ICQ, was the incredible seriousness on the part of event organizers and concert goers. "You have to respect your culture / You must honestly answer for it / With your conscience, ribs, and armature"— as one of the main hits of Proverochnaia Lineika claimed.

Active participants in closed DIY punk concerts did not perceive their participation in them as entertainment (what they were and should be in the rest of the world). They understood themselves as representatives of a secret society, which was in rather severe conflict with the outside world. In principle, this can be understood—there was not much fun in war, but there was a need to raise and maintain morale.

The vocalist of Lineika, Pjtor, brought shamanistic rituals to punk concerts, the participants of which, like a wild tribe, sank into a trance while dancing under the enchanting music ("For this purpose there was a special rhythm—the rhythm of 'D'"—Pjtor said laughing). "Rhythm D" as he called it, is easy to guess—d-beat.

Each concert seemed to me a kind of training before what was to come after it. Going to a private show, you realized that the program included far more than music—the evening inevitably turned out to be one of wandering in industrial zones or forests, with high energy that at any moment would induce flight or fight: fear, excitement and an incredible feeling of catharsis, which occurs when, at last, you managed to tumble into a large crowd in the subway car. This final event meant that at that moment the likeliness of combat ceased. Not all of them, however, were successful. Once our friends were attacked in the train, when we were traveling to a hardcore concert, which was held in one of the suburban regions. Our small company miraculously managed to escape into the woods directly across the railway lines, and most of the punks were in the train and on the platform ready to fight. Some got a concussion and others badly injured. We were glad that at least no one died.

One of the toughest disputes about whether it was possible to have fun at shows, broke out at a Moscow concert in memory of Timur Kacharava, a member of the St. Petersburg band Sandinista! in 2005. He was the first, and unfortunately not the last, victim of a street war between the nascent antifa movement and neo-Nazis. The concert in his memory took place a few days after the tragedy.

"Mod, poser, feed homeless people! Clean evil's clock with an argument!"—words from the same song by Lineika. It was believed that all the normal guys dressed in secondhand clothes. And all participants were required to take part in socially important initiatives like Food Not Bombs. Of course, many tried to look stylish, but it was not always welcomed.

My first years at the institute, where I arrived in 2004, were for me a living hell. I was trapped, surrounded by dull people talking about dull subjects. The alternative was the army, so I had to endure. You can imagine my joy when, soon after the concert at Jerry Rubin, I accidentally collided with the vocalist of Lineika in the institute's hallway. The question of my future participation in private concerts was settled in that moment.

Pjtor was one grade higher and studied in the religious studies department. He, as an intelligent person, captured the attention of the entire department. Even the 50 year old faculty head of the department followed the adventures of the leader of Lineika, which Pjtor wrote in a closed blog. Alas, it was Pjtor who was the one fan of Banda Chetyrekh, who in school with football friends went to concerts, where the whole hall went crazy and made the nazi salutes.

Pjtor recounted his reasons for joining hardcore in his own book. I note only that his interpretation of punk was really more than music, or more precisely, in the first place, not music at all; he treated subculture primarily as a conduit for his insane energy, and as a means of transforming himself and the social atmosphere around. This approach was unusual for Moscow DIY activists who were staring at the West. I would even say, revolutionary. Craig O'Hara didn't even write about such things.

Pjtor was young blood. He burst into the hardcore world of Moscow and quickly realized that the rules that existed before him did not apply to him. He began to bend the rules. What was Moscow hardcore before Pjtor?

At the end of the '90s to the beginning of 2000s, Moscow's DIY punk community gathered around the label Old Skool Records (OSK), the largest and most active of its kind. Its head, Sergey Voloshin, formed the first metropolitan straight edge hardcore band B'67 (Brutal 67, the year of the singer's birth). Sergey's brother, Pavel, played on the drums, and on the guitar was Kirill Tolkachev nicknamed "Student," and the leader of Skygrain, an important Moscow hardcore band of the 1990s. B'67 produced two demos, which are primarily of historical value. To seriously listen to these recordings is impossible today, mainly because of the terrible quality of both the recordings and material.

However, unlike most of their peers, the brothers Voloshin and their friends by the '90s already dealt with Western DIY punk. In 2000, their song "Ne Meshay Mne Dyshat" was published in an international collection "More Than The X On Our Hands," put out by a landmark Dutch hardcore label, Commitment.

Representatives of the Moscow Hardcore Crew, as they called themselves, gathered around B'67, OSK, and Skygrain, and they tried to adapt Western hardcore standards to Russian realities as hard as they could.

In late '90, this crew published a fanzine called *Punk Hardcore Magazine*, and in 1999 they published the first and, unfortunately, only magazine of Old Skool Kids (today it can be found on the site DIY-zine.com). In those same years, Pavel Voloshin played a short while without recording any records in Cheese Balls Punx with Sergey "Bay" Baybakov—one of the first SHARP skinheads of Moscow and one of the first members of the band Distemper. This band, which started as crossover style in the spirit of the DRI, quickly evolved into a ska-punk project, becoming Russia's main group in this genre and one of the most popular local punk bands. Distemper still holds that title, along with Tarakany! and Naïve.

Through OSK's back-catalog, one can trace the events that were fashionable in the underground world in the early 2000s— screamo, modern hardcore, thrashcore-revival, crust. Members of the Moscow Hardcore Crew looked only abroad and fumbled at the very bottom, because all that existed in the mainstead was Russian rock bands catered for the domestic market, and local imitators of popular foreign punk bands, whom they rightly considered as govnopank.

The boys proudly hung on to this little subcultural ghetto, largely because the reality of Russia at the end of the '90s was totally unprepared for such unusual, radical, and unusual music.

Kirill "Student" said that during the first concert of Skygrain, there were no more than 10 people who knew about stage diving and crowd surfing. Someone jumped off the stage and was supported by some guys, who then ran around the room. Nobody ever saw this before. He told me another story about a festival where his band Tri Kresta was invited to play in a provincial town.[272] The provincials had a very clear attitude toward those who looked and acted differently (even today), and descended on the festival with chains and all but shovels and pitchforks.

The police, trying to keep order, quickly realized that they were outnumbered by combattants. According to Kirill, when Tri Kresta came out on stage and started playing, the provincial youth didn't understand at all what was going on—and only this fact saved the band members from a brutal beating.

Aggressive-minded guys expected that there would be painted punks with mohawks, but instead they saw neat kids in skate rags playing some kind of noise. The audience could perceive

272 Tri Kresta—Three Crosses.

the emotion of Tri Kresta simply as a weird noise; they did not know that it was possible to play that way and that there was such music. Many thought Kirill's band was a foreign group.

By the middle of 2000s Sergey Voloshin had checked out of playing music, concentrating instead on his label and distro. He produced not only local, but also foreign groups. His brother Pasha, on the other hand, played drums for at least three other bands at the same time. Former Skygrain, Tri Kresta, and B'67 member Kirill sang in the band Argument 5.45, which united not only hardcore, but also nu-metal fans (nu-metal was much more popular in those days). Besides OSK, it is worth mentioning some other labels like Homo Sentimentalis Recordings, led by the first singer of the Moscow screamo band Marschak Andrey Otshivalov. For many of my peers who discovered DIY around the same time as me, the debut album *Marschak* became perhaps the first serious rendition of this music. Unfortunately, by 2005 the band already broken up.

If *Marschak* managed to re-assemble in the middle 2000s, I'm sure they would have found serious success. Russia was captivated by the "black and pink plague"— mainstream emo revival with all these bangs, badges, and very bad music. Marschak could have become the heroes of this generation, if they wanted, but members of the DIY community doggedly kept faithful to the ideals of the underground. The guitarist, Timur, even tried to bash the face of a journalist, who wrote a review of Marschak's debut album for Playboy magazine.

According to one version, Tarakany!'s vocalist Dmitry Spirin dedicated the song "Real Punk" to the "OSK records crew," who had been ridiculing him for "corruptness" in fighting for the ideals of DIY.

Another sister label of OSK was the S/T Demo Records, run by Sasha Lyubomudrov, who lived on the same street as me. At the beginning the 2000s, he sang in a punk band called No Copies, and managed to release songs on two punk-collections and a tribute album to Khimera. Sasha was the same age as the representatives of Moscow Hardcore Crew, but only joined their company in the second half of the 2000s.

"We talked with Voloshin and others from OSK when we were in No Copies. The band broke up shortly after boneheads beat some musician in the train; there were a lot of such cases. We signed up to play a benefit concert together with Argument 5.45, Pasha Voloshin made a poster, and it was an obvious anti-fascist concert. The opinions in the group about our participation in it were divided. Some musicians were afraid to speak out against the fascist problem. I then gave them an ultimatum: either play, or disintegrate. And we decided to break up, but then the concert was canceled anyway. We played our last show, and that was it," says Lyubomudrov.

In 2004 Sasha formed a new group, the Back Weapon Ricochet (later shortened to Ricochet) with tireless Pasha Voloshin on drums and former bassist of Marschak, Timur. The material of Ricochet was much more elaborate and complex than the straightforward punk of No Copies. Lyubomudrov's lyrics, paired with the unique and rather difficult music of Timur, formed one of the most interesting and intelligent punk bands of our time.

The peak activity of Sasha and his friends came in the second half of the 2000s, and I believe that without his efforts the Moscow punk scene would have been much different. He was involved in so many activities, including the expansion of acceptable boundaries, which inspired many, and continues to inspire to this day.

In addition to participating in Ricochet and releasing records on his label, Lyubomudrov played bass in two groups— Montfaucon and Salpetriere. Also, together with friends, he published the fanzine *Insomnia*, which unlike most of the samizdat publications of the time, was professionally drawn up and printed on newsprint. In fact, it was a clone of the American fanzine *HeartAttack* (with all its pluses and minuses).

In addition, being almost 10 years older than the vast majority of DIY punk concert-goers, Lyubomudrov became a moral authority for the youth, speaking between songs on important topics of the day. He had a real job at a telecommunications company, which allowed him to do what the majority of people did not have the money to do. Ricochet was probably the first underground Moscow band with its own equipment, which the group leader carried in a minivan he borrowed from work. The same minivan served as the band member's tour bus. Lyubomudrov organized concerts almost every two weeks, not only for local groups but visitors from neighboring countries such as Balts Tesa, When My Authorities Fall, and others. It was even he who first brought Vitamin X to Russia, Lack (Denmark), Warcry and Tragedy (United States), establishing a record not beaten until now, for most of these groups it was the first and last visit to our country.

Crossing the nihilist aesthetics of Lineika, and their affiliation with more affluent and older "punks from the day," OSK and Ricochet came out in a united anti-fascist front dedicated to social activism. In the middle of the 2000s they sponsored Food not Bombs events and trips to orphanages.

According to Lyubomudrov, he met Pjtor at a rehearsal place near the Belorusskaia metro station, which Sasha with friends dubbed "Doktor Zhopa."[273] The entire core of the capital's hardcore entourage rehearsed there: Marschak, Ricochet, Loa Loa, and, as it turned out, Lineika (the only exception was the "professional" bands Unconform and Argument 5.45). Lyubomudrov later, as the owner of the minivan, frequently participated in scouting—tracking down nazis before concerts.

Unfortunately, it was anti-fascism, or rather the sad consequences of the clash between the ultra-right and punk that became the main reason for the outside world to give attention to the DIY community. At the beginning of the 2000s, neo-Nazis began to commit high profile crimes.

---

273 *Doktor Zhopa*—Dr. Ass.

In 2002, there was a massacre of migrants at Tsaritsynsky market, which resulted in three deaths. In 2004 in St. Petersburg there was the murder of a Tajik girl Khursheda Sultonova. Also in 2004 the ethnographer, anti-fascist and human rights defender Nikolay Girenko was shot through a door.

In 2005, the year when the nazis killed Timur Kacharava, the authorities decided to toy with the idea of "managed nationalism," which meant that the ultra right was allowed to hold a patriotic "Russian march" outside the Kremlin walls. The apotheosis of this strategy was the open concert on Bolotnaia Square, in the heart of Moscow, hosting the openly fascist group Kolovrat.

It took more than five years for the authorities to recognize that "managed nationalism" was spiraling out of control. During this time, the right had killed at least eight people, not even counting Timur. Two of them were a journalist and human rights activist, the rest were punks and SHARP skinheads.

On April 16, 2006 six nazis attacked 19 year old Sasha Riukhin, who accompanied a friend to a punk concert. Riukhin died on the spot from a knife wound. The concert was assembled by Igor "Tankist" Mineev, the bassist for the hardcore band What We Feel, another important member of the Moscow DIY scene in the 2000s.

Tankist had a pop punk background; from 2001 to 2004 he played in the metropolitan Deutsch-punk band Der Steinkopf. "Ideological" hardcore bands looked down on such "unserious" groups at the time. Then Tankist disbanded the Deutsch-punk band and created the short lived group Burn in Hell. Punk forums were riddled with arguments where representatives of OSK's crew accused the Tankists of wanting to jump on a trendy bandwagon in order to earn money.

Compared to other representatives of the DIY underground, Igor stood out as a good entrepreneur. Not only did he play in a hardcore band, but he also arranged concerts, including some with representatives of the OSK crew. Every day Igor had to reiterate that he did not do it for money, and that it was completely normal to include his band on the concerts he organized. Lyubomudrov was especially indignant with regards to the actions of the Tankist.

In 2004 Tankist formed the group What We Feel, playing straightforward hardcore songs on all topical themes of the time—nazis, the police, animal protection, and so on. Soon title of "most important" (read—a model, a reference) hardcore group became vacant, at least in Moscow. In 2005 Lineika toured Russia, Belarus, and Ukraine, and made sure that their activity produced significant results—in every city they played, Pjtor and friends were supported by several crews of like-minded fans. When he returned Pjtor ended Lineika, declaring his mission fulfilled. Most likely, unconsciously, What We Feel replaced Lineika as the "most ideological" Moscow hardcore band.

The murder of Riukhin, which occurred just prior to his concert, severely hit Tankist. When the murder became known, the concert still went on. Igor decided not to stop the show, judging that there was nothing to be done and not wanting to make the already terrible evening worse. Of course, this act was actively discussed and condemned in punk forums, which added oil to the fire of Igor's depression. Later he collected money for Sasha's funeral, went to his parents, and regularly wrote in Livejournal about his experiences. It seems to me that this was the moment that Igor felt that anti-fascist hardcore was a mission and a matter of life and death.

A month after the murder of Riukhin, Igor and the band recorded the first demo of What We Feel in St. Petersburg, which later came out as a split with the German band The Force Within. In 2007, What We Feel went on their first European tour, setting the stage for their normal trips abroad as representatives of Russian anti-fascism. If memory serves me right, the group has not given an open concert in Russia since the end of the 2000s. There are a number of disappointing reasons for this.

For one, Tsentr "E" began to pursue the musicians of What We Feel along with other anti-fascists. The group rarely appeared under its own name (they usually appeared on posters as "special guests," so as not to attract the attention of the right). Once the ultra-right and police started to persecute members of the band, they stopped giving concerts in Russia. Today What We Feel is a great name, at least in Germany, where they perform at major festivals with world-famous bands. The band gives part of whatever money they earn to the families of friends that were killed by fascists. Recently (in the spring of 2017) I heard that Igor, who had been working alone on the management of the band for the last few years, took up the bass again and acted as part of What We Feel. Unfortunately, uneasy relations with him do not allow me to learn the details.

On October 10, 2008 one of the leaders of the antifa movement, the SHARP-skinhead Fedor Filatov, was killed. He died as a result of more than 30 stab wounds. Just a few months before Pjtor, who was a close friend of Fedor, returned from a European tour with his new band Ted Kaczynski. The dashing quartet played dirty crust music with apocalyptic texts and, according to Pjtor, was created solely to travel to Europe, where the ex-leader of Lineika had never been.

Yura Div, a truly remarkable character, played guitar in Ted Kaczynski. Before joining he played in a parody homosexual nazi group Evil Oh!, which sang songs from the perspective of homosexual patriots, bitterly mocking the right. The group called themselves "national nationalists," and wrote on the internet with such seriousness that both punks and rightists could not ascertain whether it was a joke. At one point, a rumor of the existence of homosexual nazis reached journalists of one of the largest Russian tabloids, *Moskovsky Komsomolets*.[274] The paper published a photo of Yura in women's shorts, which can still be found on the internet. Of course, such jokes were extremely dangerous in the second half of the 2000s. Members of Evil Oh! received threats, people tried to beat

274 Literally "Young Moscow Komsomol Member" (for a definition of Komsomol, see footnote 26, Part One).

them on the street, and they were shot at. The band finally broke up when the musicians realized that jokes about nazi homosexuals could cost them their lives.

The murder of Filatov deeply depressed Pjtor. After October 2008 he no longer participated in the punk scene, and disappeared from subculture for almost two years. In 2009, under the pseudonym *DJ Stalingrad*, Pjtor released an extremely gloomy tale, *Iskhod*, considered a comprehensive view of his five-year experience of street fighting.[275] On the last page Pjtor included a photo of Filatov, under whose jacket a cat peered out. Pjtor recalled that his brigade would also warm up cats stuck on the cold train platforms.

On November 16, 2009 another "leader of the anti-fascists," as it was written in the media, was shot in the head. Ivan Khutorskoy, nicknamed "Kostolom," was a very kind SHARP skinhead who worked as a lawyer at a children's center.[276] According to many his murder ushered in the end of an era. In its wake came a new, terrible one. By that time, the DIY community managed to create a well-established infrastructure for concerts, bringing groups, organizing tours, rehearsals, and legal actions. For many, the need for all this movement disappeared when the high price became absolutely clear.

According to Pjtor, some time after the release of *Iskhod* he went to a concert of the band The Cavestompers, whose drummer, Grisha Yeniosov, was at that time his only remaining friend in the scene, and he told Grisha he felt like he wanted to die. "I did not understand what was going on there, why all this," recalls Pjtor. "And then Grisha's friend said: 'Then let's go to the Khimki camp to go on duty' in an effort to rekindle my energy and enthusiasm. That was the first time I heard about the Khimki camp. And when the Gladiators smashed the camp, it became apparent that it is generally what we needed at the moment."[277]

275 *Iskhod*—Exodus.
276 *Kostolom*—Bonecrusher.
277 An ultra right group, fans of the Moscow soccer team Spartak.

By the summer of 2010 the struggle over the deforestation in the Moscow region of Khimki, which had been going on for years, had finally reached its climax. Ecologists and hippies were on duty in tents with equipment that was supposed to cut down the forest. On one July night, ultra-right-wing fans of the group Gladiators, beat up protesters and attacked peaceful representatives hired by the mayor of Khimki.

A couple of days after the incident a flyer reading "Proverechnaia Lineika Reunion" appeared on the internet, "Gather at the metro station Trubnaia." I had not seen Pjtor for a long time, and I immediately realized that there was some hidden agenda. Something was bound to happen.

At the appointed time about a hundred people gathered near Trubnaia. Everyone waited but did not understand what was going on. Suddenly, from the crowd Pjtor appeared in sunglasses. In his hands he had a megaphone: "I hope there are no idiots who thought there would be a reunion?" Pjtor asked the audience. All were silent. Of course, everyone was waiting for the reunion, but to admit so was to expose yourself as a fool.

"Now we will go to Khimki and hold a beautiful action there," declared Pjtor. All without question, by order, boarded the train and went to the suburbs. At the protest site Pjtor and his friends from the group Moscow Death Brigade unfurled banners "Let's clean the forest from nazi occupation," lit fireworks, and chanted "Stop deforestation," finally moving to the local administration building. Participants of the action unleashed all their anger at the unfortunate building; they cut the door with an axe, there were shots from a stun gun, broken class, and scribbled graffiti.

The Khimki initiative remains the loudest and largest direct action organized by Moscow punks. It was a brighter finale to the 2000s than one might have thought possible.

For the less radical camp of Moscow punks, 2010 also provided a sort-of finale. Many representatives of the OSK crew had children, causing many groups to disappear at once. Lyubomudrov and his wife Vera had a son, Yasha, who, unfortunately, was born deaf. A terrible diagnosis turned the life of the vocalist of Ricochet and his family upside down. Benefit concerts, several operations in Germany, loans and debts became his new life. As a result, fortunately, Yasha found some help. He can hear and speak. Ricochet gave their farewell concert in 2013.

Here, perhaps, it is appropriate to say where all these people are now. Lyubomudrov and his family moved to Canada. Shortly after the Khimki initiative Pjtor was granted political asylum in Finland, where he graduated from university. The founder of OSK Records, Sergey Voloshin, closed the label and currently upholds his name as a techno and punk DJ. His brother Pavel and his family live outside the city, a couple of times a year performing at reunion concerts of his past groups. Kirill "Student" sings in the black hardcore group Bandarlog. The Moscow punk scene is experiencing a period of calm after the tumultuous 2000s. The street wars between nazis and anti-fascists are in the past— Tsentr "E" did their job. Closed concerts are a thing of the past, and it seems the danger is gone once and for all.

There is a lot I haven't talked about. The wonderful punk scene near Zhukovsky, the summer concerts there, and the emergence of a large crust and oi! Scene in the middle of the 2000s. In any case, it is impossible to consolidate everything within a framework of one article. Honestly, if you have any questions my email is listed in the introduction.

SELECT BIBLIOGRAPHY

Fanzines Alphabetized (Russian)

Antifashistskii Motiv

Armatura (Moscow Ob. 2005)

Arteriia (Nizhny Novgorod, 2006)

BorisBreetBrosvi (Chita, 2005)

Britva (Moscow, 2006)

Brutto Netto (Vladimirskaya Ob., 2000)

Bumazhnye Uzhasy (Kirov, 2002)

V moem Supe Pechen'e v Forme Zveriushek (St. Petersburg, 1999)

Veselye Botinki (St. Petersburg, 1999)

Vzorvannoe Nebo (Moscow, 1997)

Vintovka, (St. Petersburg, 2003)

Vozdukh (St. Petersburg, 1998)

Vse Vmeste (Petrozavodsk, 2006)

Geni!al'nyi Iashchur (Velikii Novgorod, 2001)

Diversiia (St. Petersburg, 2007)

Evrobytylka (Moscow/ St. Petersburg/ Minsk/ Gusev, 2001)

Zlye Ulitsy (Tatarstan, 2013)

IMKhO (Moscow, 2005)

Imkhopang (Moscow, 2006)

Kamardzhoba (Nizhny Novgorod, 2006)

Kontr Kul't UR'a (Moscow, 1989)

Kocheryga (Moscow, 2014)

Kremen' (St. Peterburg 2010)

Krik (Tomsk, 2005)

Liniia Fronta (St. Petersburg, 2006)

Listochek (Vladimirskaya ob., 1999)

Moi Papa Sobaka (Moscow, 2005)

Mu-khu-khu (Krasnodarskii krai, 2004)

My vse eshche tam? (Novgorodskaya ob., 2009)

Mysli Vslukh (Tambov, 2008)

Nastoiashchee Iskusstvo (Volgograd, 1999)

Ne-Nenormal (Volgograd, 1999)

Ne Stesniaisia-Sdelai kopiui (Leningradskaya ob., 2002)

Nevroz (Moscow, 2007)

Neformat (Moscow, 2000)

Nozhi i Vilki (St. Petersburg, 1998)

Paddington (St. Petersburg, 2008)

Parovozopuskatel' (Krasnodar, 1998)

PliusMinusBeskonechnost' (Volgogradskaya ob., 1997)

Proiskhodiashchee (Volgogradskaya ob., 2016)

Prokliatiia is Pauchei Banki (St. Petersburg, 2016)

Pushkinist (St. Petersburg, 2011)

S Nulia! (St. Petersburg, 2005)

Slomannye Igrushki (Krasnodar, 2007)

SXEma (Tomsk, 2007)

Tochka Zreniia (Krasnodar, 1999)

Ten-Chan (St. Petersburg, 1999)

Fakfood (Irkutsk, 2004)

Khakhariashka (Moscow, 2007)

Khigglidi-Pigglidi (Cheliabinskaya Ob., 1997)

Cheburashka (Irkutsk, 2007)

Shon Penn (St. Petersburg, 2002)

Ekho-Kamera (Volgogradskaya ob., 1998)

Fanzines Alphabetized (English)

A-Bomb (Moscovskaya ob., 2009)

Again 25 (Moscow, 2010)

Always At War (Smolensk, 2000)

Anders Leben (Kirov, 2008)

Backyard Zombies (St. Petersburg, 2007)

Barbed Wire Letter (Barnaul, 1999)

Bella Normal (Volgograd, 2001)

Blah-Blah-Blood (St. Petersburg, 2002)

Boiling Point (Riazan', 2011)

Born To Crash (Murmanskaya Ob., 2006)

Bull-Bull Russia (Moscow, 2005)

Bullshitdozer! (Kaliningraskaya ob., 1998)

Ca-Pusto Punkka (Perm', 2007)

Despertar (St. Petersburg, 2007)

DIY Punkcore Bulletin (Kirovskaya ob., 1995)

Elefantboy (St. Petersburg, 1997)

Explosive (Moscow, 1998)

Fast Music (Penza, 2000)

Get Up! (St. Petersburg, 2004)

Go Scum Go! (Kaluzhskaya ob., 2010)

Goodbye My Cruel World (Barnaul, 2008)

Grindcore/Noise Newsletter (Moscow, 1998)

Homo Punk (St. Petersburg, 1999)

I.Q. Party (Novosibirskaya ob., 1997.)

In A Free Land (St. Petersburg, 1999)

Insomnia (Moscow, 2006)

Interpretation (Moscow, 2006)

Made In Moscow (Moscow, 2009)

Meatzine (Volgograd, 2005)

Message? (Tomsk, 2004)

Musketeer (Moscow, 2005)

My Riot Inward (Petrozavodsk, 2009)

New Blood (Samara, 2008)

No Borders (St. Petersburg, 2007)

Noise Music (Petrozavodsk, 2007

Old Skool Kids (Moscow, 1999)

On The Edge (Moscow, 2003)

Paranoid (St. Petersburg, 2010)

Plastic Bullets (Moscow, 2008)

Play Hooky! (Kirov, 1995)

Positive (Moscow, 1999)

Punk Hardcore Magazine (Moscow, 1996)

Punk-A-Burg (Ekaterinburg, 2005)

Punk Massacre (Nizhny Novgorod, 2017)

Röd-Svart (Perm', 2006)

SeryogaRocker (Volgograd, 2006)

Skunx Times (Kirov, 2004)

Spunkcore (Voronezh, 2006)

Stand Your Ground (St. Petersburg, 2006)

Sticky Bubblegum Zine (Moscow, 2011)

Stokers (Ekaterinburg, 2006)

Street Print (Permskaya Ob., 2005)

Summer Holidays And The Punk Routine (St. Petersburg, 2006)

Tommy's (Kraznoiarskii krai 2001)

Totalka Kiselica (Moscow, 2007)

Unname Shit (Tomsk, 2010)

Voice (St. Petersburg, 2000)

Well Ask Ass (Kazan, 2007)

Xerotika (Kaliningradskaya ob., 1998)

Yes Future! Bulletin (Novosibirskaya ob., 1998)

Zine X (Petrozavodsk, 2006)

Zorry For The Delay (St. Petersburg, 1999)

Monographs

Aksiutina, Olga. *Pank-virus v rossii.* Moscow: Bukinisticheskoe izdanie, 1999

Alekseev, A., A. Burlaka and A. Sidorov. *Kto est' kto v sovetskom roke.* Moscow: Izdatel'stvo MP "Ostankino," 1991.

Alekseev, Denis and Petr Psymuline. *Gazelle of Death.* Moscow, 2017.

Balunov, Aleksandr. *Korol' i shut mezhdu Kupchino I Rzhevkoi.* Moscow: Izdatel'stvo AST, 2016.

D.J. Stalingrad. *Iskhod.* St. Petersburg: Azbuka, 2011.

Ermichev, Kirill. *Russkaia psikhataka: zapiski v stile psychobilly.* Moscow: Tverdyi pereplet, 2007.

Gololobov, Ivan, Hilary Pilkington and Yngvar B. Steinholt. *Punk in Russia: Cultural Mutation from the 'useless' to the 'moronic.'* London: Routledge, 2014.

Gorbachev, Aleksandr and Ilya Zinin. *Pesni v pustotu: poteriannoe pokolenie russkogo roka 90-kh.* Moscow: Tverdyi pereplet, 2014.

Kalgin, Vitalii. *Viktor Tsoi.* Moscow: Molodia gvardiia, 2015.

Kochetkov, Maksim and Ruslana Stupina. *Naïv: Istoriia gruppy v fotografiiakh.* Moscow, 2013.

Kosovo, Petia. *Korrespondent Gaskarov v adu, i drugie isyorii.* Moscow: Creative Commons, 2014.

Libabova, Evgeniia. *Korol' i shut: Angely Panka.* St Petersburg: Amfora, 2014.

Pilkington, Hilary. *Russia's Youth and Its Culture: A Nation's Constructors and Constructed.* London: Routledge, 1994.

Pilkington, Hilary, Al'bina Garifzianova, Elena Omel'chenko. *Russia's Skinheads: Exploring and Rethinking Subcultural Lives.* London: Routledge, 2010.

Ryback, Timothy W. *Rock Around the Bloc: A History of Rock Music in Eastern Europe and the Soviet Union.* New York: Oxford University Press, 1990.

Sandalov, Feliks. *Formeishen: istoriia odnoi stseny.* Moscow: Creative Commons, 2016.

Spirin, D. Tupoi *pank-rok dlia intellektualov.* Moscow: AST, 2014.

Stogoff, Ilya. *Greshniki.* St. Petersburg: Amfora, 2006.

_____. *Anarkhiia v RF: Pervaia polnaia istoriia russkogo panka.* St. Petersburg: Amfora, 2007.

The Feminist Press. *Pussy Riot! A punk prayer for Freedom: Letters from Prison, Songs, Poems, and Courtroom Statements, Plus Tributes to the Punk band that Shook the World.* New York: The Feminist Press, 2013.

Troitsky, Artemy. *Back in the USSR: The True Story of Rock in Russia.* Boston: Faber and Faber, 1987.

Resource Websites

Joannastingray.com
Sadwave.ru
Negativecreep.ru

Articles and Zine Issues

Bernstein, Anya. "An Inadvertent Sacrifice: Body Politics and Sovereign Power in the Pussy Riot Affair." *Critical Inquiry.* Volume 40, Number 1 (Autumn 2013).

Herbert, Alex. "A Brief History of Punk in Izhevsk: Resisting Monotony in an Industrial Wasteland." Razorcake. July 2, 2015. http://razorcake.org/archive-a-brief-history-of-punk-in-izhevsk-russia/

Kozlov, Vladimir. "Allowed for Performance: Punk and Rebellion in the 1980s Siberia." Vice Noisey. March, 2015. https://noisey.vice.com/en_au/article/r3zq9w/siberian-punk-scene-in-the-1980s

Maximum Rocknroll #96, May 1991

Maximum Rocknroll #170, July 1997

Maximum Rocknroll #177, February 1998

Maximum Rocknroll #261, February 2005

Maximum Rocknroll #270, November 2005

Maximum Rocknroll #355, December 2012

Maximum Rocknroll #375, August 2014

Maximum Rocknroll #385, June 2015

Meduza. "Russia's lost punks: Squatting in homes, breaking each other's faces, and living the hardcore life. A photo series." Photos by Ksenia Ivanova. July 23, 2015.

Shumov, Vasily. "Russian punks: The ideology, music, and lifestyle." Russia Beyond. August 18, 2013. https://www.rbth.com/arts/2013/08/18/russian_punks_the_ideology_music_and_lifestyle_28995.html

Videos

Baragozin, Boris. *Goriachee Vremia*. Published July 9, 2017. https://www.youtube.com/watch?v=5ty6rVpcMPg&t=252s

Bortnikov, Ivan. *TAMTAM: Muzyka smutnogo vremeni (2017) dok.film.* Khushchevka org. Published March 5, 2018. https://www.youtube.com/watch?v=oto38dC1Fy0

Khimera. *Vsevolod Gakkel' o klube TaMtAm i Edike Starkove*. Published May 2, 2016. https://www.youtube.com/watch?v=9Czh-azwk6I

Kozlov, Vladimir. *Sledy na snegy*. Platzkart Productions. Published September 8 2017 https://www.youtube.com/watch?v=c1CrPFcvKi4&feature=youtu.be&app=desktop

Molnar, Ingrid. *TaMtAm - The St. Petersburg Music Club*. EEfilmsEvgenijKozlov Published May 23, 2014. https://www.youtube.com/watch?v=sthSTL78S40&t=1141s

Obyekt Nasmeshek – Epokha dlya nas + Interv'iu na angliyskom. Pengvin86. Published January 7, 2009, https://www.youtube.com/watch?v=Csh4PLX22d4.

Sad But True. *Ivan. In Memory of Our Friend*. Published August 31, 2015. https://www.youtube.com/watch?v=P_pfgPf3PG0&t=1807s

Zinin, Ilya. *"TamTam": Dokumental'nyi fil'm o klube "tam-tam," 1993 god*. Published April 5, 2016. https://www.youtube.com/watch?v=14ciYUtTZ2I

ABOUT THE AUTHOR

Alexander Herbert is a doctoral student at Brandeis University focusing on the history of the late Soviet Union. His research interests include social movements, youth culture, macabre film, music, and politics toward the end of the socialist experiment. He is a devoted father to a beautiful daughter, veteran vegan, self-ascribed environmentalist, occasional musician, opportunistic freelance writer and translator, and fan of beet and pickle pizza.